Evolutionary
Explanation
in the
Social Sciences

PHILOSOPHY AND SOCIETY
General Editor: Marshall Cohen

Evolutionary Explanation in the Social Sciences

AN EMERGING PARADIGM

Philippe Van Parijs

ROWMAN AND LITTLEFIELD
Totowa, New Jersey

For Jean Ladrière

Copyright © 1981 by Philippe Van Parijs

First published in the United States 1981 by Rowman and Littlefield,
81 Adams Drive, Totowa, New Jersey 07512.

LIBRARY OF CONGRESS CATALOGING IN PUBLICATION DATA

Van Parijs, Philippe, 1951-
  Evolutionary explanation in the social sciences.

  (Philosophy and society)
  Bibliography: p.
  Includes index.
  1. Social sciences. I. Title. II. Series.
H61.V36   300'.1   80–18316
ISBN 0–8476–6288–8

Printed in the United States of America

Contents

Acknowledgments

This book owes so much to so many people that there is a good deal of unfairness involved in calling just one of them its author.

In particular, had it not been (1) for the mixture of peace and stimulation which I found at the Queen's College, Oxford, amidst the dominican community of Froidmont Farm, Rixensart, and even, later, with my wife and baby, (2) for liberal financial support from the Leverhulme Trust (through a Florey European Studentship awarded by the Queen's College) and from the Belgian taxpayer (through two successive Research Fellowships with the Fonds National de la Recherche Scientifique), this book might never have been written.

Had it not been (1) for the thoroughness with which Jean Ladrière supervised the two Louvain theses in which part of the material used here underwent a preliminary analysis, (2) for the stimulating supervision of my Oxford D.Phil. thesis (which this book follows closely) by Rom Harré and, for shorter periods, by Brian Barry and Jonathan Barnes, (3) for instructive and/or clarifying discussions with Marie-Claire Beck, Arnold Burms, G. A. Cohen, Peter Halfpenny, Peter Lipton, Steven Lukes, David McFarland, Herminio Martins, Alan Montefiore, Talcott Parsons, Peter Vipond and Georg Zilian, (4) for the critical reactions of the various audiences to which I submitted some of the ideas put forward in the following pages, and in particular (5) for an unknown

Asian graduate student's apparently absurd remark (at the end of a seminar paper I gave in Oxford in 1976), which I finally took over, after much struggling, as my central claim, this book would be much more obscure and more naïve, much looser and much duller than it actually is.

Finally, without my wife's patient scrutiny and the competent assistance of Rowman and Littlefield's staff, this book would also be much more unpleasant to read.

Centre de Philosophie des Sciences
Collège Thomas More
Louvain-la-Neuve
December 12, 1980

Introduction

Summary

The introduction specifies the status claimed by the following chapters. As a contribution to the philosophy of science, they attempt a systematic description of some of the rules which govern scientific practice (section 1). As a contribution to the philosophy of the (stigmatized and pre-paradigmatic) social sciences, such a systematic description may help shape scientific practice, by mediating the emergence of a new paradigm (section 2). The method adopted rests on the analysis of a wide variety of concrete examples, in a way which combines a clarification of what is asserted and assumed in them with an attempt to make sense of them (section 3).

1. The philosopher of science as a grammarian

The philosopher of science, the epistemologist, is in no way qualified to tell scientists what they ought to do and ought not to do. His primary task is just one of parasitic clarification.[1] And most of his efforts are therefore directed towards the systematic description of actual scientific practices. This conception of philosophy of science as a descriptive activity immediately suggests an analogy with descriptive linguistics. Is not scientific practice governed by the social rules of scientific communities, in much the same way as speech is governed by the social rules of speech communities? If this is so, the object of the epistemologist's description can conveniently be characterized as the scientists' *competence,* i.e. the socially shared system of rules which underlies the scientists' actual *performances,* for example their explanations or their experiments. And the epistemologist's task is to produce a descriptively adequate *reconstructed grammar,* i.e. a system of explicit rules which yields the same judgements about what is "right" or "wrong", as does the scientists' *grammar in use,* their implicit competence.[2]

The conditions under which the systematic description of a practice can adopt such a grammatical method are by no means trivial. The language of rules can only be useful if there is a broad (implicit) consensus, in the community concerned, about what ought to be done and not done, and if this conception of what ought to be done and not done is a powerful factor in shaping the community's practice. If these two conditions—of *homogeneity* and of *nomicity*—are only poorly satisfied, the language of rules is, at the very least, misleading, and the grammatical approach breaks down. The systematic description of very heterogeneous or anomic communities is then more conveniently conducted in terms of interests and strategies.[3] It is worth stressing, however, that what needs to be shared and operative is not the scientists' proclaimed conception of their competence—what they publicly claim ought to be done—, but only their actual competence—what they feel they ought to do when they are faced with a concrete problem. When reference is clearly made to the latter, not to the former, both homogeneity and nomicity may be sufficiently plausible for us to be able to adopt a grammatical approach without too many qualms.

In the process of reconstructing some scientific (or linguistic) community's competence, the observation of actual performances plays a central role, but not a decisive one. Consistency with observed performances is neither strictly necessary nor strictly sufficient for a particular reconstruction to be singled out as adequate. On the one hand, some performances may be "deviant", "ungrammatical" by reference to their own performer's competence, and cannot therefore count as a refutation of the reconstruction. And on the other hand, several rival reconstructions may be able to accommodate all observed performances which are uncontroversially "grammatical", while ruling out all those which are uncontroversially "ungrammatical". In the latter situation, which is most likely to arise when the intuition on which judgements of "grammaticalness" are based is blunted, the criterion of descriptive adequacy leaves the choice of a grammar underdetermined. One must then bring in additional criteria, whose nature depends on the purpose for which the grammar is intended. When faced with such a situation of underdetermination, the epistemologist will have to ask: how much light does each of the descriptively adequate alternatives shed on actual scientific practice? The reconstruction which performs best in this respect is the one which he will have to choose.

This is the perspective from which this book has been written and from which it asks to be judged. The two questions presented in its first two chapters are meant as grammatical questions about some aspects of some scientific practices. Bearing in mind the two qualifications just made—descriptive adequacy does not refer to all actual performances and it is not the only relevant consideration—, the answers given to these two questions in subsequent chapters are claimed to be descriptively adequate. They have been chosen for this reason and will be vindicated on these grounds.

2. The philosopher of the social sciences as a midwife

In a way, however, this book does not reduce to a descriptive, grammatical inquiry along the lines sketched in the previous section. Two interconnected features of the scientific practices which form its subject-matter—the fact that they are both "stigmatized" and "pre-paradigmatic"—open up the possibility that it may contribute to *shaping* the disciplines whose practices it claims to describe. By *stigmatized* I mean a scientific practice which enjoys a comparatively low social status, even in the eyes of its own performers. By *pre-paradigmatic* I mean a scientific practice in which there are no "standard ways of doing things". Both stigmatization and pre-paradigmaticity are much more prominent in the social sciences than in the natural sciences. But this fact is not an epistemological necessity, and there are notorious exceptions, such as microeconomics and, arguably, meteorology.

The connection between the two features is not due only to the fact that the impression of confusion given by a pre-paradigmatic practice detracts from its scientific prestige. More important for our purposes, it is due to the fact that a paradigm—a set of standard ways of doing things—may be hindered in its emergence by the stigmatized nature of the practice involved. This point can be clarified with the help of an analogy to the case of a stigmatized dialect. A native speaker of such a dialect is typically confused, not only in the sense that his explicit statements about his competence do not reflect his actual competence—a situation which is by no means restricted to stigmatized dialects—, but also in the sense that even his most concrete judgements become dubious. Stigmatization breeds insecurity, and insecurity prevents the competence from displaying itself in a consistent, reliable fashion.[4] In such a situation, the descriptive linguist may be driven to a prescriptive stance, feeling compelled to assure the native speaker that there is nothing intrinsically wrong or inferior about the way the latter would spontaneously speak and judge. As a result of this "hand-holding" operation, performances may become less erratic, and competence less confused. Similarly, the stigmatization of a scientific practice may generate such insecurity among its practitioners that their intuition will often get muddled.[5] Although this may not prevent things from being done "properly" most of the time, it may well prevent standard ways of doing things from appearing as clearly as they could. In other words, it may keep the scientific practice at a pre-paradigmatic stage.

The import of these remarks is that there is a way in which

this work can be more than just descriptive. In the case of a prestigious, paradigmatic scientific practice, the philosopher of science can have little hope of leaving his mark. Only the scientists themselves, by scrutinizing anomalies and working out alternatives, can effect paradigm shifts. In the case of a stigmatized, pre-paradigmatic scientific practice, however, the philosopher of science is entitled to expect a more significant impact. His systematic descriptions may reveal a network of analogies between areas apparently very remote from one another. In this way, not only can isolated sketches and hesitant allusions be integrated into a consistent whole, but assurance can spread throughout the network. Standard ways of doing things cease to be problematic, and the scientific practice concerned stops looking a mess, both to insiders and to outsiders. A paradigm, in other words, is allowed to emerge.

In such stigmatized disciplines as most of the social sciences, therefore, the philosopher of science may play an important role in shaping scientific practice. This does not require his being prescriptive in any strong sense. He does not need to give arrogant advice nor to develop his own alternative research programmes. In a pre-paradigmatic situation, the *maieutic* impact of his work, its contribution to the birth of a paradigm, stems directly from its descriptive dimension. This point will be illustrated by this book, where the attempt to answer the two grammatical questions asked at the start is indissociably linked to the elaboration of a paradigm. It will be shown how, with the ambition of an underlabourer and the method of a grammarian, the philosopher of science can end up as a midwife.

3. Clarity and charity

The first two sections of the introduction have stated the purposes of this book. On the one hand, the book can be seen as an attempt to answer two distinct "grammatical" questions, the nature of which will be specified in the first two chapters. On the other hand, it can also be seen as an attempt to formulate an evolutionary paradigm for the social sciences—or more precisely, as we shall see, two "evolutionary patterns of explanation". For both purposes, it has seemed more fruitful to look at a wide variety of concrete examples drawn from actual scientific practices, rather than to concentrate on a handful of outworn illustrations for tired philosophers. As an aid to the presentation of the argument or as evidence for its validity, a large number of "classics" and "exemplars" have been borrowed from various social sciences. In many cases, this borrowing has been coupled with a great deal of simplification. Not only did it seem important that readers who were unfamiliar with the field from which the example was taken should be enabled, without too long a digression, to follow the argument. Trimming the examples down to their essentials also seemed a useful way of bringing out most clearly the bare bones of the arguments they contained. Whatever point is made in this work about the simplified versions of the examples can also be made, in principle, about their original, more complex versions. This does not imply, however, that any point which can be made *against* a simple version can also be made against a more complex one. Fairness to the examples used demands this word of caution.

More important is the fact that, in the actual analysis of the examples, I have constantly tried to reconcile two principles: clarity and charity. That *clarity* should count as an important consideration is obvious enough. If the epistemologist's job is one of "parasitic clarification", he is committed to the never-ending task of making clear exactly what scientists mean, what they imply, what they assume, what they exclude. Clarity, however, does not mean reduction to simplistic positivist clichés. The recent literature on explanation, causality, teleology or functions provides a stock of analytical tools which make it easier to be clear without needing to be simple-minded.

The principle of *charity,* on the other hand, forces one to resist a temptation to which those who care about clarity are prone to yield. It demands that apparently unsound aspects of a scientific practice should not be dismissed offhand, but that they should rather be approached in a sympathetic mood. In particular, most of the concrete analyses proposed in the following pages can be seen as attempts to *make sense* of puzzling explanations. This "making sense" will most of the time consist in providing the explanations under consideration with a plausible mechanism. But it may also occasionally consist in exhibiting the logical structure of an explanation, in showing that it can be tested, or that it is free of "ideological bias".

My attempt to reconcile clarity with charity is obviously open to objections on two fronts. Those who think that I give too much weight to charity will wonder why I bother with explanations which they judge inconsistent or exceedingly obscure. Those who find that I give too much weight to clarity, on the other hand, will complain that I flatten or trivialize what is subtle and profound. All I can say to the former, is that I do indeed think that there is something of value in the problematic explanations I examine, although this does not mean that I agree with every one of them, nor even with any of them.[6] If there is something fundamentally wrong with the kind of explanation I consider, it is for the critics to say what it is. And all I can say to those who find that I overemphasize clarity, is that I do indeed think that the reconstruction I propose by way of clarification is the only possible way, or at least the best possible way, of making sense of the explanations examined. If there is anything important in these explanations which my reconstruction is unable to capture, it is for the critics to show what it is.

With these methodological warnings in mind, let us now turn to the two "grammatical" questions which constitute our starting point.

1

The Deep Structure of the Social Sciences

Summary

Chapter 1 presents the first question which this book hopes to help solve: beneath the chaotic appearance of the social sciences, is it possible to reveal an underlying order? (section 4)

This can only be done by focusing on explanation, i.e. the operation by which one answers why-questions about empirical facts (section 5). Explanation is governed by two formal conditions, a condition of causality and a condition of intelligibility. The former asserts that one cannot explain without asserting the existence of a causal link, understood as a production relationship between two facts (section 6). Its fulfilment requires, but does not reduce to, the existence of regularities (section 7). The condition of intelligibility, on the other hand, asserts that one cannot explain an empirical fact without making it intelligible, by suggesting the nature of the mechanism through which it is produced (section 8). In any scientific community, one or several types of mechanisms are recognized as being plausible, and any non-black-box explanation conforms to a pattern of intelligibility defined by one of them (section 9).

In the social sciences, one pattern which is obviously of great importance is the action pattern, defined by reference to the generation of actions on the basis of the agents' subjective situation (section 10). A standard doctrine, here labelled methodological actionalism, claims that all legitimate social-scientific explanations conform to this pattern (section 11). By putting this claim to the test, one can hope to reveal alternative patterns of explanation whose description, together with that of the action pattern, would provide a rough outline of the deep structure of the social sciences (section 12).

4. *Underneath the chaos*

Let us face it. With few local exceptions, the social sciences are very far from presenting the image of a tidy, neatly organized field. The raging conflicts between rival Schools, and the competing claims of overlapping disciplines, reinforce each other in generating an impression of total chaos, which is a headache for students, a nightmare for teachers, a source of despair for textbook writers, and one reason for the scorn of many outsiders.

To be fair, this deplorable situation cannot be ascribed to the lack of attempts to tidy up the house, to order the immensely varied things which are being done by social scientists. Such attempts take two typical forms. On the one hand, one finds systematic surveys which bring together the various existing approaches to social phenomena, as they present themselves. And on the other hand, one finds ambitious frescoes which try to show how the various existing approaches constitute theses and antitheses in a development whose synthesis is provided by the approach which the author of the fresco happens to promote.[1] The trouble with attempts of the first kind, is that they juxtapose the various approaches far more than they connect them together or integrate them into a unified picture. And the trouble with attempts of the second kind is that the legitimatory motivation behind them is so strong that they tend to seriously disfigure the various approaches which they try to fit into their apologetic systems of symmetries.

The unsatisfactory nature of both kinds of attempts may make us doubt the very possibility of revealing what one could call a *deep structure of the social sciences,* an underlying order behind their chaotic appearance. There would be no satisfactory way of truly "articulating" the various approaches, of neatly showing how they differ from each other and complement each other, without doing them violence. Such a scepticism is only warranted, however, if one misplaces the locus of the deep structure, the point at which the articulation of the various approaches can be perceived.

This privileged point is not to be found at the level of the "conceptual frameworks" which the various approaches set up, nor at the level of the "laws" which some of them claim to establish. Nor can it be found in the way in which the various approaches relate to formalization, to empirical verification or to political action. This book's first important claim is that this privileged point can only be found if one focuses on one particular operation which can be called *explanation,* or more precisely on one particular aspect of it, which will be called the *morphology* of explanation. Only in this way can one try to reveal the deep structure of the social sciences without being led to desperation or trickery. Although this claim can gain some plausibility from a demonstration of the central role which explanation plays in relation to other scientific operations, it can only be decisively established or refuted by looking at the fruits of the inquiry it inspires.

5. A privileged operation

One does not need to start such an inquiry with a thorough analysis of the meaning of the term "explanation", as it is used in scientific or everyday language.[2] The operation we are interested in will be called "explanation" because, in actual fact, the term is often used to refer to the operation. But we do not need to assert that, whenever the term is used, the operation is meant. It is therefore as a postulational definition that I state: *explaining an empirical fact x* consists in answering the question "why x ?" in an appropriate way. Taking this for granted, one can then try to spell out the conditions which determine what counts as "appropriate". Before doing so, however, several remarks are required to clarify this definition.

First of all, note that the definition is restricted to the case of empirical facts. With this restriction, I mean to exclude answers to why-questions about epistemic facts (Why do I or should I believe this?) as well as about normative facts (Why should I do this?), which are more aptly called "justifications" than "explanations". And I also want to exclude the case of logical and mathematical facts, where answers to why-questions can be expected to be governed by different rules. But I do *not* mean to exclude facts which are not directly observable. Consequently, I shall consider it perfectly meaningful to speak of empirical facts whose description makes an essential use of theoretical constructs ("theoretical facts"), quantifiers ("universalities" and "existences") or modal operators (possibilities, necessities, causal relationships).

Secondly, the grammatical point of view outlined in the introduction (section 1) implies that the term "appropriate" refers to the implicit rules which govern the practice of scientific communities. Some of these rules may govern the use of the pair "Why?/Because" in all communities in which the latter is used, and could therefore be said to explicate its meaning. Others may be specific to particular communities. But for the grammatical approach to be fruitful, one must in *both* cases be able to assume a reasonable. level of homogeneity within the relevant scientific community.

Thirdly, the answer which the relevant community considers to be the *true* answer must also be regarded as an appropriate answer. But in principle nothing prevents a false answer from being appropriate. Appropriateness, in other words, is broader than truth. It is exclusively concerned with *formal* conditions of acceptability, as opposed to *material* conditions, which refer to the truth or falsity (and perhaps to the verifiability or falsifiability) of the answers provided. Such material conditions are obviously not negligible. But their examination is of no use in the attempt to state the specific features of the operation we are concerned with. Material conditions of acceptability, in other words, play a part in the determination of what counts as the right explanation, or as a scientific explanation, but not of what counts as an explanation.

Fourthly, formal and material conditions of acceptability can both be formulated in an *ontological* mood, as conditions which have to be fulfilled by the world for the answer to the why-question to be acceptable, and in an *epistemic* (or subjectivist) mood, as conditions which have to be fulfilled by the beliefs of the community considered, for the answer to the why-question to be acceptable. *Both* formulations, not only the latter, are compatible with the adoption of the descriptive-grammatical perspective sketched in the introduction. And in both cases, the adoption of such a perspective implies that the set of reconstructed rules provides an answer to a *sociographic* question about the implicit competence which underlies the operation here called "explanation".

Finally, it is worth stressing that the rules or conditions we are concerned with are imposed on what is *meant,* rather than on what is said, when a why-question is answered. This means that the conditions may often be satisfied at the level of what is implied or presupposed in the answer, rather than at the level of what is explicitly asserted.

The primary object of a "grammatical" inquiry focusing on the operation of explanation can now be formulated as follows. We are looking for a set of (necessary and sufficient) conditions which must be fulfilled (explicitly or implicitly) by answers to why-questions about empirical (possibly not observable) facts, if such answers are to be considered as formally acceptable by the community in which they are offered.

Whether self-consciously or not, the problem of specifying this set of conditions—rather than the problem of analyzing the meaning of the word "explanation"—has formed the core of the philosophical discussion about scientific explanation.

6. *Explanation as accusation*

The solution to this problem which I shall adopt, consists in two conditions, which will be briefly introduced in this section and in section 8, respectively. On the one hand, I claim that any explanation, in the sense defined, asserts the existence of a *causal link*. And on the other hand, I claim that any explanation assumes the operation of an *underlying mechanism*. I cannot hope, in a few pages, to defend these two conditions against all possible misunderstandings and objections. I shall only aim to make them sufficiently clear and plausible, by reference to a single example, to be able to use them in the subsequent, more specific discussion. The way in which they are used should then further contribute, I hope, both to clarifying their meaning and to vindicating their validity.

To illustrate the first condition, suppose, for example, that we want to explain the social unrest which affected the capitalist world towards the end of the nineteenth century by the fact that the world's real GNP (roughly, the amount of goods and services produced) was growing much faster than the world money supply (roughly determined, at that time, by the amount of gold produced).[3] What the first condition asserts is that it is impossible to mean this as an answer to a why-question without asserting the existence of a *causal link* between the fact(s) mentioned in the explanation—here, the fact that real growth was faster than monetary growth—and the fact to be explained, as described in the *explanandum*—here, the widespread occurrence of social unrest towards the end of the nineteenth century. Using the etymological connection between "cause" and "accusation," one can also say, more compactly, that explaining an empirical fact necessarily involves *accusing* some other fact(s).

Obviously, this stipulation remains rather vacuous as long as the concept of "causality" is not further analyzed. It is useful to state straight away that the kind of causality concept we need must be general enough in three distinct senses. Firstly, it must be free of "physicalistic" or "mechanistic" connotations. It must be able to accommodate cases where intentions, decisions and actions, for example, play a crucial role in the link which the explanation asserts. In other words, it must not commit us to a particular kind of mechanism. Secondly, it must not be restricted to the case of events. It is crucial to our subsequent discussion, for example, that the presence of a feature (not just the occurrence of an event) can be explained by reference to the presence of another feature. And thirdly, it must not be restricted to the deterministic case. Explanation, in the sense defined, should be possible in situations where the variables involved are not perfectly correlated.

The so-called *Humean* account of causality in terms of regular succession between events constitutes a simple and classic candidate for the analysis we need. It is certainly general enough in the first sense. And, when suitably reformulated, it can also to some extent be made general enough in the other two senses, by being extended to facts which are not events and to statistical regularities. Such an account, however, does not only raise comparatively minor difficulties of formulation (which will be touched upon in the next section). In so far as it claims to capture the nature of the link between an explanandum and the facts by reference to which it is explained, the Humean account also raises a much more fundamental difficulty, which is most clearly illustrated by so-called *twofold-symptom* situations.

Take again the example introduced above. In a Humean interpretation, the causal claim which is being made in the explanation can be restated along the following lines: an insufficient growth in the money supply (relative to the growth of the real GNP) is regularly followed (under certain conditions to be specified) by social unrest. Suppose, however, that (under the same conditions) an insufficient growth in the money supply also causes, and more rapidly, but independently, a swelling of the profits cashed by mining companies. The swelling of these profits (providing it does not arise from any other cause) would then be regularly followed by social unrest throughout the capitalist world, and a Humean would be forced to say that the former causes the latter, just as he is forced to say that one symptom of an illness causes another if they regularly come in sequence. Clearly, while one can safely predict a fact (the second symptom) on the basis of another fact related to it in this way (the first symptom), the same relationship cannot possibly warrant an explanation of that fact, in the sense of an appropriate answer to a why-question about it. Humean causality, therefore, is not strong enough to characterize the general nature of the link between the fact which is being explained and the facts by reference to which it is being explained.[4]

The only real alternative to the Humean account consists in refusing the reduction to regularities which it proposes. Causation can then be paraphrased as *production*, action, influence. And one can state that a fact is causally dependent on another if and only if by modifying the latter, one can affect the former. Such an account of causality is general, firstly in the sense that it can apply to all kinds of facts, not just to events, secondly in the sense that it does not imply anything about the nature of the underlying mechanism, and thirdly in the sense that it can easily be extended to cover probabilistic influences. At the same time, it is narrow enough to prevent twofold-symptom relationships from being causal: the first symptom does not bring about the second one. It may well be, therefore, that this "production" analysis of causality adequately captures the nature of the link whose existence is asserted in any explanation. But one can challenge the claim that it actually provides an *analysis* of the concept in more than a purely circular way: a clarification of what is meant by such terms as "produce", "affect", "bring about" would soon lead us back to causality.[5]

This is not to say, however, that such an explication of "causality" in terms of "production" and related concepts is useless as a way of clarifying the meaning of "causal". Indeed, I shall consider the concept of causality to be sufficiently disambiguated by such paraphrases for us to be able to formulate our first condition as follows, without much risk of being misunderstood. Any explanation asserts the existence of a causal link, in the sense that the fact to be explained is brought about by the other fact(s) mentioned in the explanation. In other words, any explanation is an accusation, in the sense that it ascribes to the facts it mentions some part in the production of the fact it explains. I shall call *logic of explanation* the study of the various ways in which this condition is fulfilled.

7. *Where regularities come in*

Even if Humeans are wrong, as argued above, about what the causal claim made by any explanation *means,* they may still be right about what, in such a claim, can be *tested*—and they would consequently be right about its meaning too, if we were unable to mean something that could not be tested. Regular successions, in other words, may well be closely connected to causal claims ("productively" interpreted), in the sense that the latter's validity can only be established (or refuted) by observing (or failing to observe) the former.

That we should be interested in regular *successions* follows from the fact that production, influence, etc. is bound to take some time, however short. Nevertheless, whereas the very notion of production excludes backward causation, we may well sometimes be willing to allow simultaneous causation, at least in the case of persistent features, not in the case of events. Two sets of situations in which we may be willing to do so are particularly important for our purposes. We may want to say that there is an (admittedly very special) causal dependence, on the one hand, between a dispositional feature of a set-up and an underlying categorical (or non-dispositional) one, and, on the other hand, between the equilibrium state of a system (or of its endogenous variables) and the values taken by its parameters (or exogenous variables). Both kinds of situations will be abundantly illustrated in subsequent chapters.

Thus the fact to be explained may be posterior to (as always in the case of events) or simultaneous with (as sometimes in the case of persistent features) the facts adduced in its explanation. But in either case—and at least as long as the exact nature of the underlying mechanism is not specified—the only way of checking the existence of a causal link is to look for *regularities*. This connection between causal claims and the commitment to the existence of some regularities can be highlighted by examining the *counterfactual* implications of our "production" concept of causality. Although the ability to support counterfactuals cannot characterize causal claims uniquely—it is also associated with other law-like statements, for example of an analytic or "two-gold symptom" kind—it is certainly an important feature of any such claim.[6]

If I say, for example, that the social unrest at the end of the nineteenth century was brought about by a gap between real and monetary growth, I am committed to the following counterfactual claim. Suppose that the situation were unchanged, except for the absence of both social unrest and the gap between real and monetary growth. Then, if such a gap were to arise, social unrest would follow. Consequently, we can often loosely, but usefully, paraphrase as follows the accusation of fact A for fact B: if fact A is or were present, fact B will or would be present as well. The ideal test of such a claim is obviously experimental. If experiment is impossible, one can resort to the observation of other, sufficiently similar situations and check whether the increase in the gap between real and monetary growth is actually followed by social unrest. Whether we use observation or experiment, however, we are recording regularities, and not "production" itself. This brings out the valid core of the Humean account.

It must be stressed here that, even when the causal claim takes a very simple form, the regularities implied may be very complex indeed. An explanation which mentions a single fact does not imply that this fact can on its own bring about the fact to be explained. First of all, explanations are often requested with a *contrast class* in mind, which shares a number of background conditions with the situation we want to explain. We may want to know, for example, why social unrest arose at the end and not, say, in the middle of the nineteenth century, when working conditions were no better. An appropriate answer to this why-question does not involve enumerating all the background conditions shared by the situation at hand and the contrast class. It rather consists in pointing to crucial differences between the two situations. This is why the explanation proposed refers to the rate of growth of the money supply, and not to working conditions in factories. Secondly, even bearing these shared background conditions in mind, one does not need to claim that the fact mentioned in the explanation is sufficient to produce the fact to be explained. Other conditions may be required, which we may not realize until we are faced with counterexamples. Someone may point out, for example, that there are situations which share all the relevant background conditions with both the situation we want to explain and with our contrast class, but in which there is no social unrest in spite of a large gap between real and monetary growth. This clearly means that the simple regularity suggested is false, and we shall have to correct it by introducing further variables, such as, say, the "degree of maturity" of working-class consciousness. But it does not need to mean that our original explanation was false, although it must then be seen as an *explanation sketch*, which can be filled in with a (possibly long) list of additional differences between the situation to be explained and the contrast class.[7]

What the previous paragraph suggests is that the regularity

implied is often only very elliptically suggested, and that it is often not clear what must count as an "otherwise unchanged" or "sufficiently similar" situation in the experimental or observational test of a causal claim. However, if our concept of causality has the counterfactual implications mentioned above, one cannot escape the conclusion that some regularity, however complex, is implied. Together with a description of the fact referred to (explicitly or implicitly) in the explanation, the statement of the regularity implied entails the explanandum. This indicates the valid core in the deductivist (or "deductive-nomological") account of explanation. Like the Humean conception of causation, with which it is closely associated, it does not catch the full force of the causal claim contained in any explanation. But it correctly spells out some of its implications. The deducibility of the explanandum, in our perspective, is only a by-product of the presence of a causal claim. And it could not have been introduced separately as a weaker requirement (to be complemented by another requirement dealing with whatever there is in causality which is not reducible to deducibility) because the validity of deductive arguments cannot always be determined independently of the assumptions made about the nature, causal or otherwise, of the regularities asserted in the premises.[8]

8. Explanation as causal understanding

In section 6, I have briefly introduced the claim that one cannot explain without accusing. And we have just seen, in section 7, how this claim is related to the weaker, orthodox condition, which stipulates, roughly, that any explanation must provide a deduction from a regularity. I shall argue, however, that even the stronger condition—explanation is accusation—is not strong enough to capture what is needed for an answer to a why-question to be (formally) appropriate. One needs a second, complementary condition, which can be formulated as follows: one cannot explain without understanding.

To illustrate this point, let us return to our example: social unrest broke out towards the end of the nineteenth century because the world's real GNP was growing much faster than the world's money supply. To the layman at least, the mechanism (if any) through which the latter fact is supposed to exert its causal action on social unrest is rather obscure. As long as the nature of the underlying mechanism is left unspecified, our explanation remains a (clearly not fully satisfactory) *black-box explanation*. One way of expressing our dissatisfaction with explanations of this kind consists in saying that they are mere accusations, not genuine explanations. As an accusation, a black-box explanation can be made very plausible by accumulating overwhelming evidence to the effect that an insufficient growth in the money supply is systematically followed by social unrest. But, however impressive the evidence, as long as one does not say *how* the money supply's failure to grow fast enough can generate social unrest, one does not really answer the why-question, because the fact to be explained is not rendered intelligible.

A mere accusation, however, can be transformed into a genuine explanation by the specification of a plausible mechanism. In this case, one can imagine the following story.[9] If the world's money supply (represented, under a gold-standard system, by the world's stock of gold) grows much more slowly than the mass of commodities whose circulation it is supposed to secure, then (with an unchanged velocity of circulation of money), prices and wages, expressed in money terms, must fall substantially. Falling money wages (even with falling prices) breed resentment, encourage labour militancy and so generate social unrest. It is only when such a scenario is provided—or tacitly taken for granted, if it is obvious enough—that the relevant scientific community feels comfortable enough with the accusation made, to consider it a genuine explanation, possibly false but formally appropriate.

When formulating the additional condition illustrated in this example as a condition of *intelligibility*, or when stipulating that one cannot explain without *understanding*, it is important to be clear about which sense of "understanding" is meant. For the term "understanding" is commonly used to denote very different operations. It may refer to the *hermeneutic* understanding of a sentence, a text, a gesture or an action, through the discovery of the meaning it expresses. Or it may refer to the *globalizing* understanding of, say, a historical process or a society, through grasping the "unifying principle" which lies behind its outward appearance. The kind of "understanding" which we are interested in here, rather consists in imagining a plausible mechanism through which the empirical fact to be explained is brought about, produced, caused. And I therefore suggest that we call it *causal* understanding.[10]

Variants of the "dual" conception of explanation— sketched here in terms of causality and (causal) intelligibility—can be found in the writings of many recent philosophers of science. On the one hand, those whom we could call "historicists" have emphasized that genuine explanations must not, or must not only, point out causes or regularities. Explanation rather consists in making reality intelligible, and what counts as "intelligible" in a scientific community is historically variable.[11] Those who call themselves "realists", on the other hand, insist that genuine explanations must specify the nature of the generative mechanism through which the fact to be explained is being produced. Proposing an explanation, in their view, essentially involves an ontological claim about the existence or operation of such real mechanisms.[12] The two schools may differ from each other by the mood, epistemic or ontological (in the language of section 5), in which they tend to express themselves. But, as has been pointed out above, there is a close connection between intelligibility and mechanism. To the extent that both schools claim to deal with the same "descriptive" question about the implicit rules which actually govern scientific practices, therefore, the historicist and realist versions of the claim that causality, if relevant at all, is not enough for explanation, can be considered as roughly equivalent.

Whatever formulation is adopted, however, the "dual" conception of explanation is open to the objection that it does not provide the only way of capturing a scientific community's intuition that "black-box explanations" are not quite satisfactory. It is perfectly possible to admit the epistemological (not just psychological) desirability of causal intelligibility in the sense indicated, without making it a condition for explanation. In particular, it is possible to argue that a large number of black-box theories—from Newtonian mechanics to behaviourist psychology—have been persistently used by scientific communities to provide answers to why-questions. One can concede that such answers are not as "full", as "deep", as satisfactory as they would be if the underlying mechanism were specified, while maintaining that they are nevertheless formally appropriate, and therefore explanations in our sense. [13]

I do not think that an appeal to a scientific community's intuition is sufficient to discriminate between the two rival reconstructions of the underlying competence, between the claim that "black-box explanations" are not genuine explanations—they do not *really* tell us why the facts are what they are—and the claim that they are just not satisfactory explanations—they really tell us why the facts are what they are, but in a somewhat defective way. As I find the former reconstruction slightly more convenient, I shall adopt it here. But nothing in what follows hinges on this choice, and those who prefer the latter reconstruction should feel perfectly comfortable if they keep interpreting my "accusations" as their "explanations" and my "explanations" as their "satisfactory explanations". The important point, which can be expressed in both perspectives, is that the explanatory practice of scientific communities is not just governed by a condition of causality, but also by a condition of intelligibility in the sense indicated. For reasons which will become clear in the next section, I shall call *morphology* of explanation the study of the ways in which this second condition is fulfilled.

9. *Patterns of intelligibility*

As long as our condition of intelligibility is formulated at the general level at which it has been discussed in the previous section, it may be doubted whether, in practice, it really adds anything to our condition of causality. To assert the existence of a causal mechanism of some sort, loosely defined as a structured sequence of events, seems hardly more restrictive than to assert the existence of an (abstractly defined) causal link. For the condition of intelligibility to be met, however, it is crucial that the suggested mechanism should be considered *plausible* by the scientific community in which the explanation is proposed. And in any given scientific community, only certain *types* of mechanisms are considered plausible. We could therefore rephrase our condition of intelligibility as demanding that any explanation should conform to one of the legitimate *patterns of intelligibility*, each of them defined by a type of mechanism recognized as plausible in the scientific community concerned. Requiring conformity to a particular pattern of intelligibility—defined, say, by molecular interaction or natural selection—does definitely add something to the mere requirement of a causal link.

Such patterns of intelligibility play a very important role in shaping both the "empirical" and the "theoretical" aspects of scientific practice. As far as empirical analysis is concerned, they operate as sifting devices. Among innumerable possible candidates, they indicate which variables should be picked out to be controlled, experimentally or statistically, in order to bring out existing causal links and regularities. And in the process of interpreting observed regularities, they determine where the analysis is allowed to stop: they are what enables us to discriminate between relationships which can safely be considered meaningful and relationships whose presumed spuriousness must be disclosed by further analysis.

The theoretical component of scientific practice, on the other hand, essentially consists in articulating particular patterns of intelligibility. Although a fully elaborated (micro) theory is not necessary for the condition of intelligibility to be fulfilled, it is true that whenever a (micro) theory from which the postulated causal link can be derived is available, the explanandum, ipso facto, is made intelligible. This brings out the grain of truth in the deductivists' suggestion that "depth" or "fullness" of explanation is just a matter of second-order deducibility: an explanation can be made "deeper" or "fuller" by deducing from a "theory" the regularity with the help of which the initial explanandum has been deduced. But it is important to note, firstly, that this is only valid if a "theory" is not conceived as any old generalization or set of generalizations, but as one which articulates a pattern of intelligibility; and, secondly, that very often, especially in historical disciplines, why-questions are answered in a fully satisfactory way without there being any explicit "theory" from which the implied (but often unknown) regularity can be deduced.

It is now clear that the central task of the morphology of explanation—the study of the ways in which the intelligibility condition is fulfilled—consists in investigating the nature of the various patterns of intelligibility which various scientific communities consider legitimate. And it is also clear that such an investigation provides a criterion for the classification of all explanations—all accusations for which a mechanism is specified—according to the *pattern* to which they conform. What will count as different patterns of intelligibility (or of explanation) obviously depends on what one wants to consider as different types of mechanisms. For a meaningful typology of mechanisms to be possible, one need not assume that there is an absolute basis—for example a set of absolutely elementary mechanisms—which would enable us to construct a fully "objective" classification. Types of mechanisms should rather be defined in terms of *constellations* of more elementary mechanisms—for example, heredity + mutations + recombinations + natural selection—which are routinely assumed in the explanations proposed by a scientific community.

Nevertheless, it is the central claim of this chapter that a "morphological" classification of explanations, an inventory of the legitimate patterns to which they conform, gives the key to the "deep structure" of science in general, and of the social sciences in particular. Admittedly, the logic of explanation—the study of the ways in which explanations fulfil our condition of causality—also provides a criterion of classification. Explanations can be classified according to the *form* which the causal claim takes: from a system of differential equations to a historical narrative, from equilibrium laws to regression analyses. However, although the frequencies with which various forms of explanation, in this sense, are used by different disciplines and by different approaches to a discipline, may vary considerably, each form can, in principle, be found in every one of them, and explanations of very different forms can often easily be seen to imply or directly suggest each other. This is not the case with *patterns* of explanation, which are much more narrowly confined to particular disciplines or approaches, and which differ from each other in such a way that explanations which conform to different patterns cannot possibly imply or directly suggest one another. Consequently, a "morphological" classification cal" classification, as far as our attempt to reveal the "deep structure of science" is concerned. In particular, it is much more likely to provide us with the privileged vantage point from which the social sciences can cease to look a mess.

10. The action pattern

The discussion so far has remained at such an abstract level that nothing has been said which is not claimed to apply equally to all empirical sciences, whether natural or social. The rules which govern explanation, as defined in section 5, have been specified firstly in terms of a condition of causality (sections 6–7), and secondly in terms of a condition of intelligibility (sections 8–9). But it has just been suggested that the classification of explanations connected with this second condition provides us with what we need to tackle the problem with which we started, the question of the "deep structure" of the social sciences. Consequently, we must now lower the level of abstraction and examine more specifically which patterns of intelligibility govern the practice of the social sciences.

Even a casual look at the latter reveals that there is one pattern which is of paramount importance. I shall call it the *action pattern* and define it by the class of mechanisms which generate an action on the basis of the subjective situation of an agent. One can distinguish elementary and complex instances of this pattern and, among elementary instances, "pure", "degenerate" and "intermediate" cases.

In the *pure* case, the agent's action is the subjectively rational outcome of a decision process, which can conveniently be described in the terminology of decision theory. In the course of the decision process, the agent considers a set of alternatives, ascribes consequences to them, orders these consequences according to his preferences, and performs an optimal choice among available alternatives. The optimality principle which guides the choice—utility maximization, probability-weighted utility maximization or maximization of minimum utility—depends on whether the agent can associate with each alternative one particular consequence (certainty), a distribution of subjective probabilities over a set of alternative consequences (risk), or just a set of possible consequences (uncertainty). Whenever a particular action is explained in terms of reasons or motives, in terms of means and ends, or in terms of the "logic of the situation", the explanation can, in principle, be translated into this decision-theoretical language. And it can therefore be said to constitute a pure instance of the action pattern.

In the *degenerate* case, at the other extreme, the agent's action is the mere execution of a programme he has learned. As the set of (perceived) available alternatives is here reduced to a single element, one cannot conveniently speak of "decision" or "deliberation". In most cases, the "programme" can be formulated as a set of rules. Role analysis, the explanation of linguistic or ritual performance by the corresponding competence, accounts of social practices in terms of "class habitus" all exemplify this degenerate case of the action pattern.

Between these two extremes, there is room for a continuum of cases where more than one alternative is subjectively available, but where the decision process does not conform to the rationalistic model of pure optimization, but rather to what H. A. Simon has called a *satisficing* model. Typically, the agent examines a small subject of the alternatives he knows are available. He roughly estimates their consequences. And if one of the alternatives considered has consequences which he finds satisfactory, he chooses it. If not, he keeps considering more alternatives until he finds a satisfactory one. And this may not be possible unless he adjusts his aspiration level. From chess playing to mate selection, this picture of the process by which a course of action is selected is often more realistic than both extreme cases. The latter, however, have the advantage of picking out (in general) a single course of action as *the* utility-maximizing or rule-abiding one, whereas the intermediate model, by giving a crucial role to the search process, leaves (in general) a wide margin of indeterminacy.

In all these cases, a human action is explained by reference to the subjective situation of the agent. In most social-scientific explanations, however, the explanandum does not describe a single individual action, but rather a complex social phenomenon—for example social unrest at the end of the nineteenth century—, which is to be explained by reference to another complex social phenomenon—for example a gap between real and monetary growth. Such complex explanations can also be accommodated by the action pattern, to the extent that the mechanism whose operation they assume consists solely in aggregating elementary action-generation mechanisms. Among complex instances of the action pattern, some are systematically articulated by such theories as micro-economic theory in the case of market models and game theory in the case of conflict models. Most of them, however, are informal, in the sense that they form no part of any explicit theory.

I shall call *actional explanation* any explanation which conforms to the action pattern, whether simple or complex, pure or degenerate, informal or theoretically articulated.

11. *Methodological actionalism and cognates*

As defined in the previous section, the action pattern of explanation obviously covers a very large number of social-scientific explanations. It accommodates very easily, for example, any explanation of a social fact as the unintended consequence of the intentional actions of a large number of individual agents, which is often cited as the "paradigmatic" type of (good) social-scientific explanation. Not surprisingly, this has led many authors to claim that the action pattern is the only (legitimate) pattern of intelligibility in the social sciences. In so far as it is meant to be a descriptively adequate reconstruction of social-scientific explanatory competence, I shall call this claim *methodological actionalism*. Max Weber, for instance, in a language easily translatable into ours, states that "causal explanations" must fulfil two conditions, which he calls "causal adequacy" and "meaning adequacy": they must be based on an observable regularity and also be interpretable in action terms.[14]

Other authors have tried to formulate the same intuition by proposing alternative, narrower versions of the actionalist claim. Popper and his followers demand that social-scientific explanations be expressed in terms of "logic of the situation".[15] Homans and other social-exchange theorists maintain that satisfactory explanations of social phenomena must be derivable from fundamental propositions which, in Skinnerian terms, express a principle of rationality.[16] Others have suggested that the social sciences can and should be integrated on the basis of a theory of rational choice.[17] Whatever the language used, these various positions tend to restrict their attention to the "pure" case of the action pattern, i.e. to deliberate decisions rather than, say, the performance of a programme. I shall therefore interpret them as different variants of *methodological rationalism*, which implies methodological actionalism without being implied by it.

Methodological psychologism, on the other hand, can be introduced as a more liberal doctrine, which is implied by methodological actionalism without implying it. All it claims is that all satisfactory explanations in the social sciences assume some sort of psychological mechanism, whether or not it is of the action-generation type.[18] Finally, *methodological individualism* is the (apparently) even weaker claim that the underlying mechanism operates on the level of the individuals involved, whether or not it operates through their minds.[19] This claim remains stronger than the mere assertion that all social-scientific explanations fulfil our condition of intelligibility, because the mechanism which one needs to specify in order to fulfil this condition may conceivably operate on the level of social groups, rather than on the level of their individual members.

All these claims are potential components of the morphology of explanation in the social sciences. They constitute hypotheses about the condition which an accusation needs to meet in order to be considered a genuine explanation (or a "full" explanation, if one wants to make room for the possibility of a real answer to a why-question which leaves the mechanism unspecified). When ordered according to increasing strength, they state that all genuine (or "full") social-scientific explanations assume the operation (1) of some sort of mechanism (condition of intelligibility), (2) of a mechanism operating through individuals (methodological individualism), (3) of a psychological mechanism (methodological psychologism), (4) of some sort of action-generation mechanism (methodological actionalism), and (5) of a mechanism which consists ultimately in rational decisions (methodological rationalism). Note that none of these propositions is concerned with imposing conditions on the nature of the facts which must be explained or on the nature of the facts by which they must be explained. Consequently, however strict the condition it imposes on the underlying mechanism, each of them is perfectly compatible with the Durkheimian maxim that a social fact must be explained by another social fact.

12. Exploring a residue

One might want to systematically test the descriptive adequacy of each of the five propositions listed in the previous paragraph. In what follows, however, I shall take it for granted that the first proposition is correct, bearing in mind the reservations expressed above (at the end of section 8) about making intelligibility a condition for "genuine" explanations, rather than just for "satisfactory" ones. I shall also take it for granted that the fifth proposition, methodological rationalism, is incorrect: the very description of the action pattern (in section 10) presupposes that it is refuted. I shall consequently focus on the remaining three propositions. Are there social-scientific explanations which do not conform to the action pattern? And, if so, do they assume another type of psychological mechanism or a non-psychological one? Do they assume another type of individualistic mechanism or a holistic one? Providing the answer to the first of these three questions is in the affirmative—i.e. providing the action pattern leaves an irreducible residue—, the investigation of the other two should provide us with a rough outline of what I have called the "deep structure of the social sciences", i.e. with a rough characterization of the explanation patterns which the social sciences use. The detailed structure of each of the patterns would still have to be explored. But this exploration could then take place on the background of a known landscape.

Admittedly, it follows from what has been said previously that some aspects of the social sciences will be left out of the picture. For instance, because black-box explanations, or mere accusations, fail to fulfil our condition of intelligibility, there is no way of fitting them in, unless they are reinterpreted by reading into them the assumption of a particular kind of mechanism. It is possible to argue, however, that pure black-box explanations have a very shaky and loose status as long as no such reinterpretation has allocated them a place in the body of social-scientific knowledge.

More importantly, a substantial part of what bears the label "social science" may not be in the least bit concerned with the explanation of social phenomena. As was briefly suggested above (section 8), the form of understanding it seeks may be "globalizing" rather than causal. And "globalizing" understanding cannot by any means be seen as an auxiliary operation for explanation. It seems impossible to make sense of the bulk of Parsons', Luhmann's or Touraine's sociological theories, for example, if one restricts the purpose of the "social sciences" to the answering of why-questions about empirical phenomena. If one is reluctant to reject such theories as sheer nonsense, it is crucial to broaden the purpose of the "social sciences" in such a way that it includes the task of constructing all-embracing, unified pictures of society and/or history. Here again, however, it can plausibly be argued that this important aspect of the social sciences which is left out of the picture I shall try to draw, must indeed be left out. For sociological theories which aim at a unifying understanding of reality share with philosophical theories a totalitarian ambition which makes them unsuitable for being fitted into any larger construction. A discipline which is made up of such theories cannot have any more of a "deep structure" than the history of philosophy.

For these reasons, a description of the patterns of intelligibility under which social-scientific explanations fall, can justifiably be said to provide an outline of the deep structure of the social sciences. More specifically, granted the central importance of the action pattern, the crucial task consists in testing the descriptive adequacy of methodological actionalism, by systematically exploring the potential residue.

One way of expressing the aim of this book is by saying that it attempts to take one step in this direction. As we shall see, it does not claim to offer a complete map of the peripheral explanation patterns which cover this residue. But it claims to give a well-founded and unambiguously affirmative answer to the question of whether there are such patterns, and to analyze the most significant one among them.

Before embarking on our exploration, however, we need to find a useful starting point. For reasons which will shortly become clear, a promising one is provided by a particular form of explanation which I shall call "function explanation". One *prima facie* reason why this should constitute a good starting point can be expressed as follows. On the one hand, function explanations are frequently used by social scientists —not only by so-called "functionalists", but to no lesser extent by "structuralists", "Marxists", "interactionists" and many others. On the other hand, their use is often criticized on methodological grounds, precisely by the proponents of such doctrines as methodological actionalism or methodological individualism. However, this debate around the legitimacy of function explanations is important in its own right, quite apart from its connection with the question of the deep structure of the social sciences. And it therefore provides us with an alternative way into the rest of this book.

2

The Legitimacy of Function Explanations

Summary

Chapter 2 presents the second question which this book hopes to help solve: how is it possible for function statements to be explanatory in the social sciences? As far as the nature of the postulated *causal link* is concerned, this problem is solved by showing that function explanations, like other consequence explanations, causally ascribe the presence of an item, not to its consequences, but to a dispositional property of the situation in which it appears (section 13).

As far as the nature of the underlying *mechanism* is concerned, the solution of this problem requires an analysis of what distinguishes a function explanation from other consequence explanations (section 14). The traditional view singles out a reference to the *welfare* of some entity as the crucial distinguishing feature: the function of an item is its contribution to the survival or proper working of the entity of which the item is a part (section 15). Function explanations, if one adopts this view, can only be legitimated if one can assume the operation of cybernetic mechanisms. But cybernetic mechanisms only enable us to make sense of very few function explanations, and of many consequence explanations which are not function explanations (section 16).

As an alternative to the traditional view, one can point out that typical function explanations are concerned with explaining the presence of *persistent* features rather than events (section 17), by reference to consequences which are *good* according to some criterion and whose "goodness" matters to the explanation (section 18). Explanations of this sort can only be legitimated by reference to optimization mechanisms, and more precisely, if one leaves aside the possibility of omniscient agents, mechanisms of local optimization (section 19). These mechanisms, which can be called evolutionary, are processes of trial-and-error in which the criterion of selection makes reference to the consequences associated with the various alternatives (section 20). Whether such mechanisms operate in the social realm is not only relevant to the question of whether function explanations are legitimate in the social sciences; in so far as evolutionary mechanisms can legitimate latent-functional, and not only manifest-functional, explanations, it is also relevant to the question of whether all legitimate social-scientific explanations conform to the action pattern (section 21).

13. *The logical-mistake argument*

Chapter 1 took as its point of departure the chaotic appearance of the social sciences. This chapter starts with the apparently problematic status of one particular kind of claim which is often made in the social sciences. This kind of claim, which has been at the centre of the long methodological debate on "functionalism", often takes the form of statements which ascribe a function to some item, for example: "The function of religious ritual is to maintain social cohesion" or "The function of the capitalist State is to protect the long-run interests of the bourgeoisie". I shall call such statements *function statements*. Some statements in which the word "function" occurs—for example "The suicide rate is a function of the degree of anomie"—are clearly not function statements in this sense. And other statements in which the term does not occur—for example "The role of ritual is to maintain cohesion"—may be assimilated to function statements, to the extent that they can be accurately translated into canonic function statements of the kind exemplified above. Very often, if not always, such function statements are made by social scientists with the clear intention of *explaining,* or of contributing to explaining, the item's presence. Radcliffe-Brown (1952, 152), to quote just one example, laid much emphasis on the distinction between "accidental results" of rituals and beliefs and "their essential function and the ultimate reason for their existence". When a function statement carries such an explanatory claim, I shall speak, by definition, of a *function explanation.* [1]

The question with which this chapter is concerned can then simply be formulated as follows. Are function explanations legitimate? Does it make sense to answer a why-question with a function statement? If the analysis presented in the preceding chapter is correct, this question has two components. As far as the logic of explanation is concerned, one must inquire into the nature of the *causal link* whose existence is asserted by a function explanation. As far as the morphology of explanation is concerned, one must inquire into the nature of the *mechanism* whose operation is assumed when a function explanation is proposed. The first component of the question will be dealt with in this section, and the second in the rest of this chapter.

The logic of function explanations, at first sight, is paradoxical. Whatever else one may mean when ascribing a function to some item, it is generally clear that one is pointing out some (actual) consequences of the item's presence—at least if one is willing to use the term "presence" in a generic fashion to cover cases where such terms as "performance", "activity", "functioning", "use", "occurrence", etc. would be more appropriate. There may be some cases where the consequences pointed out are expected or intended consequences, rather than actual ones. For example, one may want to say that the function of university lectures is to facilitate the absorption of knowledge by students, even if no one believes them to have any degree of success in this respect. However, such uses of the term can be safely discarded as "deviant" or, at least, as "marginal".[2] I shall therefore accept that the statement

(1) The function of i is c,

implies the assertion that the presence (or occurrence etc.) of *c* results from the presence (or occurrence etc.) of *i*, or

(2) i's presence → c's presence,

where → denotes a causal link (as characterized in sections 6–7). Any function statement, in other words, is a consequence statement about it, any function explanation is a consequence explanation.[3]

Now, what is sometimes called the *logical mistake argument* claims that there is something intrinsically inconsistent about explaining a fact by reference to its consequences.[4] The argument can be stated as follows. Any explanation, as we have seen above (section 6), asserts the causal dependence of the fact to be explained on the fact by which it is being explained. It asserts, in other words, that the former is an (empirical) consequence of the latter. But in a function explanation, as we have just seen, the fact by reference to which one explains is also a consequence of the fact to be explained. Therefore, unless we allow for backward causation (which was excluded in section 7), there seems to be a basic flaw in any attempt to explain by pointing out consequences. And if this is so, the legitimacy of function explanations is shaken at the level of their very logic.

Fortunately, there is a very simple way of getting round this objection. When one claims to explain an item's presence *by reference to* some of its consequences, the fact *by which* one claims to explain the item's presence is *not* the occurrence of its consequences. It is rather the fact that, should the item be present, its presence would have these consequences. And this fact, unlike the occurrence of the consequences, is a fact about the situation prior to (or in some cases simultaneous with) the item's presence. If *i*, *c* and → stand for the item, its consequences and the causal link, respectively, the structure of the explanations in question is given by:

(3) (i's presence → c's presence) → i's presence.

For example, if one explains the existence of religious ritual by reference to its consequence of maintaining social cohesion, the causal claim implied is not that the ritual's presence is produced by the cohesion it produces. It is rather that the ritual's presence is produced by the fact that (the situation is such that) if it is or were present, it will or would produce cohesion.[5] The fact by which the item's presence is explained is not the presence of its consequences, but a *dispositional property* of the situation, whose display condition is the presence of the item.[6]

As soon as this point is fully realized, the "logical mistake" argument collapses, and the paradox with which we started vanishes. As far as the logic of explanation is concerned, there is nothing illegitimate about function explanations.

14. *Function statements and consequence explanations*

We can now turn to the second, less trivial, component of our initial question: what sort of mechanism is assumed to operate when a function explanation is proposed? If the assumed mechanism is deemed plausible, the legitimacy of function explanations is not problematic. If it is not, function explanations could only claim the shaky status of mere accusations. The question of the nature of the mechanisms assumed can only be answered fully by proceeding "inductively", i.e. by analysing what is asserted and assumed in concrete instances —which will be attempted in the following chapters. In this chapter, however, I shall proceed "deductively" and try to specify *a priori* the formal features which any mechanism which can legitimate a function explanation must possess.

Clearly, the cornerstone of such a "deduction" can only be the use which is made of the term "function", whether in scientific or in everyday language. And one may question the wisdom of choosing such a shaky starting point. Not only must the use of the term be sufficiently homogeneous (and uncorrupted by philosophical discussion) to allow a precise analysis, but above all, if this analysis is to be fruitful in the present context, the term must also be used in such a way that function explanations constitute a sufficiently homogeneous class, as far as underlying mechanisms are concerned. However dubious this may seem *a priori,* I shall work on the assumption that the set of function statements is homogeneous enough in this respect. I shall assume, in other words, that it is not "by chance" that, among all possible consequence explanations, function explanations have played such a conspicuous role in scientific practice and in methodological debates. By examining what the use of the word "function" implies, it is possible to arrive at a broad characterization of the type of mechanism which is needed (under some plausible assumptions) to legitimate any particular function explanation.

It is clear, in this perspective, that the analysis of "function" will not be conducted for its own sake.[7] The difference between *typical* function statements and other consequence statements is rather used as a useful clue for the specification of the set of mechanisms which are in principle capable of legitimating function explanations. Consequently, I need offer no apologies for occasionally being somewhat ruthless in discarding counterexamples as "marginal" or "deviant". In trying to clarify the common core of meaning in all typical uses of the word "function", I do not attempt to find a firm basis on which to build the subsequent arguments. But it is interesting to see how the common features of the set of mechanisms which will be explored in the following chapters in connection with specific function explanations can be derived from what is typically meant by the word "function".

In the following sections, I shall briefly review the traditional discussion on function explanation as an attempt to provide an analogous derivation (sections 15–16), and then propose an alternative point of view (sections 17–20). Before doing so, however, I need to say a few words about the so-called *etiological* analysis of function statements, which has been implicitly rejected in the previous discussion.[8]

It has already been argued (in the previous section) that function statements are consequence statements. Not all consequence statements, on the other hand, are function statements. The destruction of a town may be the result of an earthquake, for example, but it does not follow that the *function* of the earthquake is to destroy the town. Consequently, it makes sense to investigate what distinguishes function statements from other consequence statements. But such an investigation can only be of some use to the attempt to discover something specific about function *explanations*—in particular, what kind of mechanisms they are bound to presuppose—if function statements are not just consequence explanations. Now, the central claim of the etiological analysis of function statements is precisely that function statements are just explanatory (or at least "accusatory") consequence statements. What it adds to *(2)* in the explication of *(1)* is precisely *(3)*.

This kind of analysis has repeatedly been attacked both on the grounds that it is too strong and on the grounds that it is too weak. On the one hand, it is argued that there are function statements which are clearly not meant to explain the presence of the item to which they ascribe a function. When Moore and Tumin (1949) speak of the "social functions of ignorance", for example, or Kuhn (1963) about the "function of dogma in scientific research", in no way do they claim to tell us *why* ignorance exists or *why* scientists are dogmatic. Similarly, it is generally recognized that function statements in physiology do not carry any explanatory connotation in the strong sense of the word.[9] However, one could possibly dismiss such counterexamples as "marginal". And in any case, it does not matter for our purposes whether function statements, when they are function explanations (and therefore consequence explanations) are so by virtue of their meaning or not. I shall assume that they are not, but nothing in what follows hinges on this assumption.

What does matter for our purposes is that the etiological view is too weak. It is important, in other words, that not all explanatory consequence statements should be function statements. Otherwise, concentrating on "functions", as opposed to "mere consequences", would be of no use in our attempt to narrow down the range of relevant mechanisms. Consequence explanations which are clearly not function explanations fall into two main categories, which can be illustrated by the following two examples. Firstly, suppose a pendulum is pushed in such a way that it is displaced from its equilibrium position of minimum potential energy. The pendulum then finds itself in a situation in which returning to its initial position would have the result of restoring equilibrium, and this is what explains the pendulum's return. In other words:

(4) (pendulum's return → restoration of equilibrium)
→ pendulum's return.

Secondly, suppose a particular country is plagued with terrorism, that terrorism breeds repression, and that this repression is what keeps terrorism alive, by unwittingly feeding it with a constant flow of defensible pretexts. Somewhat elliptically, one could then say:

(5) (terrorism → repression) → terrorism.

Both examples undoubtedly satisfy conditions (2) and (3) imposed by the etiological analysis. Nevertheless, it would sound rather strange to say that the *function* of the pendulum's return is to restore equilibrium, or that the *function* of terrorism is to generate repression—at least if one bears in mind the scenario sketched above.[10]

One could argue, admittedly, that speaking of "functions" in such cases is at least conceivable, although everyone is likely to agree that doing so would not provide us with "typical" uses of the term. As will be argued below (sections 17–20), failing to distinguish between such statements and typical function statements would make us miss a precious clue about the specific nature of the mechanisms which function statements must presuppose, when they are meant to be explanatory. Before showing this in detail, let us turn briefly to the traditional debate on so-called "functionalism", which demonstrates how picking out the wrong clue can make function explanations look much more problematic than they actually are.

15. *The welfare view*

According to what I shall call the traditional view, the use which physiologists make of the term "function" provides us with the "hard core" of function statements which we are looking for. Physiologists typically ascribe functions to organs and processes. For example: "The function of the heart, or of the heartbeat, is to circulate blood." What the term "function" conveys in addition to the notion of "consequence", according to this view, is the notion that the circulation of blood constitutes a *functional imperative,* i.e. a "need" of the organism, a necessary condition for its *welfare.* The term "welfare", in turn, can be interpreted either strictly as "survival" or more broadly as "proper working" of the organism. More formally, the statement

 (6) The function of item i in entity e is c

can be analyzed as the conjunction of

 (7) i's presence $\rightarrow$ c's presence (in entity e),

where $\rightarrow$ denotes a causal link, and

(8) c's presence is required for entity e to be in a state of welfare.

Following Nagel (1977, 290), I shall call this analysis of function statements the *welfare view.* [11]

The extension of this analysis from physiology to the social sciences has been greatly facilitated by the fact that a physiological analogy has often explicitly been present in the use and discussion of social-scientific function statements.

Radcliffe-Brown, for example, attempts to explain the ceremonial customs of the Andaman Islanders by their function of maintaining feelings of dependence on the social group and of attachment to it. And when doing so, he systematically stresses the fact that such feelings are essential for the continuing existence of society.[12] Clearly, the function c thus ascribed to custom i in society e can easily be analysed as a consequence of the presence of c in e, and one which is required for society e to "fare well".

When thus extended beyond physiology, the welfare view gives rise to a number of tricky conceptual difficulties, which have been abundantly discussed in the methodological literature about functionalism. In particular, is it possible to find a clear and non-tautological criterion of what is to count as a social entity's "welfare" (as its "survival" or its "proper working") and, accordingly, as its "functional imperatives"? And what determines the boundaries of the "social entity" which needs to be taken into consideration? The crucial difficulty for our purposes, however, concerns how function statements (whether physiological or sociological), when analyzed in this way, can be explanatory. In other words, how is it possible to say why an item is present by pointing out that one of its consequences is required for some entity's "welfare"?

In the discussion about functionalism, the deductivist misconception of explanation has often led people to mistake this question for another one: how is it possible to deduce the statement that item i is present from a set of premises which includes the statement *(7)* that i's presence has consequence c and the statement *(8)* that c's presence is required for entity x's welfare? The simplest answer to the latter question consists in adding to the two premises mentioned the further premises that nothing other than i's presence can secure c's presence and that entity e is actually in a state of welfare. The first of the additional premises and the first of the initial premises jointly imply that

(9) i's presence is required to produce *c*.

Together with the second of the initial premises, this guarantees that

(10) i's presence is required for *e* to be in a state of welfare.

And if we know that *e* is in a state of welfare—our second additional premise—, we can obviously conclude that *i* must be present.

One may want to question the realism of the "postulate of indispensability" expressed in *(10)*. The two premises *(8)* and *(9)* on which it rests are related in such a way that, with a given item *i*, whatever plausibility is gained on one side is automatically lost on the other: the more narrowly we specify our function c, the more unlikely the item is to have "functional equivalents"—i.e. the more *likely* the satisfaction of *(9)*—but the more unlikely the function is to constitute a "functional imperative"—i.e. the more *unlikely* the satisfaction of *(8)*—; and the other way round. For the sake of the argument, however, let us suppose that the item *i* has been chosen in such a way that both *(8)* and *(9)*, and therefore also *(10)*, can be made plausible.[13] The crucial question which one needs to ask, then, is how one can possibly *explain* the presence of *i* by reference to the fact stated in *(10)*, i.e. the fact that *i*'s presence is required for *e*'s welfare. If, as has been argued above (section 6), any explanation involves a causal claim in the sense indicated (or even in the weaker, Humean sense of regular succession), it is obviously irrelevant to mention the fact that entity *e* is in a state of welfare at a time at which *i*'s presence has had the time to produce its effects. Although the mentioning of this fact enables us to *deduce* from *(10)* that *i* must have been present, it does not help us one bit to show how *i*'s presence may have been *brought about* by the fact stated in *(10)*, i.e. by the fact that *i*'s presence is required for the welfare of *e*. This is the question we have to solve if we want to show how function statements, in the welfare interpretation, can be explanatory. And it can only be solved by suggesting underlying causal mechanisms, not by fiddling with syllogisms.

16. Cybernetic mechanisms

This point has been more or less clearly grasped by most proponents of the welfare view. And the traditional discussion on function explanations has consequently tended to focus on whether one can conceive of mechanisms which make an item present when its presence is required for some entity to be in a state of welfare. What we need to look at is the way in which so-called "goal-directed" entities manage to keep producing the conditions under which their "goal state" can be maintained.

Here again, physiological examples provide the main source of inspiration. Take the case of thermoregulation in warm-blooded animals. The human body (entity e), for instance, tends to maintain itself at a temperature of 37°C (state g). It may be displaced from this "goal state" as a result of external disturbances, e.g. a draught. But it then reacts by shivering (item i), which results in the restoration of state g. In the hypothesized circumstances, shivering is (arguably) required to restore a temperature of 37°C. And this fact about the situation prior to the shivering is what brings the latter about. In other circumstances (say, after a physical exertion), sweating may be required to restore the temperature of 37°C In either case, however, the underlying mechanism consists in the operation of a *homeostatic* or negative-feedback device, with which the human body is equipped: when an external disturbance displaces the human body from its "goal-state" of 37°C, corrective reactions are automatically triggered off. Analogously, one might want to conceive of Society as a "goal-directed" entity, which maintains its "goal-states" with the help of such homeostatic devices. The punishment of a crime, for example, could be seen as the restoration of a state of "welfare". By destroying or encapsulating the deviant individual, or perhaps by reviving the whole community's attachment to the social norms, it removes the disruption which the crime has created. Similarly, a mourning ritual could be seen as the restoration of society's "euphoria" after it has been shaken by the death of one of its members.[14]

Admittedly, not all entities are "goal-directed" in the sense indicated, and when some entity is goal-directed, it may not be so in every respect. However, to the extent to which an entity is goal-directed and to which the respect in which it is goal-directed has something to do with its "welfare", the supposition of such *cybernetic* mechanisms can make function statements explanatory. If it is cold and I shiver, I can say that my shivering has the function of restoring a temperature of 37°C, and by saying so I can claim to say why I shivered, because I can assume the operation of a homeostatic device. A similar reasoning may apply if I explain a particular mourning ceremony by its function of obliterating the discomfort created by a death.

It must be stressed, however, that the number of function statements which can be given explanatory force in this way is exceedingly small. Even in physiology, only very few function explanations can be legitimated in this way. The item whose presence (or rather occurrence) is being explained can only consist in a homeostatic reaction, a corrective event. When the item is an organ, an ongoing process, a behaviour pattern, there is no way in which "the item's presence" could be brought about by a cybernetic mechanism. In the social sciences, where the identification of "homeostatic devices" is much more problematic, the situation is even worse. It is rather surprising, therefore, that so much time and energy has been devoted, in the literature about "functionalism", to the discussion of this cybernetic approach. [15]

If cybernetic mechanisms are what makes function statements explanatory when they are, only very few function statements are explanatory. This may be disappointing, but true. However, there is one fact in particular which should make us suspect that the welfare view, which led us to this cybernetic perspective, did not pick out the distinguishing feature of function statements which it should have picked out. Cybernetic mechanisms, in the broad sense indicated, also give explanatory value to many other consequence statements, which are not function statements. Take, for example, the case of cold-blooded animals, such as reptiles, whose temperature simply adjusts to that of the environment. If some exogenous disturbance drives the temperature of the organism above that of the environment, a "homeostatic reaction" can be said to occur, which brings the organism's temperature back to its equilibrium level, equal to the temperature of the environment. The fact that, in some circumstances, a fall in the temperature of the animal is required to restore equilibrium, can be said to bring about such a fall—just as the fact that shivering is required to restore a temperature of 37°C in a warm-blooded animal can be said to bring about that shivering. In both cases, as in any case in which a stable equilibrium state is maintained, "cybernetic mechanisms" can be assumed to operate. Clearly, there are important differences between the two cases, and I shall return to them. Not only is the mechanism much more complex in the latter case than in the former. There is undoubtedly also a sense in which the maintained state is a "desired" one and in which the maintenance mechanism involves a homeostatic *device* in the latter and not in the former case. But in both cases, one finds the feedback loop which characterizes cybernetic mechanisms.[15]

What this means is that cybernetic mechanisms, while legitimating a few function explanations, also give explanatory value to a large number of consequence statements which are not function statements. It seems odd to say, for example, that the *function* of the fall in a reptile's temperature is to restore equilibrium with the environment, or that the *function* of the pendulum's return is to restore a situation of minimum potential energy. But the corresponding consequence statements are nevertheless made explanatory by the assumption of a cybernetic mechanism. What this suggests is that our having lost somewhere along the line a specific relevance to function explanations may well be responsible for the disappointing character of the welfare-cybernetic solution to our problem. The special position given to function explanations, as opposed to other explanations by consequences, in the biological and social sciences, may be an important clue that there must be something which makes *specifically* function statements explanatory. The fact that we end up with mechanisms which apply only very marginally to function statements is a sign that the clue, if there was one, has been missed.

17. Persistent features

After having thus pointed out the unsatisfactory nature of the traditional approach and suggested the reason for it, I can now endeavour to propose an alternative. The question to which this chapter is devoted, you will recall, is how it is possible for function statements to be explanatory. As far as the *logic* of explanation is concerned, section 13 has shown that the problem is solved once one realizes that the fact *by* which a function explanation explains is described by attributing to the situation a dispositional property. As far as the *morphology* of explanation is concerned, on the other hand, things are more complicated. If we want to systematically describe the set of mechanisms whose assumption can legitimate function explanations, we certainly need an analysis of function statements which says more than just that they are consequence statements. One analysis which is defensible—although it has difficulties in accommodating, for example, the attribution of functions to artefacts—consists in interpreting a function as a consequence which is required for some entity's welfare. But we have seen in the previous section how poor an answer to our problem this analysis generates.

In the hope of supplying a more satisfactory answer, I propose identifying in a different way the subset of consequence statements which forms the hard core of function statements. I shall want, in particular, to exclude from this hard core the two examples which have been used above (section 14) to suggest the potential usefulness of distinguishing between function statements and other consequence statements in the investigation of underlying mechanisms. We need an analysis which does not allow us to say that the *function* of the pendulum's return is to minimize the level of potential energy, nor that the *function* of terrorism is to breed repression (bearing in mind the scenario sketched in section 14).

A first important fact to note—and one which gets rid of the first kind of example—is that functions are typically attributed to *persistent features*, whether organs, ongoing processes, artefacts, behaviour patterns, etc., rather than to events.[17] Undoubtedly, there are counterexamples. Indeed, we have just seen in the discussion of cybernetic mechanisms that some hemeostatic reactions (such as my shivering) can be explained by function statements, although most of them (such as the pendulum's return) cannot. However, the difference between the two kinds of homeostatic reactions is precisely that the former is the manifestation of a persistent feature—namely a homeostatic *device*—which can itself be the object of a function statement, whereas the latter is not. The fact that my shivering here and now can be said to have the *function* of restoring a temperature of 37°C, derives from the fact that the whole machinery which maintains the human body at a certain ("desirable") temperature can itself be said to have the function of making some aspects of the metabolism possible. If this is true, the mechanism which makes a function statement about homeostatic reactions explanatory *qua* function statement must be the same as the one which makes the function statement about the whole homeostatic device explanatory, rather than the cybernetic mechanism. Even to the limited extent that it seemed to provide an answer to our problem, therefore, the cybernetic perspective appears to be misguided.

The fact that function statements are typically connected with persistent features has another, more important consequence, as far as the nature of the underlying mechanism is concerned. When persistent features or events are explained by reference to their consequences, this means first of all, as we have seen above (section 13), that they are explained by a dispositional fact about the situation in which they appear: the fact that, should they appear, their presence (or occurrence) would have certain consequences. However, this reference to consequences is dispensable, and in this sense superficial, because the same situation could also be described in purely categorical, non-dispositional terms. The pendulum's return, for example, could also be explained by reference to the fact that, just before it moved, the pendulum was in such and such a position. By concentrating on persistent features, however, one makes room for the possibility that reference to consequences may be explanatory in a deeper sense. Whereas the consequences of the occurrence of an event cannot, barring backward causation, form part of the mechanism through which that occurrence is produced, the consequences of the presence of a persistent feature can, in principle, be part of the mechanism through which that presence is produced. Admittedly, the feature's presence at a certain time cannot be influenced by consequences it will have in the future, but only by consequences which the presence of the feature has had in the past. But the feature can remain the same, and the consequences remain the same, at least if there is no change in the situation or, as I shall say in the case of persistent features, in the *context*. In this way, it is possible for a reference to consequences to be essential to the description of the causal *mechanism* which produces the presence of a persistent feature, but not of the mechanism which produces the occurrence of an event—even though, as mentioned above, such a reference is never essential to the description of the causing *fact*.

A related difference, and a very important one for our purposes, is that the presence of persistent features, unlike the occurrence of events, can be the object of so-called *static* (or synchronic) explanations. Let us first get the terminology straight. The explanandum of a static explanation states that some system, at equilibrium, is in a certain state. The state of a system can be described by the values taken by its various endogenous *behaviour variables* (or state variables). An *equilibrium state* of a system is a combination of values of its behaviour variables which, under certain conditions, is invariant with respect to time. The explanans of a static explanation, on the other hand, states the values taken by some exogenous *control variables* (or parameters). For a static explanation to have any "grip" on reality, the equilibrium state it explains must be at least *locally stable*, in the sense that, after slight disturbances and with invariant control variables, the system returns to it. I shall call *attractor* a locally stable equilibrium state. It can be depicted as a point in the behaviour space of the system, i.e. in the set of all its possible states.[18] Any static explanation is closely associated with *comparative-static* explanations of diversity or change. A comparative-static explanation explains differences in the equilibrium values of the behaviour variables of a system by differences in the values of its control variables. A standard example of static and comparative-static explanation is provided by Boyle's law. If we take the volume and the temperature of a mass of gas as the control variables, manipulated from outside, pressure is the behaviour variable. Given values of the control variables determine an attractor in the behaviour space constituted by the set of possible values of the variable "pressure". A change in the value of one of the control variables generates a change in the position of the attractor, i.e. of the position in which the system can settle.

Once we restrict outselves to persistent features, it becomes possible to interpret function statements, in so far as they are explanatory, as giving static explanations, and suggesting comparative-static explanations, in the sense indicated. The control variable would consist in whether or not the context is such that, should the feature be present, its presence would have certain consequences. And the behaviour variable would consist in whether or not the feature is present. Suppose, for example, that the white colouring of the polar bear is explained by reference to its function of camouflage. If our "static" interpretation is correct, this could be paraphrased as follows. The fact that the context is such that white colouring has (or would have) a camouflage effect (given value of the control variable) makes whiteness an attractor as far as the bear's colouring is concerned (equilibrium value of the behaviour variable). Such a paraphrase immediately suggests a comparative-static correlate. By altering the control variable —say, by removing the snow in such a way that white colouring ceases to have a camouflage effect—one can modify the position of the attractor, here the polar bear's colouring *at equilibrium*.

Let us now return to our question: what makes a function statement explanatory at the "morphological" level? This section started with the clue that function statements, as opposed to other consequence statements, are typically concerned with persistent features. Being concerned with persistent features rather than with events, it has been argued, opens up two important possibilities: one is that consequences may actually be part of the underlying mechanism, and the other that the explanation may be a "static" one and that the underlying mechanism may therefore consist in some kind of "equilibration". If what makes a function statement explanatory has something to do with what makes it a function statement, these two suggestions may provide important elements of the underlying mechanism we want to characterize.

18. Good consequences

The pendulum example has led us to restrict the scope of function explanations to persistent features. Let us now turn to the second kind of example we want to eliminate, to our explanation of terrorism by the fact that it breeds repression (and that repression in turn fosters terrorism). If any explanation of a persistent feature by the fact that it has certain consequences were a function explanation, this would have to be one too. The fact that the function language does not seem appropriate in this case provides us, I shall argue, with a second important clue about the nature of the mechanisms which can make function statements explanatory.

One easy way of dealing with such an example consists in adopting the good old "benefit theory" of functions and pointing out that functions are typically *good*, beneficial or useful consequences.[19] Obviously, what counts as "good" or "useful" is rather relative, but so is, one could argue, what counts as "function"—and to exactly the same extent. It seems reasonable to claim, in any case, that the hard core of function statements consists of statements which attribute good consequences to persistent features. And since repression is not a "good consequence", saying that the function of terrorism is to breed repression falls outside this hard core. Similarly, if John's obesity makes him lazy and if this laziness is what keeps him obese, we can explain John's obesity by the fact that it makes him lazy, but we cannot say that the function of his obesity is to make him lazy—so the argument goes—because laziness is not a good consequence. However, even leaving aside the point that some people may fail to see anything wrong with repression or laziness, this analysis can be challenged by choosing another example of the same family where the consequence is as unambiguously good as it can be. Suppose, for example, that the quality of some area's soil accounts for its beautiful vegetation, and that this vegetation, in turn, is what prevents that soil from being eroded away. Producing beautiful vegetation is a good consequence of the quality of the soil, but it does not seem to be its function.

There is one way of reconciling this kind of counter-example—which shows that some good-consequence statements about persistent features do not belong to the "hard core" of function *statements*—with the idea that what is decisive in making the explanation of the presence of a persistent feature by its consequences a function *explanation*, is the fact that the consequences are good. It consists in restricting function explanations to cases where the following holds: not only is the feature present because its presence has certain consequences, not only are these consequences good, but the feature is present *because these consequences are good* according to some criterion. In our terrorism example, after all, someone may well find that repression is a good thing, but given our scenario (in which it is crucial that repression, in turn, fosters terrorism), this fact is irrelevant to the explanation. If one changes the underlying scenario, however, by suggesting, for example, that someone has an interest in repression and therefore engineers whatever is likely to provoke it, the fact that the consequences of terrorism are good from some point of view is no longer irrelevant. At the same time, if one bears this modified scenario in mind, it becomes much more plausible to say that the *function* of terrorism is to breed repression, or that terrorism can be explained by its function of breeding repression. To the extent that no such reinterpretation is available in the obesity or vegetation examples, applying a function language to them cannot but remain strange.

Unlike the rather incidental difference between consequences and good consequences, the difference between cases where the "goodness" of the explanation matters to the explanation and cases where it does not is of great significance to our inquiry about the nature of the mechanisms which make a function statement explanatory when it is. Before examining why, however, note that the latter difference is closely connected with another important one. In cases where "goodness" does not matter, the presence of the feature can and must not only be explained by its propensity to have certain consequences, but also by the presence of these consequences taken separately. John's obesity, for example, can be accounted for by its propensity to make him lazy only because it can also be accounted for by his being lazy. And terrorism, in the first scenario, can only result from its propensity to breed repression because it results from repression. In cases where "goodness" does matter, on the other hand, the presence of the feature does *not* result from the presence of the consequences, but only from its own propensity to produce them. The whiteness of the polar bear's fur, for example, may be accounted for by its propensity to conceal, but it is not a result of the concealment. And the presence of terrorism, in our second scenario, may be said to result from its propensity to breed repression, but it is not generated by repression itself. Put differently, the explanation of the presence of a persistent feature refers to its consequences *qua* consequences in cases of the latter kind, where function language is appropriate, and not in cases of the former kind.

19. Local optimization

The clues discussed in the last two sections, enable us now to formulate our question in a fruitful way and start answering it. As far as the form of the postulated causal link is concerned, the question of what makes a consequence statement explanatory can be given the same answer, whether or not we are dealing with a function statement. As far as the nature of the underlying mechanism is concerned, on the other hand, the question can only be given a very heterogeneous answer, unless it is restricted to function statements. This makes it necessary to have an idea of what distinguishes a "function" from a mere "consequence". The traditional approach picked out the connection between function and welfare and was thus led onto the disappointing cybernetic path. The approach adopted in the preceding two sections, on the other hand, suggests the following reformulation of our question: By reference to what type of mechanism is it possible to legitimate a function explanation, i.e. the explanation of the presence of a persistent feature by the fact that it has certain consequences and that these consequences are good (according to some criterion)? My contention is that this is the question which the whole debate on "functionalism" is really about, and that it can be given a unified answer, in the form of a homogeneous class of mechanisms.

A first important feature which characterizes this class of

mechanisms is that they are mechanisms of *optimization*. By this I mean no more and no less than that the feature whose presence is being explained has been selected from a set of alternatives, whether actual or potential, which can appear in the same context, and that the criterion of this selection is some evaluation of the (actual) consequences associated with the various alternatives.

I shall call *optimum explanation* an explanation of a persistent feature which is directly formulated in terms of such a criterion, for example the explanation of the whiteness of the polar bear's fur by the fact that it maximizes the bear's chances of reproduction. I shall call, and (if the above analysis is correct) I have already called, *function explanation* an explanation of a persistent feature by consequences which are good according to such a criterion, for example the explanation of the whiteness of the polar bear's fur by its having a camouflage function.[20] And I shall call *functional explanation* any explanation which is either an optimum explanation or a function explanation. The fact that optimum explanations have not been discussed so far (and have not been called function explanations) is due to the fact that although one can say, for example, that the maximization of chances of reproduction is a consequence of the bear's fur being white, one never says that it is its *function*. Finally, the comparative correlates of functional explanations I shall call *adaptational explanations*: they explain changes or differences in persistent features by changes or differences in the context, which affect their being optimal or their having certain functions. For example, one may explain a difference in the bear's colouring (say, white or brown) by a difference in the environment which gives whiteness a camouflage function in one case, and brownness in the other.

The nature of optimization mechanisms implies that the (functional as well as adaptational) explanations which they underlie are essentially *comparative* in a different sense, in a way which sets them clearly apart from other consequence explanations of persistent features, for example those (of the obesity type) discussed in the previous section. This comparative dimension is reflected, first of all, in the fact that the consequences by reference to which the presence of a feature is explained are *differential* consequences. This is clear enough in the case of optimum explanations, where the term "maximization" contains a direct reference to the consequences associated with other alternatives which could appear in the same context. But it is equally important in the case of function explanations. It is impossible to explain the whiteness of the bear's fur by its function of camouflage, for example, without comparing it implicitly to other possible colourings and claiming that they would conceal the bear less well than whiteness does. Secondly and no less importantly, the essentially comparative aspect of these explanations is reflected in the fact that they can only be complete explanations if the feature whose presence they explain is the only one whose presence has the consequences ascribed to it. In other words, the presence of the feature must be required for the production of the consequences. This is clear enough, again, in the case of optimum explanations: if several colourings maximize the chances of reproduction (in the given context), it is obvious that the optimum explanation of the bear's whiteness leaves the optimal solution underdetermined. And it also applies in the case of function explanations, though often in a more complex way (see section 25).

It is important, at this point, to stress two aspects of the notion of optimization mechanism which has been introduced above. Firstly, this notion does not presuppose any conscious decision-making process. The optimization in terms of actual consequences which we are concerned with here should not be conflated with the optimization in terms of expected consequences which has been briefly discussed earlier (section 10). Secondly, the notion of optimization which is relevant here is sufficiently loose to accommodate what one might want to call *satisficing* mechanisms, in analogy with the decision-making case. Whether the mechanism can be said to pick out the "best" alternative ("optimization") or just one that is "good enough" ("satisficing") is largely a matter of how the alternatives are defined. If, in the polar bear example, we have a detailed classification of colourings, which distinguishes for instance various shades of white, we may be tempted to say that the underlying mechanism is only of the "satisficing" kind. But if we adopt a rougher classification, if we lump together the various shades of white, the same mechanism can be said to be of the "optimizing" kind. What is crucial to the notion of optimization which is relevant here, therefore, is not that the selection process should operate in a very precise fashion, but only that its criterion should refer to the consequences of the various alternatives.

Optimization mechanisms, as discussed so far, can in principle apply to events as well as to persistent features, but only under one condition. There must be an agent who decides whether the event will occur or not, and who anticipates perfectly what its actual consequences will be. As soon as this assumption is dropped, optimization and the explanations by *actual* consequences which it underlies, can only apply to persistent features. Optimization then acquires the two features which, as has been noted above (section 17), are made possible by such a shift from events to persistent features: the consequences can actually *be part of* the mechanism, and what is being explained is the presence of persistent features *at equilibrium*. If one rules out the possibility of an omniscient agent, in other words, optimization necessarily becomes a process of "equilibration through consequences". When consequence-anticipation is excluded, one is left with consequence-feedback.[21]

As a matter of fact (not of logic), it is difficult to conceive of such a mechanism of "equilibration through consequences" which would optimize over the whole range of possible alternatives. Barring foresight, the domain on which selection can operate is restricted to chance deviations, and these are much more likely to involve "neighbouring" alternatives than more "remote" ones. In other words, equilibration through consequences will consist in *local optimization*, not only in the sense that optimality (with a given criterion) is relative to the context in which the feature appears (because it is the context which determines what consequences its presence has), but also in the sense that the "best" alternative which the mechanism picks out need only be the "best" one among alternatives which are close enough to the starting point to be accessible by chance.[22] For reasons which I must now explain, I shall call *evolutionary* such mechanisms of local optimization.

20. *Evolutionary mechanisms*

The term "evolution" is sometimes used to refer to any succession of changes which affect a system through time.[23] More often, it is restricted to successions of changes which are characterized either by their overall *direction* or by the underlying *mechanism*. A perspective centred around the former concept, I shall call *evolutionist*. A perspective centred around the latter, I shall call *evolutionary*. An evolutionist perspective essentially consists in looking at history (whether biological or social) as development, as progress, as a succession of stages of increasing complexity or perfection. Its explanatory claims are often restricted to spelling out a *logic* of development: the succession of stages which it presents only reflects the fact that one stage is a precondition for the next one. But sometimes its claims extend to the *dynamics* of development: the succession of stages which it presents then corresponds to a path on which species or societies are "dragged forward" towards some "End of History" by reference to which the various stages need to be explained. Whether in its weaker or in its stronger version, this evolutionist perspective has nothing to do with the topic of this chapter and of this book. To the extent that it suggests the opposite, the etymological connection between "evolutionist" and "evolutionary" is very misleading.[24]

An evolutionary perspective, on the other hand, focuses on mechanisms of *filtering* or *trial-and-error*, i.e. on mechanisms of selection between actual (as opposed to potential) alternatives. Even in the pure case, the variation on which the selection operates need not be random. It can be biased. But it must be *blind*, in the sense that the bias must not be connected with the criterion of selection. The evolutionary perspective can also be said to apply to impure cases, where the (spontaneous) direction of variation is more or less loosely *coupled* with the criterion of selection. As long as there is some "blindness" involved, the selection component is, in the last analysis, the decisive one. The bias in variation can facilitate selection and accelerate evolution, but the end result is determined by the criterion of selection. At the end of this continuum, where "blindness" is totally removed, however, there is no room left for the selection component to operate—nothing to filter out, no error among the trials—, and the evolutionary perspective accordingly loses its relevance.[25]

Nothing has been said so far about the nature of the criterion of selection. The evolutionary perspective, as characterized above, would apply to the sorting of pebbles by the waves on the shore according to their sizes, as well as to the trial-and-error search for beauty in art or for truth in science. A definition of "evolutionary" which covers all these cases is perfectly defensible. However, here I shall prefer to restrict the term to cases where the criterion of selection refers to the actual (as opposed to potential) empirical (as opposed to logical) *consequences* of the presence of the features which are being selected. This implies that I shall not call "evolutionary", for example, a theory of scientific practice which focuses on the selection of propositions according to the degree to which they (and their logical consequences) approximate the truth.[26]

The mechanisms of "filtering by reference to consequences" which we end up with here are no different from the mechanisms of "equilibration through the consequences" on which the previous section closed. Evolutionary mechanisms constitute the intersection of the set of optimization mechanisms with which the previous section started and the set of trial-and-error mechanisms with which we started here. The need to discard perfectly "coupled" situations mirrors the exclusion, in the previous section, of an omniscient agent. And the need to take consequences into account in the filtering process reflects the notion of optimization.

I shall call *evolutionary* a pattern of explanation which is defined by reference to evolutionary mechanisms in the sense indicated. If it turns out to be useful to distinguish between various types of such mechanisms, there may accordingly be various evolutionary patterns of explanation. Explanations which conform to an evolutionary pattern can be called *evolutionary explanations*. Such explanations will often take the form of functional or adaptational explanations, to be interpreted as static and comparative-static, respectively, since the underlying mechanism is one of equilibration. However, evolutionary explanations need not have the dispositional structure characteristic of both functional and adaptational explanations. For example, I can explain the whiteness of the polar bear's fur by the fact that the environment is covered with snow as well as by the fact that whiteness maximizes the bear's chances of reproduction, while assuming exactly the same mechanism. Such "categorical" (or non-dispositional) evolutionary explanations, however, are as static or comparative-static as their dispositional counterparts, since they assume the operation of the same mechanisms of "equilibration through consequences".

The attractors, or locally stable equilibrium states, corresponding to such mechanisms will be called *evolutionary attractors*. They coincide with the local optima briefly discussed at the end of the previous section.

21. Latent functions and the action pattern

By introducing the notion of evolutionary mechanism, this chapter does not intend to answer the question of whether function explanations are legitimate in the social sciences. It only aims to prepare the ground for such an answer, by showing that the latter basically hinges on whether evolutionary mechanisms, in the sense indicated, can be plausibly assumed to operate in the social realm. In the process, it has elaborated an abstract conceptual framework, which applies to any type of evolutionary mechanism and to the explanations which it underlies. Only concrete analyses of the kind proposed in the following chapters, however, can really tackle the question of the legitimacy of function explanations, about which this chapter has only offered preliminary remarks.

Before switching to those more concrete analyses, however, it is useful to ask how the question with which this chapter has been concerned is connected with the question to which the previous chapter was devoted. How can the answers to these two questions possibly be interdependent? How can an inquiry into the deep structure of the social sciences be closely related to an inquiry into the status of function explanations? What are the interconnections between the adequacy of "actionalism" and the legitimacy of "functionalism"? What needs to be examined, in order to clarify these interconnections, is the nature of the relationship between, on the one hand, the action pattern of explanation, whose residue must be systematically explored if one is to be able to answer the first question, and, on the other hand, the evolutionary patterns(s), whose significance must be systematically assessed if one is to be able to answer the second question.

The nature of this relationship can conveniently be sketched in the following table (Table 2.1), bearing in mind that both the action pattern and the evolutionary pattern(s) cover many more explanations than those represented in the table. The set of explanations which is being classified includes any explanation of the presence of a persistent feature which refers directly to the "goodness" of the consequences of that presence, or else to some specific good consequences with the implication that their "goodness" matters to the explanation (in the sense discussed in section 18). Out of the eight possible combinations of properties, only the four mentioned are meaningful. The first two, which refer to anticipated consequences, can be said to cover *intentional explanations*. The last three, which refer to actual consequences, correspond to *functional explanations*, as defined above (section 19). Depending on whether the actual consequences need to be recognized by the agents *(ii* and *iii)* or not *(iv)*, I shall call these explanations manifest-functional or, for short, *M-functional* and latent-functional or, for short, *L-functional*, respectively.[27] The plus sign indicates that the subset of explanations which it helps to define demands that the consequences to which they refer should possess the property mentioned. The minus sign indicates that, although the consequences referred to may happen to have the property mentioned, their actually having it is not required by the explanation.

In subset *i,* the presence of a feature is explained by the fact that certain consequences were expected from it by some agents before its introduction. Whether these consequences turn out to be the actual ones (and can then be recognized as such) is irrelevant. Subset *ii* corresponds to the omniscient agent, whose existence was briefly discussed and dismissed

Table 2.1. Types of "consequence explanations"

Explanations		Consequences			
		Actual	Recognized	Anticipated	
Intentional	i	−	−	+	Action pattern
M-functional	ii	+	+	+	Action pattern
	iii	+	+	−	Evolutionary patterns
L-functional	iv	+	−	−	Evolutionary patterns

above (section 19) An explanation by reference to actual consequences is possible, but only because the agent is assumed to anticipate them perfectly. Both subsets *i* and *ii* constitute unproblematic instances of the action pattern in its non-degenerate form (see section 10). Subset *iv*, on the other hand, if it is not empty, contains (*L*-functional) explanations which fall unambiguously outside the action pattern. There is no way in which the latter can accommodate the causal role of consequences (qua consequences) which are neither anticipated nor recognized by some agents.

The status of subset *iii*, finally, is ambiguous. Here, the presence of a feature is being explained by reference to its actual consequences. The latter need not be anticipated, but they must be recognized by the agents who maintain the feature. Such explanations do not fit into the action pattern *sensu stricto* as it has been defined above. However, since patterns of explanation are not .defined by (mutually exclusive) elementary types of mechanisms, but rather by typical constellations of mechanisms, it may be argued that the action pattern can be slightly extended to cover the following: action-generation processes which combine with the processes through which agents become aware of the actual consequences of the presence of features which they control. The elements of subset *iii*, though they would still be evolutionary explanations, could then also be said to conform to this action pattern *sensu lato*.

As we have seen above (sections 19–20), on the other hand, explanations of subsets *iii* and *iv* (unlike those of subsets *i* and *ii*), if they can be legitimated at all, must conform to an evolutionary pattern, in the sense defined. Consequently, if by investigating the evolutionary pattern(s) of explanation one wants to explore the residue of the action pattern, it is essential that evolutionary mechanisms should enable us to make sense, in the social sciences, of L-functional explanations (subset *iv*). If it turns out that although evolutionary mechanisms are plausible in the social realm, they can only legitimate M-functional explanations (subset *iii*), investigating them would still be relevant to the question presented in this chapter, but not to the question presented in the previous one. As we shall see, however, and as is suggested by the fact that social scientists who propose function explanations often stress the "latent" nature of the functions they point out, the opposite will turn out to be true. This is why this book can try to shed light simultaneously on both the deep structure of the social sciences and the legitimacy of function explanations.

3

The Sociobiological Model

Summary

Natural selection consists in the selection of features through the differential survival and/or reproduction of the entities which they characterize. Depending on whether the features are biological characteristics or cultural traits and on whether the entities are individuals or groups, one can distinguish four forms of natural selection, which together constitute what is here called the sociobiological model (section 22).

The *logic* of the explanations legitimated by natural selection can most conveniently be clarified in the case of the standard form of natural selection, the selection of biological characteristics through the differential reproduction of individual organisms. This type of mechanism legitimates, first of all, optimum explanations in terms of adaptiveness (section 23), which can usefully be reformulated in terms of evolutionary attractors (section 24). It also legitimates, though more loosely, function explanations in terms of specific contributions to reproductive success (section 25). Between these two kinds of explanations and the general principles of universal optimalism and universal functionalism, there is a close link which is clearly revealed by an analysis of the way in which such explanations can be tested (section 26).

Kin selection and so-called reciprocal altruism provide two ways in which the standard form of natural selection can accommodate the existence of some *specifically social* features (section 27). For the explanation of other such features, however, it seems possible, though for various reasons highly problematic, to move from the differential reproduction of organisms to the differential survival of groups (section 28) or from the selection of biological characteristics to the selection of cultural traits (section 29). The most promising line of inquiry, however, consists in combining these two moves to consider the selection of cultural traits through the differential survival of social groups. Such a mechanism is still very implausible in the case of total societies (section 30), but it need not be so in the case of subsocieties such as firms or sects (section 31). This makes some room for an evolutionary pattern of explanation which would not just be a part of biology. But its scope is so restricted that having shown its existence is of little more than anecdotal interest (section 32).

22. Four forms of natural selection

There are two, and only two, basic types of evolutionary mechanisms, in the sense defined in the preceding chapter. The first one, which will be examined in this chapter, I shall call *natural selection*. Accordingly, I shall call *NS-evolutionary* the explanations which this type of mechanism legitimates, the pattern of explanation which it defines, and the attractors which it determines. The crucial defining property of natural selection is that the features whose presence is being explained are selected through the differential survival and/or reproduction of the entities which the features characterize. By "differential", I mean that the probability of survival and/or reproduction of the entities depends causally on whether or not the features which are being explained are present.

This definition has two important implications. Firstly, natural selection is restricted to *living* entities, which are capable of dying or surviving. It is also preferable, though not strictly required, for these entities to be capable of *reproduction*, i.e. of generating other entities which share a large number of features with them. Otherwise, either natural selection would soon be left with very little to select between, or it would have to keep starting its work from scratch with newly created entities. Secondly, natural selection involves an essentially *populational* point of view. The object of the explanations which it legitimates is not the presence of some feature (at equilibrium) in some *particular* entity, but rather the presence of that feature (at equilibrium) in a *typical* member of a population of such entities. Consequently, NS-evolutionary explanations can only *seem* to explain the presence of a feature in a specific member of a population, and this only when it can explain its presence in all of the latter's members. Furthermore, the changes which they can explain are never changes in the features of a particular entity, but only changes in the distribution of some features in a population of entities.

According to the nature of the entities (the "unit of selection") and the nature of the features (the "unit of variation"), I shall distinguish four subtypes of natural selection (Table 3.1). The labels used to refer to them will be clarified in due course.

Table 3.1. Forms of natural selection

	Entities	
Features	Individuals	Groups
Biological characteristics	1 "Neo-Darwinian Synthesis" (sections 23-27)	2 "Group Selection" (section 28)
Cultural traits	3 "Cultural Ethology" (section 29)	4 "System Functionalism" (sections 30-31)

Subtypes *1* and *2* assume the existence of genetically controlled features, which I shall call *(biological) characteristics*. It will be convenient to view these as phenotypic features—e.g. brown colouring-, rather than as the underlying genotypic features—e.g. the gene(s) responsible for the brown colouring. However, it must be clear that phenotypic features are here called characteristics only if, and to the extent that, they are genetically controlled. Subtypes 3 and 4, on the other hand, assume the existence of socially controlled features, which I shall call *(cultural) traits*. Subtypes 1 and 3 operate through differential reproduction (and survival) of individual organisms, whereas subtypes 2 and 4 operate through the differential survival (and reproduction) of groups of organisms.

Subtype 1 constitutes the standard and least problematic form of natural selection. Its relevance to the explanation of social phenomena has recently been vindicated by sociobiology. In the following sections, I shall start by discussing the "bare bones" of this standard form of natural selection, without any specific reference to social phenomena. This will enable us to illustrate the abstract notions about evolutionary mechanisms and evolutionary explanations introduced in the previous chapter. Afterwards, I shall briefly discuss the way in which sociobiology has used (and slightly modified) the standard conception of natural selection in order to deal with specifically social phenomena. And finally, I shall turn to the non-standard forms of natural selection, i.e. to the extension of the standard form either to group selection or to cultural traits or to both. I shall loosely speak of a "sociobiological model" when referring to any NS-evolutionary explanation of social facts, whether or not the standard form of natural selection is assumed to operate.

23. *Adaptiveness as local optimality*

The standard form of natural selection—the selection of biological characteristics through the differential reproduction of individual organisms—constitutes the core of what is often called the "Neo-Darwinian Synthesis". The variation component of the mechanism has been studied by Mendelian genetics. Variation must at the same time be large enough for selection to have raw material on which it can operate, and small enough to prevent the effects of selection from being erased straight away. Hereditary transmission ensures the latter, while mutations, i.e. occasional errors in the course of hereditary transmission, are the major source of new variation. In the case of species which reproduce sexually, mutations are supplemented with recombinations of the genetic material inherited from the parent organisms. And migrations from one environment into another may marginally increase the amount of variation available for selection. Whether variation is created by mutations, recombinations or migrations, however, it is assumed to be "blind". And if the presence of a biological characteristic is to be explained by its differential consequences, this is entirely due to the operation of the selection component of the mechanism.

The fact that the characteristics are assumed to be selected through the differential reproduction of individual organisms, determines the criterion in terms of which both optimum explanations and, implicitly, function explanations have to be formulated, if they are to be legitimated by this standard form of natural selection. This criterion, which will be slightly modified later (section 27), is often called *adaptiveness*. A characteristic is *adaptive* if and only if its presence locally maximizes the chances of reproduction of the kind of organism in which it appears. Strictly speaking, the chances of reproduction are given by the mathematical expectation of reproduction after several generations in the same environment. For most practical purposes, however, the average number of viable offspring at the first generation provides a sufficiently accurate estimate. The presence of an adaptive characteristic maximizes these chances of reproduction *locally* in two distinct senses.

Firstly, adaptiveness is *relative to a given context*. This context encompasses not only the physical and biological environment of the organisms concerned, but also all the latter's features, whether hereditary or not, which are not part of the characteristic which is being explained. Whereas taking the environment as given is usually unproblematic, incorporating some characteristics of the organism into the context relative to which the adaptiveness of other characteristics is assessed, will often seem arbitrary. Take the following example. Many species of fish have a dark back and a light belly. The adaptiveness of this characteristic is obvious enough once one realizes that the fish are thus made less conspicuous when looked at from below as well as from above. However, it is clear that the adaptiveness of this characteristic is contingent upon another characteristics of the organisms concerned, namely the genetically controlled habit of swimming on their bellies. Indeed, fish of other species have a light back and a dark belly, and then also the habit of swimming on their backs.[1] In this kind of situation, it seems equally arbitrary to pick out the colouring as the characteristic to be explained, while taking the swimming habits as given, and to pick out the swimming habits, while incorporating the colouring into the context. Clearly, the more characteristics have to be taken as given, the more arbitrary the choice is likely to be. And it seems better, therefore, that the characteristic's adaptiveness should be as little local as possible in this first sense.

Adaptiveness is not only local in the sense that it is relative to a given context, but also in the sense that it is *relative to neighbouring alternatives*. The notion of "neighbourhood" can obviously only be meaningful if some measure of distance is conceivable. In the case of genetically controlled features, this measure is given by the number of (discrete) genic mutations which are needed to go from one alternative to another. Even if the exact nature of the relationship between characteristics and genes is not known, one can safely say, in the above example, that the complex characteristic "dark-back/light-belly/swimming-on-the-belly" is more remote from the characteristic "light-back/dark-belly/swimming-on-the-back" than from the characteristic "dark-back/light-belly/swimming-on-the-back". A neighbouring alternative, then, is one that is sufficiently close to be arrived at "by chance". And a characteristic is adaptive when there are higher chances of reproduction associated with it than with such neighbouring alternatives. Clearly, the more complex the characteristics which are being explained—and hence the more numerous the dimensions which are not frozen into the context—the longer the distances can be between alternatives which can appear in the same context, and the more likely it is, therefore, that there will be more than one adaptive characteristic. In the above example, the distance between "dark-back/light-belly/swimming-on-the-belly" and "light-back/dark-belly/swimming-on-the-back" is sufficiently long for both of them to be able to constitute adaptive characteristics. Removing a dimension from the context unavoidably increases the probability that there will be several locally adaptive characteristics in the second sense. In so far as this is undesirable, it is therefore better to keep the number of free dimensions as low as possible. This highlights the trade-off which cannot be avoided if one wants to have adaptive characteristics which are at the same time as little local as possible (in the first sense) and as few in number as possible.

The central kind of explanation which is legitimated by the standard form of natural selection is optimum explanation (as defined in section 19), which can here be described as follows. The fact which is being explained is the fact that, at equilibrium, a particular characteristic *(i)* is present in all the organisms of a population. The fact by which it is being explained is the fact that *i* is adaptive.[2] The latter fact is a dispositional fact about the context in which *i* appears. It can be more fully described as follows: the context is such that, should *i* be present, its presence would locally maximize the organisms's chances of reproduction. The explanation asserts the existence of a causal link between this latter fact and *i*'s presence at equilibrium. If the context is defined in such a way that several characteristics are adaptive, the explanation obviously remains incomplete. And if the context is changing so rapidly that there is no time for equilibration to take place, this kind of explanation, like any other static explanation, is obviously pointless. If the context changes sufficiently slowly, on the other hand, there is room for an adaptational explanation of a change in the characteristic which is present at equilibrium, by a change in relevant aspects of the context.

24. NS-evolutionary attractors

It is useful, at this point, to introduce a spatial representation, which will help make the argument of the rest of this chapter more intuitive. First of all, the presence of a characteristic in an organism can be represented as a point in the behaviour space of a system, with as many dimensions as there are predicates which are needed to describe the characteristic. Suppose, for simplicity's sake, that we are concerned with a single dimension—for example the length of a bird's wings— and that this dimension can be considered continuous. It is important that distances in this one-dimensional space should be assumed to reflect the number of mutation steps which are required to get from one point to another. Taking a particular context for granted—including, for example, the strength of the bird's wings or its flying habits—one can then associate with each wing length the chances of reproduction which its presence confers upon the organism which it characterizes (Fig. 3.1 or 3.2). A particular wing length (i^*) is, by definition, adaptive, if it corresponds to a local maximum of such a function. Even in a one-dimensional case, it is not excluded that there should be several such maxima (Fig. 3.2). The likelihood of such a situation increases with the number of dimensions of the behaviour space. In the two-dimensional case, each of these local maxima corresponds to the top of a hill above the plane which represents the behaviour space. This fact suggests the term *adaptive landscape* for this kind of representation.[3]

Any individual organism corresponds to a point in the

Figure 3.1. Unimodal adaptive landscape

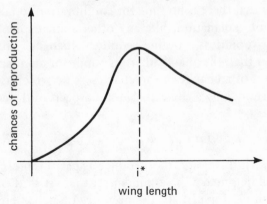

Figure 3.2. Bimodal adaptive landscape

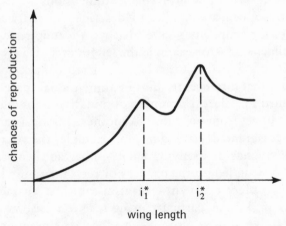

behaviour space, in this case along the horizontal axis of the
diagrams (Fig. 3.1 and 3.2). A population of organisms,
assumed to be homogeneous as far as the (relevant) context is
concerned, corresponds, at any given time, to a set of such
points. Blind mutations, recombinations and migrations tend
to spread the population at random in the behaviour space.
The differential reproduction of organisms, however, keeps
pushing the population up the hills, in such a way that, in the
long run and with an unchanged context, only the hill tops are

occupied. It is this process of local optimization—"local" because blind variation is unlikely to "jump" very far—which makes the presence of an adaptive characteristic (in all members of a population) an attractor, or more precisely an NS-evolutionary attractor, of the system concerned. The presence of an adaptive characteristic maximizes locally the chances of reproduction in the same two senses of "locally" as an attractor constitutes a locally stable equilibrium state.

Whether a characteristic is adaptive or not depends on the nature of the context. This implies, given what has just been said, that a modification in the control variables (which describe the context) can induce a shift in the position of the (NS-evolutionary) attractors in the behaviour space. Suppose, for example, that the average power of the wind increases substantially (as a result, say, of the population's migration to the other side of a mountain), while every other relevant aspect of the context remains unchanged. The adaptive landscape may then be modified in such a way that shorter wings now correspond to the attractor. It is possible to draw the (potential) adaptive landscape corresponding to each possible value of the control variable. By aggregating all such landscapes together, one obtains a more complex three-dimensional diagram (Fig. 3.3), where the altitude of the relief reflects the chances of reproduction of an organism of a certain kind (specified by the behaviour variable) in a context of a certain kind (specified by the control variable). The projection of the crest line of this relief on the plane gives the set of attractors as a function of the control variable (Fig. 3.4).

When more than one characteristic is adaptive (as in Fig. 3.2) for at least some values of the control variable, there is a *conflict* between NS-evolutionary attractors. There is then more than one crest line (as in Fig. 3.5), and the projection of the crest lines on the combined behaviour-and-control space may then form what is sometimes called a "catastrophe surface" (as in Fig. 3.6). Suppose, for example, that the trough between the two peaks, in Fig. 3.2, is due to the presence, in the given context, of a large number of predators

Figure 3.3. Unimodal adaptive landscape with control variable

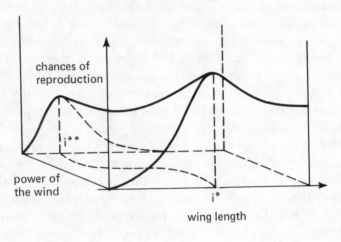

Figure 3.4. Single-sheeted attractor line

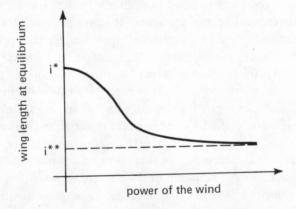

which aim preferably for medium-sized birds. As the extent of this type of predation diminishes, a point will be reached where the trough will be smoothed out (Fig. 3.5). The barrier which prevented local optimization from taking the system from a low to a high wing length would then be removed, and we would be left with a single attractor. This is clearly shown by the projection of the relief's highest and lowest points on the plane (Fig. 3.6). The line which emerges from this projection is sometimes called a *fold catastrophe*. The term "fold" is suggested by its folded shape, and the term "catastrophe" by the fact that, when moving gradually along the control vari-

Figure 3.5. Bimodal adaptive landscape with control variable

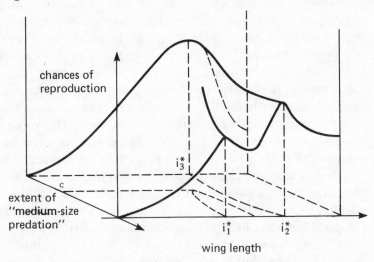

Figure 3.6. Catastrophic attractor line

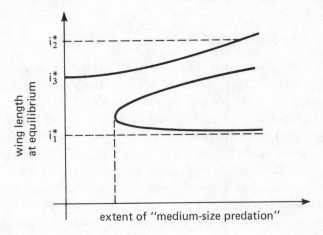

able (from right to left on the lower curve of Fig. 3.6), the possibility suddenly arises (at point c, where the trough vanishes) for the behaviour variable to move to a non-adjacent attractor (from around i_1^* to around i_2^*).

The importance of this rudimentary and very idealized representation is that it gives an intuitive, though abstract, framework into which one can fit any explanation of a characteristic by reference to the natural selection of organisms—and much more generally, as we shall see later, any evolutionary explanation, whatever the subtype to which it belongs. In every case, given a particular context (i.e. a value on the horizontal axis in Fig. 3.4 or Fig. 3.6), blind variation constantly tends to spread the organisms at random in the space of genetic possibilities (i.e. along the vertical dimension in Fig. 3.4 or Fig. 3.6). Natural selection, however, keeps pulling the population towards the attractor, in such a way that one can explain the widespread presence of a characteristic in a population (in the long run) by its being adaptive. Obviously, "real-life" situations are much more complex. Both the behaviour space and the control space are often multi-dimensional, and they can rarely be assumed to be anything like continuous. Nevertheless, however difficult to represent the two spaces are, the underlying logic would remain basically the same.

25. *Why bother with function explanations?*

Whether functional (and static) or adaptational (and comparative-static), evolutionary explanations may be formulated in terms of specific consequences, or functions, as well as in terms of an ultimate criterion, or optimum. The latter kind of explanation is the only one which has been considered in the preceding two sections, and, strictly speaking, it is the only one which can be legitimated by evolutionary mechanisms. However, function explanations are also often used—with good reasons, as we shall see—and their logic may therefore be worth investigating in some detail.

What is being explained by a function explanation is again the fact that, at equilibrium, a particular characteristic (*i*) is present in all the organisms of a population. But the fact by which this is explained is now the fact that *i* performs a particular function. Just like the fact that *i* is adaptive, the fact that it performs a particular function must be viewed as a dispositional fact about the context in which *i* appears: the fact that the context is such that, should *i* be present, its presence would have some specific consequence which is called its function. A function explanation asserts the existence of a causal link between this fact about the context and *i*'s presence at equilibrium.

It is clear (from section 23) that the operation of natural selection can only legitimate such an explanation if the consequence singled out by the latter is *decisive* in making *i* adaptive. More precisely, the context must be such that *i* is adaptive if and only if *i*'s presence has this consequence.[4] Strictly speaking, however, this is never the case. Take the explanation of the male bird's song in springtime by its function of attracting a sexual partner. It is easy to conceive of a context in which the bird's song would still potentially have this consequence, while no longer being adaptive: for example, due to the immigration of a new species, the likelihood of the song attracting the attention of predators may increase substantially. And it is also possible to conceive of a context in which the bird's song has lost this function, while still being adaptive because of other favourable consequences it may have, such as protecting the bird's territory from the intrusion of other males. A function explanation, therefore, is at best justified as an approximation to the corresponding optimum explanation.

Furthermore, there is often a good deal of arbitrariness involved in the choice of the function in terms of which the characteristic's presence is explained. On the one hand, there may be a multiplicity of functions *in series*. For example, one may want to explain a male bird's aggressive behaviour at one and the same time by its function of territory protection, by its function of spacing out the population at the reproduction period and by its function of reducing the efficiency of predation at a time when the population is particularly vulnerable.[5] Each of these functions describes the way in which the next one is supposed to be performed, except for the last one, which indicates the way in which chances of reproduction are locally maximized. On the other hand, there may also be a multiplicity of functions *in parallel.* For example, within the same context, the male bird's song may both keep other males away and attract a female, and so help to enhance the bird's chances of reproduction in (at least) two parallel ways. In general, therefore, function explanations of the presence of biological characteristics are not only mere approximations to the "real" explanation in terms of adaptiveness, but they also reflect an arbitrary choice among the various ways in which the characteristic's presence contributes to an organism's reproductive success.

Nevertheless, function explanations may be quite useful, for two main reasons. Firstly, they are more specific than optimum explanations about the nature of the mechanism of "consequence equilibration" which produced the presence of the characteristic (at equilibrium), and thereby make the latter more intelligible. For example, an explanation of dreaming in man and other species by its being adaptive sheds less light on the existence of dreaming than would an explanation which could point out its specific function. The former explanation suggests that the mechanism is one of differential reproduction, but the latter would indicate more precisely which differential consequences played a crucial role. Secondly, function explanations are also more helpful than optimum explanations in pointing out which features of the context, described in categorical terms, are causally relevant to i's presence (at equilibrium). For example, if instead of simply saying that the whiteness of the polar bear's fur is adaptive, one claims that it has the function of concealing the bear from its prey, it becomes much more obvious which aspects of the context—such as the bear's hunting habits or the fact that the environment is covered with snow—account for the fact that polar bears are white. Taken together, these two features make function explanations a useful, though loose, form of NS-evolutionary explanation.

26. *Universal optimalism and universal functionalism*

The use of optimum and function explanations is closely associated with two principles, which can be called *universal optimalism* and *universal functionalism*.[6] In our NS-evolutionary case, these principles assert that every existing characteristic is adaptive and that every existing characteristic performs a function, respectively. They are not simply related to the corresponding explanations in the way in which any heuristic principle is. Whenever one attempts to explain reality by means of a certain type of explanation, for example a particular behaviour in terms of the class origin of its performer, one might be said to be using an approach which rests on the heuristic principle that reality can always be explained in that way, for example that any social behaviour can be explained in terms of class origin. Universal optimalism and universal functionalism, however, are more intimately connected to the kinds of explanations we have been considering. Their validity (at equilibrium) is implied by the operation of the mechanism which such explanations presuppose. This can be shown as follows.

A non-adaptive characteristic, by definition, is one which is worse, as far as reproductive success is concerned, than at least one neighbouring alternative. The natural selection of organisms, as a mechanism of local optimization, tends therefore to eliminate all non-adaptive characteristics.[7] At equilibrium, no non-adaptive characteristic can be present, or, in other words, although not all adaptive characteristics need to be present, all the characteristics which are present are adaptive. This universal optimalism implies, as a corollary, what has been called above universal functionalism, providing one makes the following two assumptions: firstly, that the presence of a characteristic always involves a *cost* (in terms of reproductive success), when compared to its absence, and secondly, that the presence and absence of the characteristic are *neighbouring* alternatives. Clearly, under these assumptions, an "a-functional" characteristic is non-adaptive, and it then follows from universal optimalism that no characteristic which is present (at equilibrium) is "a-functional", or that any characteristic which is present (at equilibrium) has at least one function.

Neither universal optimalism nor universal functionalism provides us with a genuinely testable proposition, because any alleged refutation can easily be disposed of in one of the following three ways (corresponding to situations 1, 2 and 3 in Fig. 3.7). Firstly, it is often possible to argue that one "has not looked hard enough". One might say that the human appendix, for example, only seems to be a-functional or non-adaptive because the various aspects of its significance for reproductive success have not been investigated thoroughly enough. Secondly, it is sometimes possible to argue that, although the characteristic which is actually present in the population is not the best possible one, all better alternatives are "too far away" in the space of genetic possibilities. The rudimentary social organization of some social insects, for example, may well be adaptive, or *locally* optimal, even if the

Figure 3.7. Immunizations of universal optimalism

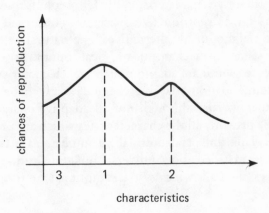

adoption of the more complex organization which some other insects have adopted would enhance chances of reproduction in the given context. Finally, it is, in principle, always possible to argue that the alleged refutation refers to a situation of disequilibrium: either the optimal mutations have not had time to take place, or the pressures of selection have not had time to favour them to a sufficient extent.

The optimum explanation and the function explanation of the presence of particular characteristics derive their legitimacy from the operation of the same mechanism as universal optimalism and universal functionalism. At the same time, however, they assert both less and more than the corresponding universal principles. They assert less, obviously, because they are exclusively concerned with one characteristic. They also assert more, first of all, because they apply to characteristics which are actually present, and not to characteristics which would be present if the situation were one of equilibrium—which excludes the third kind of immunization strategy mentioned above. Suppose, for example, one wants to explain some gulls' hereditary habit of removing eggshells as soon as the young have hatched, either by its being adaptive or by its having a function of camouflage.[8] Such an explanation entails the claim that, compared to its absence, the presence of the habit has the consequence of increasing the gulls' chances of reproduction or of reducing the probability of their nest being spotted by predators. Testing a causal claim of this kind, whether by observing the effects of spontaneous variation in the relevant characteristic or by introducing artificial variation, may require a lot of patience and ingenuity. But it is clearly possible. If the claim is refuted, it is obviously irrelevant to invoke the possibility of disequilibrium. What is claimed to be adaptive or to have a particular function is not the habit which would be present at equilibrium, but the one whose presence is being explained. This is a first reason why one can say that optimum and function explanations assert more than the corresponding (equilibrium) principles.

Secondly, and more importantly, like any other consequence explanation (see section 13), the optimum explanation and the function explanation of the presence of a characteristic entail a second causal claim. What is asserted is not just that the characteristic is present and that it is adaptive (or has a specific function), but that it is present *because* it is adaptive (or has that function). Whereas the first causal link was between the presence of the characteristic (within a given context) and the organisms' reproductive success (or some more specific consequence), the second one is between the context's having some dispositional property (that of being such that, should the characteristic be present, it would be adaptive or perform the specific function attributed to it) and the characteristic's presence at equilibrium. The simplest way of testing such a claim is to identify a categorical property of the context closely connected with the relevant dispositional property and then to investigate the effects of variation, whether synchronic or diachronic, in this property. So-called industrial melanism provides a textbook example of such an investigation.[9] The variation in the context is provided by the fact that the bark of trees is progressively covered by soot in industrializing areas. The context is thereby transformed from one in which a grey and brown colouring is adaptive for species of moths which are in the habit of resting on the bark of trees, into one in which black colouring is adaptive. With some time lag, one has actually observed the rise and spread of a new variety of black moth in the various species concern-cerned. Had one not done so, one could possibly have argued that equilibrium had not yet been reached, or that the "black" alternative was not close enough, or that—after all—the "grey and brown" variety was still adaptive (situations *3,2,1* in Fig. 3.7). The test of the second kind of causal claim, therefore, is never fully conclusive. But it may be convincing enough to shake or establish the plausibility of the explanations concerned.

This second step in the testing of any functional explanation (whether function explanation or optimum explanation) is clearly absent from the testing of universal optimalism or universal functionalism, which only claim that the characteristics which are present at equilibrium are adaptive or have a function, not that they are present *because* they are adaptive or have a function. However, should the validity of universal functionalism and, especially, of universal optimalism be sufficiently well established, this would make the second step in the testing of a function explanation or, at least, of an optimum explanation, largely redundant. If a particular characteristic which is present is shown to be adaptive, this clearly leaves open the possibility of a "preadaptation", i.e. of an adaptive characteristic whose presence is not due to its adaptiveness. But if the characteristics which are present are systematically adaptive, the possibility that the coincidence between a particular characteristic's presence and its adaptiveness be due to "chance" is practically ruled out, and showing that it is adaptive is nearly tantamount to showing that it is present because it is adaptive. It thus turns out that, although there is no strict implication in either direction, there is a very close relationship between the functional explanation of the presence of particular features (at equilibrium) and the corresponding "universal principles".

27. Kin selection and reciprocity

The aim of the previous four sections was to discuss briefly a number of notions which are central to the logic of NS-evolutionary explanations. No special attention was paid in them to behavioural characteristics, let alone to specifically social behaviour. We must now turn to the question of how the natural selection of biological characteristics through the selection of individual organisms can possibly legitimate the explanation of specifically social features. Or, in other words, how is an NS-evolutionary explanation of such features possible on the background of natural selection in its standard form? This is precisely the issue on which so-called sociobiology has focused and on which it has come up with two distinct solutions.

First of all, one may define a behaviour pattern as specifically social if it is *altruistic*, in the sense of benefitting other members of the group at the expense of the individual animal which displays it. If this "expense" is measured in terms of survival, the existence of such specifically social features need not create any special problem. The lapwing which feigns injury when its nest is threatened by a hawk, for instance, may reduce somewhat its own chances of survival, while substantially increasing those of its offspring and so increasing its own chances of reproduction. Since what matters to adaptiveness is reproduction and not survival, the possibility of such parental altruism can easily be accommodated by the standard form of natural selection. A more serious problem arises when the altruistic behaviour involves "expenses" for its performer not only in terms of chances of survival, but also in terms of chances of reproduction. The warning call uttered in many species of passerine birds when a predator is spotted, for example, does not specifically benefit the caller's offspring, and certainly does not seem to benefit them sufficiently to offset the reduction in the caller's chances of survival. By definition, altruistic behaviour in this stronger sense is not adaptive. How can its existence possibly be explained by reference to the natural selection of organisms?

It is precisely in order to answer this question that sociobiologists have introduced the related notions of kin selection and inclusive fitness.[10] The key point is that an organism does not only share genes with its offspring, but also with its parents, its siblings, its cousins, etc. By contributing to the latter's survival at the expense of its own, an organism may conceivably decrease its chances of reproduction, while increasing the probability that the genes it carries will be further transmitted. This probability defines the *inclusive fitness* associated with the presence of a particular characteristic in an organism of a certain kind. When the key point mentioned above is realized, i.e. when the reality of *kin selection* is taken into account, the natural selection of organisms must be viewed as local optimization in terms of inclusive fitness rather than in terms of chances of reproduction, and the definition of adaptiveness (section 23) must be reformulated accordingly. In order to be adaptive in the modified sense (in terms of inclusive fitness) while not being adaptive in the original sense (in terms of chances of reproduction), a characteristic must fulfil the following conditions: it must only slightly reduce its carrier's chances of reproduction, it must sufficiently increase the chances of reproduction of some other organisms, and these other organisms must be genealogically sufficiently close to the carrier. Whether such characteristics as the passerines' warning call fulfil these conditions is of course an empirical matter. But the conditions seem sufficiently stringent for the difference between the original and the modified concept of adaptiveness to be of little practical importance.

Furthermore, a characteristic which is adaptive in the modified sense but not in the initial sense is somewhat less accessible and less stable than one which is adaptive in both senses. An altruistic mutant individual will have lower chances of reproduction than its selfish siblings, although its offspring—because they will benefit from one another's altruism—may have higher chances of reproduction than its siblings' offspring. This means that, for an altruistic mutation to be able to spread, it must be given a chance for a sufficiently long time, and its universal presence in the population is therefore less easily "accessible" than that of non-altruistic adaptive characteristics. Symmetrically, a selfish mutant individual will have higher chances of reproduction than its altruistic siblings—because it will benefit from their altruism without cost—, although its offspring will have lower chances of reproduction than its siblings' offspring, at least if the altruistic characteristic possessed by the latter maximizes inclusive fitness. This means that the universal presence of an altruistic characteristic is less stable, more vulnerable to mutations, than that of non-altruistic adaptive characteristics.

Kin selection constitutes one way in which this instability can be kept within narrow limits: if the main beneficiaries of altruistic behaviour are siblings, it will take only one generation for the carrier of a mutant selfish characteristic to be at a disadvantage, compared to its altruistic cousins. Another conceivable way in which instability can be checked is provided by so-called *reciprocal altruism,* although many doubt that it has any application among non-human animals.[11] What is essential here is not that close kin should be the main beneficiaries, but that organisms should be able to recognize one another individually. Take, as a possible illustration, meat-sharing among chimpanzees. The latter give meat (when they have plenty) to kin and non-kin indiscriminately, but it seems that their doing so depends on whether the receiver reciprocates (when it has plenty). Such a behaviour pattern is not altruistic in the sense mentioned above: once established, it does not reduce the individual's chances of survival or of reproduction—on the contrary. However, like the kind of "altruistic" behaviour discussed above, and in a more acute form, it raises a problem of "accessibility". A mutant "giver" can expect little reciprocation, and it is only when "good luck" will have made the underlying characteristic sufficiently frequent, that the probability of being paid back will cease to be negligible. Only then can the behaviour pattern cease to be a liability and be imposed upon the whole population by selection pressures. The stability of such a behaviour pattern once it has spread, on the other hand, is automatically secured, at least in a sufficiently small population, by the fact that a non-reciprocator will be discriminated against. If the population is so large that the probability of two individuals interacting more than once is fairly small, however, it is possible for "genetic cheaters", i.e. non-reciprocating mutants, to get away with receiving without giving back. The situation is then equivalent to one in which individual recognition plays no role, and "reciprocal altruism" becomes exceedingly vulnerable to "selfish" mutations.

28. Group selection

Kin selection and reciprocity constitute two ways in which sociobiology has attempted to accommodate "specifically social" behaviour patterns within the framework of the natural selection of organisms. In one case, an altruistic behaviour pattern is shown to be relatively stable because the performer's siblings are its main beneficiaries. In the other case, an apparently altruistic behaviour pattern is shown to be stable because its performance is contingent upon reciprocation by an individually recognized beneficiary. However, some have maintained that there are "altruistic" behaviour patterns in animal populations, whose beneficiaries need not be closely related to the performer nor individually recognized by him. The standard example is demographic regulation through "birth control" or through "suicidal emigration", which has been alleged to take place in a number of species of rodents: before the population reaches starvation point, at which it may completely exhaust its resources, regulation sets in and enables the population to survive. Since neither of the two strategies discussed in the previous sections can be applied to this case, the natural selection of organisms cannot possibly legitimate the functional explanation of such behaviour patterns. One needs another type of mechanism, the natural selection of groups of organisms or, for short, *group selection.* [12] If there are differential rates of extinction and dissemination among groups of organisms depending on whether their members possess a particular characteristic or do not, then, at equilibrium, it seems that this characteristic should be universally present in the (meta-) population of groups of organisms. Admittedly, the differential extinction and dissemination of groups is likely to need much more time to produce its effects, than the differential reproduction of individuals—which means that equilibrium situations can only be postulated in the very long run. But one could nonetheless assert the existence of an NS-evolutionary attractor corresponding to the optimal characteristic for group survival (x_G^* in Fig. 3.8), distinct from the optimal characteristic for individual reproduction within the group (x_I^* in Fig. 3.8). It has been suggested that what individual selection is to biological functional explanations, group selection could be to sociological functional explanations.[13]

Figure 3.8. Group optimality and individual optimality

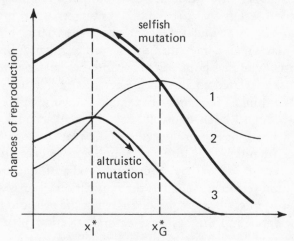

behavioural characteristics
(for example, degrees of loudness of warning call)

Note: The chances of reproduction which are represented here are those of an individual organism with characteristic x, when every other individual in the group (1) also has characteristic x, (2) has the group-optimal characteristic x_G^*, (3) has the individual-optimal characteristic x_I^*.

However, this suggestion raises two serious difficulties. First of all, group selection sharpens the problems of inaccessibility and instability, already raised by kin selection, to the point of unmanageability. The main problem, for the efficiency of group selection, is that individual selection is going on at the same time. If groups could mutate as wholes, and only as wholes, it would be possible for them to move from x_I^* to x_G^* along curve *1* (in Fig. 3.8), and impossible to move back to x_G^*. Kin selection, which can be viewed as a minimal form of group selection, corresponds precisely to the case where such an assumption is not too implausible, because individual mutations can roughly be interpreted as sibling-group mutations at the next generation. Hence the relative accessibility and stability of characteristics which are optimal for the kin group (x_G^*), while not being optimal for the individual within the kin-group (x_I^*). In the case of larger units, however, the possibility of "group mutations" (through so-called "genetic drift") becomes very problematic. When the kin group is not the crucial beneficiary, therefore, altruistic mutations (from x_I^* to x_G^*) will unambiguously move organisms and sibling groups downwards along curve *3*, rather than upwards along curve *1*, and a situation in which all members of the group share the group-optimal characteristic x_G^* becomes practically inaccessible, because of adverse selection pressures. Furthermore, mutations at a lower level than the group will constitute a permanent possibility. When the kin group is not the crucial beneficiary, therefore, selfish mutations (from x_G^* to x_I^*) will unambiguously move organisms and sibling groups upwards along curve *2*, rather than downwards along curve *1*, and a situation in which all members of the group share the group-optimal characteristic x_G^* becomes highly unstable. In the case of group selection, in other words, the difficulties of kin selection are considerably magnified. The NS-evolutionary attractors which group selection defines are so "weak" (compared to those defined by individual selection) that the presence of very few characteristics, if any, can be explained by reference to them.

The second difficulty arises from the standard version of natural selection as well as from its group-selection variant. In either case, the object of the NS-evolutionary explanation which is being legitimated can only be the presence (at equilibrium) of some hereditary biological characteristic in all the members of a population of organisms or in all the

members of all the groups of a (meta-) population of groups
of organisms. Now, it cannot be excluded *a priori* that the
pattern of explanation which covers such explanations may
rightly intrude into the field traditionally occupied by the
social sciences. But such a pattern can hardly be used to make
sense of explanations actually proposed by social scientists,
because the latter are not concerned with the explanation of
hereditary characteristics. Even when the features whose
presence they attempt to explain are universal throughout
mankind and have biological advantages, the fact that they are
culturally, rather than genetically, controlled, prevents the
operation of natural selection, as discussed so far.

Take, for example, the incest taboo, in the narrow sense of
a prohibition of sexual relationships between parents and
children and between brothers and sisters.[14] The universal
presence of this feature in man has biological advantages.
Admittedly, the fact that children born of an incestuous
relationship are more likely to be defective must be dis-
counted as irrelevant, since the increased probability of
homozygozity to which it is due can only be detrimental
because it enables more recessive genes to express themselves—and the reason why recessive genes are, in the average, less advantageous than dominant ones is precisely that
the incest taboo has partly protected them from selection
pressures. The biological advantage of the incest taboo, like
that of biparental sexual reproduction, rather consists in
securing the recombination of the existing genetic variety.
This increases substantially the population's evolutionary
adaptability and, therefore, its chances of survival in a
changing environment. However, this biological advantage
cannot form the basis of an NS-evolutionary explanation
along the lines explored above because, as anthropologists
have kept emphasizing, the incest taboo is not a (genetically
controlled) biological characteristic, but a (socially controlled) cultural trait. It does not consist in an innate motivational
structure, whether in the form of a "voice of the blood" or of
a sexual repulsion for individuals with whom one has been

brought up, but rather in a social norm, socially learned and socially enforced.[15] Consequently, even in this case, which seemed particularly favourable, and even if the first difficulty is supposed to be solved, the group-selection argument *as sketched in this section* is bound to be irrelevant to social-scientific explanations.

29. Cultural ethology

The negative conclusion to which the discussion of sociobiology and the group-selection perspective has led us must immediately be qualified. There is no *a priori* reason why the NS-evolutionary perspective should be restricted to genetically controlled characteristics. Cultural traits, whether practices or beliefs, can in principle provide natural selection with an equally sound variation basis. All that is required, as in the case of biological characteristics, is that variation should at the same time be large enough to provide selection with raw material, and small enough to enable selection to leave its mark. "Blind" innovations, immitations and migrations may ensure the former, while the traditional transmission and social enforcement of practices and beliefs may ensure the latter. It seems, therefore, that the natural selection of organisms can operate on this cultural basis, just as well as on a biological basis. In particular, if cultural traits can, by and large, be assumed to be transmitted by parents to offspring, one can expect to discover that cultural traits tend to be adaptive in the sense discussed above (sections 23 and 27).[16] More importantly, one can then explain the universal presence of a cultural trait in a population by its adaptiveness or by the fact that it has some specific consequences which are decisive in making it adaptive. And the whole discussion of the logic of this type of explanation (sections 23–26) can be applied without modification to the case of cultural traits, with only the caveat that "neighbourhood" in the space of genetic possibilities need not be identical with "neighbourhood" in the space of cultural possibilities. One can call *cultural ethology* the study of cultural traits, as shaped by such a mechanism of individual natural selection.[17]

As an illustration, take the following example. Among the !Kung Bushmen of Botswana, a foraging culture, women average four years between births, which is considerably more than in similar non-foraging cultures. This peculiarity can be related to the fact that, in a foraging culture, women have to carry their small children on their foraging trips and, given certain assumptions about child mortality, the distances to be covered, the food requirements of a family, etc., it is possible to show that a four-year birth spacing is adaptive within the given context.[18] Now, if the kind of mechanism sketched above has been operating in this case, one can explain the (universal) presence of this cultural trait in a population of !Kung Bushmen by the fact that the trait is adaptive, i.e. that it locally maximizes its carriers' chances of reproduction. Parents who have—and teach their children to have—one child every four years, will have, in the average, more surviving descendants than those who have—and teach their children to have—a larger or smaller number of children. The outcome of such a process is that individuals of the former category represent a steadily increasing proportion of the population and, at equilibrium, the whole population.

The limitations of this cultural/individual version of the NS-evolutionary approach are obvious. Firstly, it can only concern cultural traits which can affect (independently of social sanctions) an individual's chances of reproduction. It does not seem that an individual's failure to perform funeral rites for his ancestors, for example, should *per se* decrease his reproductive success. Of course, his fellowmen may ostracize him or execute him for this reason, but by taking such social consequences into account, one would blatantly beg the question. Secondly, this version of the NS-evolutionary approach can only concern cultural traits which can be carried by individuals. The fact that a society is divided into classes or that it has courts, for example, is not subject to individual variation. Furthermore, even those cultural traits which can be carried by individuals—like the spacing of births—, are usually transmitted, maintained and enforced at the level of society—school, friends, sorcerer—rather than at the level of a single family. This leaves very little room for the selection of cultural traits to operate through the differential reproduction of individuals.

30. *The natural selection of total societies*

It would seem that these difficulties can be solved if social groups, instead of individuals, are taken to be the entities on which natural selection operates. There is no problem, then, in attributing cultural traits to the social group as a whole, rather than to its individual members. And what matters is not whether the presence of those traits contributes to an individual's reproductive success, but whether it contributes to the social group's survival. The differential extinction or disbanding of social groups will operate on the pool of (blind) innovations, borrowings and migrations in such a way that, at equilibrium, those cultural traits whose presence maximizes the chances of group survival will be present in all the social groups which make up a (meta-) population of social groups. This cultural/societal form of NS-evolutionary approach seems much more congenial than the other three to the "culturalist" and "systemic" emphases of classical social-scientific "functionalism", and it is not surprising, therefore, if its potential relevance has often been pointed out in the methodological debate about "functionalism".[19]

To illustrate, take once again the example of the incest taboo. Apart from the biological advantage mentioned previously (section 28), two kinds of more specifically sociological advantages have repeatedly been attributed to the prohibition of sexual relationships between close kin. On the one hand, it prevents strife within the nuclear family. And on the other hand, in so far as it implies exogamy (i.e. *marriage* outside the nuclear family), it prevents the break-up of societies into isolated units.[20] In these various ways—which constitute what has been called above (section 25) a multiplicity of functions "in parallel"—, the presence of the trait may increase a social group's chances of survival to such an extent that only social groups which possess it will be left at equilibrium in the (meta-) population of social groups. If this is the case, the presence of the incest taboo can be said to correspond to an NS-evolutionary attractor for a population of societies, just as an adaptive biological characteristic corresponds to an NS-evolutionary attractor for a population of organisms.

One might expect group selection in the cultural realm to raise the same problems of accessibility and stability as group selection in the biological realm (section 28). But the very reasons which make cultural traits unsuitable for individual natural selection, make them particularly suitable for group selection. In particular, if cultural traits, unlike biological characteristics, are transmitted and enforced at the level of the group, individual mutations cannot undermine their evolution through group selection. The major difficulty here, at least if the social groups under consideration are taken to be total societies, is connected rather with the excessively large time scale which is required for the group selection process to operate. If the presence of the incest taboo in all societies can be accounted for by the natural selection of blindly varying societies, not only must there have been a significant rate of extinction among societies, but more precisely a significant rate of *differential* extinction: a considerable number of societies must have died out or broken up because they lacked the incest taboo. The fact that nothing like such a rate of societal mortality has been observed certainly deprives this NS-evolutionary approach of any relevance for cultural traits which change rapidly: if the pressures of selection are negligible compared to counteracting pressures of variation, there can be no evolutionary attractor in the space of cultural possibilities. Against this objection, it is possible to argue that with a cultural trait like the incest taboo, the rate of variation is also very low. Firstly, however, the NS-evolutionary "attraction" would then only work in the very long run, and its relevance would therefore be easily upset by changes in the context. And secondly, it is doubtful whether the life span of mankind has been long enough for such a slow evolutionary process to have had any significant impact on the presence or absence of cultural traits in human societies.[21]

31. Firms and sects

However insuperable this difficulty may be in the case of total societies, it does not necessarily hold in the case of smaller social groups. If the environment is sufficiently tough, the rate of differential elimination of such groups may well be far from negligible. The standard example is that of capitalist firms in a perfectly competitive market. Suppose that the production activities of capitalist firms are governed by rigid routines, subject to random modifications, rather than by rational decision-making. Suppose further that firms can only survive if they make positive profits, and that whether they do so depends on the relative efficiency of their techniques. Then, with the usual proviso that variation should be neither excessively small nor excessively large and that selection should be sufficiently harsh, one can expect the economy to move fairly rapidly towards an equilibrium state in which every surviving member of the population of firms uses locally optimal techniques.[22] The presence of such techniques can therefore be said to constitute an NS-evolutionary attractor, and it can be functionally explained by the fact that they are locally optimal, as far as a firm's chances of survival are concerned.

As in the case of populations of organisms (see section 24), changes in or differences between populations of firms can be accounted for (adaptationally) by reference to changes or differences in the relevant context, which determine changes or differences in the positions of the NS-evolutionary attractors. Suppose, for example, that money wages, in the economy, increase considerably relative to the price of capital goods. If techniques are assumed to be modified at random within each firm, one cannot predict on this basis any change in the techniques used by particular firms. But one can predict a change in the techniques used (at equilibrium) by the *typical* firm. A higher relative wage level implies that labour-intensive firms are more likely to shrink and die, while capital-intensive firms are more likely to survive and expand. One can therefore predict that the equilibrium labour/capital ratio of the economy, i.e. of the population of firms, will increase as a result of the change in the economic environment.[23]

As in the case of organisms once again, the change or difference in the context of the feature (biological characteristic or cultural trait) whose presence is being explained need not be a change or difference in the environment of the entities (organisms or firms) in which the feature is present. Take, for instance, the strong correlation which can be observed in business organizations between routine technology and authoritarian leadership on the one hand, and between creative technology and permissive leadership on the other.[24] As usual when the relevant aspect of the feature's context is not part of the entity's environment, one must here bear in mind the trade-off between arbitrariness in the choice of the context and multioptimality within the chosen context (see section 23). Suppose, however, that one can take the type of technology as given. One might then conjecture that authoritarian leadership constitutes an NS-evolutionary attractor within the context of a routine technology, while permissive leadership constitutes an NS-evolutionary attractor within the context of a creative technology. Deviations from the attractors are corrected through the competitive elimination of the deviant firms, which happen to have adopted a less effective combination of type of technology and type of leadership. At equilibrium, only those combinations which (locally) maximize a firm's chances of survival can be expected to be present.

Firms, however, are not the only kind of sub-societies to

which one may think this version of natural selection is relevant. Gangs, political parties or religious sects may also constitute populations of social groups among which differential extinction is sufficient to legitimate NS-evolutionary explanations of the presence of certain traits. Take millenarian movements, for example. Unlike many other religious groups, they are typically organized around a prophet. This feature can perhaps be explained as follows. Since millenarian movements usually arise in politically divided areas, they can only subsist if they attribute supernatural authority to a charismatic individual. Movements without a prophet, therefore, cannot really get off the ground, and they soon disappear.[25] Providing the selection pressures are sufficiently harsh to keep variation under check, it is possible to explain the presence (at equilibrium) of certain traits in a representative member of a (meta-) population of millenarian sects, by the fact that it locally maximizes a sect's chances of survival. Incidentally, function explanations are possible here, along with optimum explanations, in exactly the same way as in the standard version of the NS-evolutionary approach (see section 25). In the above example, the prophetic character of millenarian movements can be explained by its function of providing them with a cohesion they would otherwise lack.

32. *NS-evolutionary explanation in the social sciences*

Does this discussion of the sociobiological model—in a broad sense, which covers all four forms of natural selection—help us answer the two questions raised in the previous chapters? Does it shed any light on the deep structure of the social sciences and on the legitimacy of social-scientific function explanations?

Of the four forms of natural selection, the second one ("group selection") and the third one ("cultural ethology") are intrinsically problematic. It is doubtful whether there can be anything like a selection of biological characteristics through the differential extinction of groups, or a selection of cultural traits through the differential reproduction of individuals. The first form of natural selection ("Neo-Darwinian synthesis") and the fourth one ("system functionalism"), on the other hand, do not share this shaky status. The relevance of the former to the explanation of social phenomena has been emphasized by sociobiology. That of the latter has been repeatedly mentioned in the debate on "functionalism". The first and standard form of natural selection, however, because it is restricted to the explanation of genetically controlled characteristics, cannot possibly underlie the actual explanatory practice of the social sciences. The latter is concerned with features which are socially controlled and, therefore, escape the jurisdiction of biology and sociobiology *sensu stricto*. I grant that one can make it one of the objectives of sociobiology "to reformulate the foundations of the social sciences in a way that draws these subjects in the Modern Synthesis".[26] But this would be an attempt to "make nonsense" of the social sciences as they are, whereas I am concerned here with making sense of them. We are therefore left with the fourth form of natural selection as a possible basis for an NS-evolutionary pattern of explanation in the social sciences.

In a way, the existence of such a pattern provides us with a reply to the two questions which this work tries to answer. Can function explanations be legitimate in the social sciences? Yes, one seems forced to say, because, under certain conditions, some kind of evolutionary mechanism can plausibly be assumed to operate in the social realm, and we have seen (section 19) that this is enough to make room for functional explanations in general, and function explanations in particular. Does this fact shed light on the deep structure of the social sciences? Yes, one seems forced to conclude, because the functional explanations legitimated by the operation of a mechanism of natural selection are necessarily L-functional: even when the consequences which account for the entities' differential reproduction or survival happen to be recognized by the agents, this recognition is purely incidental and by no means essential to the explanation. And we have seen (section 21) that this is enough to make the corresponding pattern of explanation irreducible to the action pattern.

The questions raised in the first two chapters seem to have been answered, and one may think that this book could stop here. If it did, however, it would have failed to provide answers which are of more than anecdotal interest. True, the NS-evolutionary pattern of explanation illustrated in the previous two sections can legitimate function explanations and is irreducible to the action pattern. But the number of actual social-scientific explanations which can be fitted into this pattern is so small, and the role they play in social-scientific practice so marginal, that the answers thus given to our two initial questions are of hardly any significance beyond the realm of methodological speculation. It seems fair to say, therefore, that there is nothing in the social sciences which corresponds to natural selection in biology, and one may be tempted to conclude that very little indeed, if anything, is to be gained by the social sciences from an analogy with evolutionary biology.[27] However, if a social-scientific NS-evolutionary pattern is practically negligible, whether for the purpose of delineating a residue irreducible to the action pattern or of making room for function explanations, this does not mean that *any* evolutionary pattern of explanation, in the social sciences, is equally negligible. Let us now turn to the second basic type of evolutionary mechanism.

4

The Linguistic Model

Summary

Reinforcement is a type of evolutionary mechanism in which the selection of features does not operate through the selection of entities which they characterize, but rather within these entities. It leads to the selection of features which are functional, i.e. which maximize an entity's chances of satisfaction (section 33). It legitimates both optimum explanations, which can conveniently be reformulated in terms of evolutionary attractors, and function explanations in terms of specific consequences (section 34). Even in the animal realm, the relevance of reinforcement is not restricted to the explanation of individual habits, but extends to the explanation of cultural traits (section 35).

When trying to demonstrate the potential relevance of reinforcement to the legitimation of social-scientific explanations, however, it is most fruitful to turn to the specific case of *historical linguistics*. Not only can numerous analogies be drawn between linguistic evolution and biological evolution (section 36). But an explicitly "functionalist" approach to linguistic change has been developed, in which reference is made to reinforcement as the mechanism through which an optimal compromise is struck between cost minimization and the communication function of language (section 37). The main trouble with this approach, as with any evolutionary theory relying on reinforcement, is that the only explanations which it can generate seem to be either optimum explanations which are intrinsically circular (section 38) or function explanations whose refutation is never a threat to the theory itself (section 39). This would reduce any evolutionary theory of this type to untestable speculation, if it were not for the fact that the optimality criterion in terms of which it is formulated is one which is *specified* (in terms of cost and communication): this makes room, in principle, for a statistical test (section 40) or for one in which some components of the optimality criterion are kept constant (section 41). The same point applies to a more complex theory of linguistic change which integrates the expressive function of a language with its function of communication (section 42).

To a much more significant extent than the sociobiological model examined in the previous chapter, the linguistic model thus suggested helps to answer both the question of the deep structure of the social sciences and that of the legitimacy of function and, more generally, functional explanations (section 43).

33. *Reinforcement as an evolutionary mechanism*

Evolutionary mechanisms are mechanisms of local optimization. They operate through the selection of "blind" variants according to the consequences associated with them. The first basic type of evolutionary mechanism, natural selection, has been dealt with in the previous chapter. The second one, I shall call *reinforcement*. And accordingly, I shall call *R-evolutionary* the explanations which this type of mechanism legitimates, the pattern of explanation which it defines and the attractors which it determines. What fundamentally distinguishes reinforcement from natural selection, is that the features whose presence is being explained are no longer selected through the selection of entities which they characterize, but rather directly within those entities.

In its most elementary form, reinforcement corresponds to

operant conditioning, as studied by behaviourist psychology.[1] Take the example of the pigeon in its cage, and suppose that the context is such that, whenever the pigeon lifts its head beyond a certain level, it is given some food. After a while, it will develop the habit of lifting its head when hungry. The mechanism which brings about the presence of such a habit at equilibrium is an evolutionary mechanism in the sense specified above (section 20).[2] There is an element of blind variation which is sufficient to provide selection with its raw material: the pigeon tries new behaviour patterns. At the same time, variation is sufficiently limited to prevent the effects of selection from being erased immediately: the fact that a *habit* is being constituted indicates that there is something like a durable underlying competence which is capable of being shaped by the selection process. Finally, this selection process can be said to take the differential consequences of the alternative variants into account. It is because the pigeon "notices" a causal connection between its behaving in a certain way and its receiving food, that the conditioning can take place. Operant conditioning, therefore, is clearly an evolutionary mechanism. But it is not one of natural selection, since it does not involve the differential survival or reproduction of the organisms in which it takes place. It is rather a mechanism of reinforcement, whereby a habit is selected "within" a particular organism.

Two major consequences immediately follow from this fundamental difference between the two types of mechanisms. Firstly, whereas natural selection is restricted to entities which are capable of dying and (preferably) reproducing, reinforcement is restricted to entities which are capable of *registering* and of *feeling*, however unconsciously: if the fact that the presence of some feature has certain consequences is to play a causal role as such—and without acting through the selection of entities—, this fact must somehow be "registered" by the entity and the consequences must be "felt" to be better than those which the presence of alternative features has.[3] This means that no reinforcement can take place below the level of animals endowed with a nervous system and, therefore, with the capacity to learn. Secondly and no less importantly, whereas natural selection imposes a populational point of view, reinforcement does not. What it produces, at equilibrium, is the presence of a feature in a particular entity, not the (universal) presence of a feature in a population of entities. Consequently, it enables us to explain changes which affect a *particular* entity, not just changes which affect a population of entities or a *typical* member of it.

Just as the general nature of natural selection imposes the entity's chances of reproduction as the criterion of selection between features, the general nature of reinforcement imposes what I shall call the entity's *chances of satisfaction*. The term "satisfaction" is here used to cover every component of the entity's criterion of selection, whether learned or innate, whether culturally invariant or socially controlled. How satisfying the consequences of alternative variants are, cannot only be assessed by looking at which variants actually get established, for example by examining whether the pigeon keeps lifting its head or not. Particularly (but not exclusively) in the case of human beings, it can also be assessed directly, through the entity's "avowals" about what it finds satisfying and what not: our pigeon can scream for example. And particularly (but not exclusively) in the case of nonhuman entities, it can be assessed indirectly, by assuming that the criterion of satisfaction must have been shaped by natural selection and must therefore correspond, at least roughly, to the criterion of reproductive success imposed by the latter: the fact that eating food when hungry is good for our pigeon's reproduction, for example, is indirect evidence of its being satisfying. Without such additional evidence, whether direct or indirect, it is obviously impossible without circularity to explain the presence of a feature by its being satisfying.

Note, finally, that the term "*chances* of satisfaction" has been chosen here in order to emphasize that the consequences associated with a feature need not be deterministically connected to its presence. The entity must have at least a rough

way of balancing the degree to which alternative consequences are satisfying and the probability of their occurrence.
This would enable a pigeon, for example, to select a habit
which produces slightly satisfying consequences very frequently, rather than one which produces highly satisfying
consequences but only very rarely (or the other way round).

34. R-evolutionary attractors

Any evolutionary mechanism, as we have seen (section 19), is
a mechanism of local optimization. In the case of reinforcement, optimality is judged in terms of chances of satisfaction.
For lack of a better term, I shall call *functional* a feature which
is locally optimal in this sense, i.e. a feature whose presence
maximizes the entity's chances of satisfaction, within a given
context and relative to neighbouring alternatives in the space
of possible features.[4] As in the case of natural selection, the
main kind of explanation which can be legitimated by reference to such a mechanism is optimum explanation. The fact
which is being explained is the fact that, at equilibrium, a
particular feature has been adopted by a particular entity. A
situation of equilibrium is one in which the alternative features have had time to be tried and in which their differential
consequences have had time to be perceived by the entity
concerned. The feature consists in a behaviour pattern, in the
simplest case an individual habit. The entity consists in a
sentient being, in the simplest case an organism. The fact by
which the feature's presence is being explained is the fact that
the feature is functional, in the sense defined above. It is a
dispositional fact about the context in which the feature
appears, which can be described more fully as follows: the
context is such that, should the feature be adopted, its presence would locally maximize the entity's chances of satisfaction. An R-evolutionary optimum explanation asserts the
existence of a causal link between the latter fact and the
feature's presence at equilibrium. The presence of a functional
feature, in other words, constitutes an R-evolutionary at-

tractor in the space of features which are possible in the given context.

Under some idealizing assumptions, these notions can be represented with the help of *functional landscapes*, just as NS-evolutionary notions can be represented with the help of adaptive landscapes (section 24). Suppose that the various habits which can be adopted by the pigeon when it is hungry can be represented as a one-dimensional continuum, with each value corresponding, say, to one way of placing its head, and that distances along this continuum adequately represent the ease or difficulty with which a blind search process can lead from one habit to another. Within a given context— which includes for example the food-giving device and the pigeon's tastes—, one can associate with each position along the continuum, the chances of satisfaction which the corresponding habit confers on the pigeon. This provides us with a function, whose local maxima represent, by definition, functional habits (Fig. 4.1).

Figure 4.1. Functional landscape

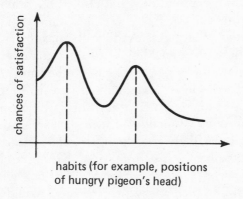

As was the case with natural selection, the selection component of reinforcement tends to push the entity's habits to the top of the hills in this functional landscape, and to keep them there. The blind-variation component, on the other hand, exerts constant pressure away from the equilibrium position. The system will not necessarily settle on the highest peak (in the given context), because the latter may be beyond the reach of blind variation. This is what restricts optimization to neighbouring alternatives.

The position of the R-evolutionary attractors depends on the nature of the context. If the food-giving device or the pigeon's tastes are modified, for example, the relief of the functional landscape is altered, and different habits may become functional. As in the NS-evolutionary case (section 24), this means that the equilibrium values of the behaviour variable, which ranges over the set of possible habits, can be given as a (possibly multi-valued) function of the control variables, which describe relevant aspects of the context. This function constitutes a matrix for comparative-static R-evolutionary explanations: a change in the habits which our pigeon adopts at equilibrium, or a difference in the habits adopted by different pigeons, can be explained by changes or differences in relevant control variables.

Like natural selection, reinforcement does not only legitimate optimum explanations, but also, though more loosely, function explanations. If, for example, the way in which the pigeon's habit of lifting its head locally maximizes its chances of satisfaction is by enabling it to open a valve and so get access to food, then one can ascribe to the habit the function of opening the valve. And one can explain its presence at equilibrium by the fact that it has the specific consequences referred to as its "function". Such an explanation is only loosely legitimated by the operation of reinforcement, because it is possible for the adoption of the habit to have other, negative consequences, which could offset the significance of its "function" in such a way that the habit would cease to be functional. And then there is no reason why one should expect reinforcement to lead to the adoption of the habit. What matters is the total balance of consequences, not a single specific one. Nevertheless, like NS-evolutionary function explanations (section 25), R-evolutionary ones may often be useful. On the one hand, they shed light on the explanandum by specifying more precisely the nature of the mechanism: pointing out that the opening of the valve plays a crucial role in the reinforcement of the habit makes the latter's presence at equilibrium more intelligible. And on the other hand, a function explanation often makes specific suggestions about which aspects of the context, described in categorical terms, are important in determining the chances of satisfaction associated with different habits: if the habit's presence is explained by its function of opening a valve, changes in the position or in the working of the valve are likely to make different habits functional.

General principles of *universal optimalism* and *universal functionalism* (at equilibrium) are connected to R-evolutionary optimum and function explanations in exactly the same way as they are in the NS-evolutionary case (section 26). The latter (and weaker) principle operates more quickly under the impulse of reinforcement than under the impulse of (the standard form of) natural selection, because the variation on which the former operates is more likely to be spontaneously biased towards "least effort" than genetic variation. The former (and stronger) principle, on the other hand, must be qualified as follows. In the case of reinforcement, the differential consequences which determine what is locally optimal (i.e. the position of the R-evolutionary attractors) must be such that their causal connection with the feature whose presence is being explained can be perceived by the entities involved. If a causal link is so subtle that its perception is beyond the latter's cognitive powers, it can play no role in reinforcement. And a feature may be present at equilibrium in spite of not being functional (i.e. locally optimal as far as chances of satisfaction are concerned), simply because some of the actual differential consequences of its presence are not and cannot be perceived as such by the entity involved. The principle of universal optimalism, which states that whatever habit is present at equilibrium is functional, i.e. locally optimal, must consequently be understood as referring only to the range of consequences which can in principle be registered by entities of the kind which upholds the habit.

35. *The evolution of animal cultures*

The relevance of reinforcement is not restricted to individual habits. It easily combines with inter-individual imitation to shape the evolution of culturally transmitted habits. The presence of some cultural traits, in other words, can be given an R-evolutionary explanation, as illustrated by the following two examples.

Once milkmen start leaving milk bottles on doorsteps in a particular village, it usually takes a fairly long time before birds (generally tits) start opening the milk bottles and drinking the cream. But once this has happened a few times, the habit spreads very quickly. It may become a real plague for the village affected, while still being unknown in a neighbouring village which has the same species of birds and the same kind of milkmen. The birds' habit is clearly a cultural one. And it is plausible to view its adoption (at equilibrium) as the product of an R-evolutionary mechanism of the following kind. On the one hand, a bird returns to places where it has found food on previous occasions (individual reinforcement), and, on the other, birds tend to come near to conspecifics which they see feeding (inter-individual imitation).[5]

The eating habits of Japanese macaques provide a similar example. Different troops of macaques have been observed to develop strikingly different food preferences, which remain stable over several generations but which cannot be attributed to different genetic endowments. In one particular colony, it was possible to observe in detail the birth and spread of one such habit. Biologists had scattered sweet potatoes on the beach in order to supplement the monkeys' diet. After some time, a young monkey started washing the potatoes in sea water before eating them. It was then imitated by its mother and playfellows and later by other members of the colony, until, after about ten years, nearly all of them had adopted it. Here again, it is a combination of individual reinforcement and inter-individual imitation which can be considered to bring about the presence of the new cultural habit.[6]

Providing the groups involved can be considered homogeneous as far as the criterion of satisfaction is concerned, this kind of mechanism enables us to explain the presence of a cultural trait by its being functional, in the sense defined above (section 34). Cultural transmission enables the R-evolutionary process to proceed, without having to start from scratch with every individual. This means that functional features which are very unlikely to be acquired by a single individual left to its own devices, are much more easily accessible (i.e. much closer in the behaviour space) when inter-individual imitation makes it possible for the trial-and-error of many individuals to be put to common use.

As usual, a relevant change in the context induces a change in the position of the R-evolutionary attractors. As a result of human activity, the habitat of a troop of Indian primates, for example, has been substantially changed. Now, fields of potatoes and cauliflowers potentially provide them with a significant additional source of food. In the space of possible foraging habits, the position of the R-evolutionary attractors has shifted. However, it takes some time before some individuals, and later the whole troop, acquire the habits which have become functional. At "equilibrium", however, all the members of the troop will have learned to explore the fields and to dig into the soil to pull up entire plants.[7] A change in a control variable will have induced, with a time lag, a change in the behaviour variable.

It may be useful to point out, at this stage, why the R-evolutionary theory of culture suggested by these elementary examples is much more likely to be relevant to explanation in the social sciences, than the two NS-evolutionary theories of culture considered in the previous chapter. Take, first of all, what has been called "cultural ethology" (section

29). Its intrinsic weakness stems from the insuperable tension between a mechanism which operates through the differential reproduction of individuals and the fact that cultural traits are constantly being shared with individuals who are not genetically related. In an R-evolutionary approach, on the other hand, not only does no tension arise from this sharing process, but the latter is even essential if specifically cultural habits are to be shaped by reinforcement. At the same time, however, an R-evolutionary approach can also easily accommodate the fact that cultural traits are often adaptive, which lent some prima facie plausibility to cultural ethology. Admittedly, the coincidence between R-evolutionary and NS-evolutionary attractors is not a necessity. Such a habit as washing potatoes in salted water may locally maximize the monkeys' chances of satisfaction without locally maximizing their chances of reproduction. But, as has been hinted at above (section 33), one can expect natural selection to have shaped the criteria by which "satisfaction" is judged.[8] And this is why the position of an R-evolutionary attractor may often coincide with the position into which natural selection would pull the system, if it were not made inoperative by the much faster operation of reinforcement.

The basic weakness of the "system-functionalist" form of natural selection (sections 30–31), on the other hand, stems from the insufficiency of the rate of differential extinction of societies and subsocieties. This strongly suggests that the evolutionary mechanisms which account for the latter's "adaptedness" must be of a kind which does not involve the selection *of* societies and subsocieties, but rather their modification through selection *within* them. Such a distinction is obviously closely parallel to the fundamental difference between natural selection and reinforcement (section 33). Since we have just seen in this section that the relevance of reinforcement can easily be extended from individual to cultural habits, an R-evolutionary reconstruction of social-scientific functional (and adaptational) explanations is bound to look more promising than an NS-evolutionary one, however rarely it has been mentioned in the methodological debate on functionalism.[9]

36. Linguistic evolution

The suggestion that reinforcement is much more significant than natural selection as far as evolutionary explanation in the social sciences is concerned, is bound to remain implausible as long as the only examples in which it is shown to operate refer to simple cultural traits developed in animal populations. The rest of this chapter will attempt to make such a suggestion more convincing, by showing how human language can be dealt with in an R-evolutionary perspective.

Numerous analogies have been drawn between the subject-matters of evolutionary biology and historical linguistics. In many respects, a language is like a species. It is made up of a set of dialects, each of which is itself made up of a set of idiolects, just as a species is made up of a set of populations, each of which is itself made up of a set of organisms. A language is defined by the potential inter-intelligibility of idiolects, and a dialect by actual (linguistic) interaction between them, just as one species is defined by the potential inter-fecundity of organisms, and a population by actual (sexual) interaction between them. Idiolects which belong to the same dialect are similar in some respects and different in others, just as organisms which belong to the same population are similar in some respects and different in others. Each dialect, like each population, therefore, is in a permanent state of heterogeneity, in spite of a substantial basis of shared features.

On this background, linguistic change, like biological change, can be seen as a gradual change in the frequency with which different variants appear. In both cases, the path followed by historical change can be reconstructed with the help of three main methods. The most obvious one is the study of material traces, written documents in the case of paleography, and fossils in the case of paleontology. The most subtle one is internal reconstruction, based on Halle's postulate of a parallelism between synchronic and diachronic rule-ordering in one case, and on Haeckel's biogenetic principle, which asserts that ontogeny repeats phylogeny, in the other. The most important one, finally, is the genealogical method, which is based on the hypothesis that similarities between languages and between species are due to common historical origins.[10]

These similarities may be deemed sufficient to allow us to speak of linguistic *evolution* in roughly the same sense as that in which we speak of biological evolution. For our purposes, however, there is a more important similarity. From Darwin onwards, it has often been suggested that linguistic change, like biological change, can be analyzed in terms of blind variation and selection: new variants are introduced inadvertently, possibly as a result of blunders or slips of the tongue, but linguistic variation is constantly subjected to a selection process, which is claimed to pick out systematically those variants which maximize either comfort or communicative efficiency, depending on the authors.[11] Clearly, if this conception is correct, language must be governed by an evolutionary mechanism in our sense (section 20), and one must be able to explain linguistic features by reference to the consequences associated with them, without needing to suppose that they have been introduced intentionally with these consequences in mind: there is a "teleology" at work in language, but it is not the "teleology of purpose".[12]

The evolutionary mechanism involved, however, cannot be of the same (NS-evolutionary) type as in the biological case. Linguistic features are cultural traits, and they do not affect to any significant extent the differential reproduction of individuals or the differential extinction of groups. Surely, the selection of linguistic variants is a selection which operates *within* idiolects, dialects and languages, rather than through the selection *of* the individuals or groups which speak them. If an evolutionary theory of language is possible, therefore, it must be an R-evolutionary one. The so-called "functionalist" approach in diachronic linguistics—also sometimes called "evolutionary structuralism"—provides precisely a theory of this kind. As sketched by Jespersen and the Prague School, it was later systematized by Martinet.[13] Its central tenets will be presented and illustrated in the next five sections.

37. *The cost/communication trade-off*

According to the pre-functionalist tradition in historical linguistics, from the Neo-Grammarians to Saussure and Bloomfield, sound change and, more generally, linguistic change, are "blind": the purposes for which a language is used are of no relevance when explaining the ways in which it is changing. According to the functionalists, on the other hand, the fact that language is primarily used for the sake of communication is of paramount importance to historical linguistics. This does not mean, even in an ideal situation in which language is used for no other purpose than communication, that the need to secure the understanding of linguistic messages is the only force at work in linguistic change. Such a need, functionalists emphasize, must constantly compromise with a twofold tendency towards least effort.

On the one hand, there is constant pressure to reduce the *articulation cost* of utterances. This tendency towards slurred pronunciation manifests itself in a wide range of phenomena. Consonants tend to lose their mark: aspirated stops, for example, lose their aspiration. The pronunciation of vowels tends to move towards a neutral position in the centre of the phonological space. Members of a sequence of sounds tend to be assimilated to one another: for example, intervocalic stops become voiced. And segments tend to be lost, especially at the end of words. On the other hand, there is constant pressure, particularly in the process of language acquisition, to reduce the *memory cost* of utterances. This tendency towards systemic simplicity also manifests itself in a wide range of phenomena. Exceptions to syntactic rules tend to be regularized. Morphological paradigms tend to be extended by analogy. The parallelism between sound and meaning tends to increase, through so-called "popular etymology" for example. And phonological systems tend to become and remain integrated, typically through the maintenance of parallel "series" of phonemes.[14]

What emerges is a picture of the evolution of language as the outcome of a conflict between two opposing forces: between communication and economy, between the clarity of the message and its ease, between the hearer's and the speaker's convenience. As one functionalist puts it, linguistic phenomena must be accounted for in terms of a "systemic optimum", which is a compromise between the "economic optimum" favoured by the twofold tendency towards least effort and the "functional optimum" associated with the requirements of communication.[15] Usually, the mechanism whose operation underlies the influence of these optimum principles on the evolution of a language is tacitly taken for granted. In their most explicit statements, however, functionalists suggest something of the following kind. If the use of a variant creates ambiguity, the probability that the speaker will not be understood or will be misunderstood is increased. When this happens, the speaker may have to repeat what he said and then tends to adopt a more careful, possibly exaggerated pronunciation. In this way, when alternative variants are available, the one which contributes better to communication will be selected and maintained, providing its cost is not too high.[16]

Such a functionalist approach to language cries out for an R-evolutionary reconstruction. One can easily identify an element of blind variation and an element of selection, even if variation is spontaneously biased (towards least effort), in a way which is not independent from the criterion of selection. The selection element operates directly on the variants, rather than through the selection of entities characterized by these variants, and the criterion it uses combines communication value, articulation cost and memory cost, here the three main factors which determine a speaker's chances of satisfaction.

The process involved is one of local optimization, whereby chances of satisfaction are maximized among neighbouring variants (i.e. variants which are accessible by chance) and within a given context (both linguistic and extra-linguistic). Providing a speech community is sufficiently homogeneous as far as the factors affecting the chances of satisfaction of its members are concerned, one can then think of the evolution of a dialect as being governed by the position of R-evolutionary attractors, or locally optimal compromises between cost and communication, in the space of linguistic possibilities. In a somewhat convoluted way, this expresses the functionalists' central emphasis on the fact that languages are shaped by complex equilibration processes.[17]

It follows that this functionalist approach can be expected to generate the standard forms of evolutionary explanations —optimum explanations and function explanations. And the mechanism by which such explanations are legitimated justifies, as usual, the two related principles of universal optimalism and universal functionalism (at equilibrium): any linguistic feature which is present at equilibrium must be functional (i.e. locally optimal) and it must serve some function. Given the particular specification of the criterion of optimality given above (in this section), the latter principle can be strengthened as follows: any linguistic feature which is present at equilibrium must contribute to communication, and this contribution must more than offset the (articulation and memory) cost of maintaining the feature.[18]

38. *The optimum explanation of linguistic features*

In this section and the next one, I shall illustrate the general approach presented in the previous section, and show that the difficulties it raises are those one should expect from an R-evolutionary theory. I shall then try to indicate, in the following two sections, how it is possible to circumvent the specific difficulty raised by R-evolutionary theories (as opposed to those they share with NS-evolutionary theories), and so to remove the major source of scepticism about functionalist historical linguistics.

As a first example, take the use of nominative-case personal pronouns in Indo-European languages. It is compulsory in French and English, optional in Italian and Spanish. This difference correlates nicely with another difference between the two groups of languages: verb endings are much more differentiated according to person in the second group of languages than in the first one.[19] It seems plausible to claim that the optional character of personal pronoun use in Italian or Spanish is functional (or locally optimal) within the context of a highly differentiated conjugation system: making the use of pronouns compulsory would increase the articulation cost of utterances while being completely redundant most of the time and, therefore, adding very little to the efficiency of communication. On the other hand, it also seems plausible to say that the compulsory use of personal pronouns in English or French is functional within the context of a poorly differentiated conjugation system: in such a context, its contribution to the clarity of messages is well worth its cost. Assuming the R-evolutionary mechanism suggested in the previous section, one may then be tempted to explain (functionally) the optional or compulsory character of pronoun use by its being optimal in the corresponding context, and to explain (adaptationally) the differences in pronoun use by the corresponding differences in the relevant context.

This leads, however, to a standard difficulty, which is likely to arise wherever an evolutionary approach is used and which has been briefly discussed in the biological case (section 23). What is it that entitles us to fix the degree of differentiation of the conjugation system as part of the context? Could we not reverse the above explanation and explain the degree of person-linked conjugational differentiation in a particular language by its being optimal within the context of optional or compulsory nominative-case personal-pronoun use? In Italian and Spanish, where pronoun use is optional, for example, one could argue that the erosion of verb endings would reduce cost, but that it is not allowed to take place because the ambiguity it would create when pronouns are not used would more than offset the reduction of cost. Incorporating a dimension of the linguistic system into the given context, in other words, seems bound to involve an arbitrary decision. In some cases—such as the gradual decline of the Indo-European declension systems, compensated for by the development of a complex prepositional system and a more rigid syntax—, an actual change can be observed, rather than just a difference. But even then, there is often no clear priority between the two dimensions, which tend to change simultaneously.[20]

As in the biological case, there is an obvious way out of this difficulty. One can simply leave both dimensions *free* at the same time, without arbitrarily freezing either of them. The trouble is that, as the number of free dimensions increases, the likelihood of multioptimality also increases, and then so does the likelihood that evolutionary explanations will have to remain incomplete. Both a highly differentiated conjugation with optional pronoun use and a poorly differentiated conjugation with compulsory pronoun use, for example, may be locally optimal (within the same context). All one can say, from an evolutionary perspective, is that local optimization will bring about (at equilibrium) one of these combinations. But which of the two will actually be selected is a matter of "historical accident". In other words (see section 24), one is here forced to acknowledge that there is a *conflict* between evolutionary attractors. Which of the two will prevail depends on where, in relation to the valley which separates the two locally optimal peaks in the functional landscape, past history will have carried the linguistic system. Although this difficulty often seriously affects the completeness of evolutionary explanations, however, it does not deprive them of all explanatory power.

A second major difficulty, this time specific to R-evolutionary explanations, seems to shake the very basis of their explanatory power. How do we know, for example, that compulsory pronoun use with a poorly differentiated conjugation (as in English and French) is functional, i.e. locally optimal, whereas compulsory pronoun use with a highly differentiated conjugation is not? It may be plausible enough to say that the former combination is less costly, while the latter leaves less room for ambiguity. But how do we know that the former combination's cost advantage overcompensates its communication disadvantage in such a way that, on the whole, higher chances of satisfaction are associated with its presence? In the NS-evolutionary case, it may in practice be very tricky to compare the chances of reproduction associated with alternative characteristics in order to determine which one is adaptive within a given context. But there is no doubt that it is in principle possible to do so. In the R-evolutionary case, on the other hand, even this possibility-in-principle is problematic. It is obviously of little help, in this case, to use either of the auxiliary strategies mentioned previously (section 33). Linguistic features do not affect chances of reproduction, and one cannot, therefore, argue indirectly that, since a feature is adaptive, it is likely to be functional. And it does not make enough sense to ask speakers of a language which variants they find most "satisfactory", for us to be able to rely directly on their "avowals". It seems, therefore, that the only way to find out whether the cost-communication compromise represented by one feature leads to higher chances of satisfaction than that represented by another (neighbouring) one, is to examine which feature gets established. Strictly speaking, this does not make the (R-evolutionary) optimum explanation of a linguistic feature tautological: we *mean* something different when saying that a particular feature is present at equilibrium and by saying that it is (R-)optimal within the given context. But if the former provides us with the only way of finding out about the latter, an (R-evolutionary) optimum explanation leaves no room whatsoever for prediction and refutation, and is therefore empirically vacuous.

39. *The function explanation of linguistic features*

In a way, precisely because they refer to specific consequences rather than to the overall balance of consequences, function explanations may be thought to escape this difficulty. Take the following very simple example. In languages where there is both a phoneme /s/ (as in "see") and a phoneme /š/ (as in "she"), the latter is pronounced with a protrusion of the lips which is not necessary to distinguish it from the former, but makes the distinction clearer. In other languages, where there is no /s/, the protrusion is absent from the pronunciation of /š/.[21] On this basis, one may want to explain the presence of the protrusion (at equilibrium) in those languages in which it is present, by its *function* of distinguishing /š/ more clearly from /s/ in a context in which both these phonemes are present. Compared to the corresponding optimum explanation, this function explanation has the usual disadvantage of being less strictly warranted by the evolutionary mechanism, and the usual advantage of being more informative both about the exact nature of the consequence-feedback and about the features of the context which may be relevant (see section 25).

The shift from optimum to function explanations, however, cannot be expected to do away with the first difficulty mentioned in the previous section. What allows us to take the presence of a /s/ phoneme as part of an exogenously given context? Could not such a presence be influenced by whether or not the /š/ phoneme is pronounced with a protrusion of the lips? As usual, the only way out of arbitrariness is to leave more dimensions free. And such a move, by increasing the probability of having several local optima, is likely to make the evolutionary explanation incomplete.

Where function explanations seem to have a decisive advantage over optimum explanations, is in connection with the other, more serious and more specific, difficulty mentioned in the previous section. R-evolutionary optimum explanations are in trouble because there seems to be no way of assessing independently whether a feature is optimal and whether it is present at equilibrium. But, clearly, whether the presence of a feature has the particular consequence which is called its function (or would have it if it were present), can and must be established independently of whether or not it is present at equilibrium. For example, it is possible to establish fairly safely whether or not the context is such that, should the protrusion be present, it would reduce the frequency of misunderstandings due to a confusion between /s/ and /š/. And one can then examine independently whether or not (at equilibrium) the feature is present. The test may remain undecisive forever, because one can never be sure that the situation observed is a situation of equilibrium. But R-evolutionary function explanations, like NS-evolutionary explanations and unlike R-evolutionary optimum explanations, make room for prediction and refutation.

So far so good. But things are not that simple. We know that function explanations are only loosely legitimated by the operation of evolutionary mechanisms. If one of them is refuted, therefore, this need not damage in the slightest the evolutionary theory from which it stems. If we find, for example, that in many languages which have both /s/ and /š/, the latter is pronounced without protrusion of the lips (at equilibrium), we may want to reject as too simplistic our explanation of the protrusion by its function of distinguishing /š/ more clearly from /s/. But we can easily do so while claiming that this very rejection is a further vindication of our general theory. The latter supports a function explanation only to the extent that the function ascribed to the feature is decisive in making it functional (i.e. locally optimal). In a context where both /s/ and /š/ are present, the protrusion (if present) would perform the function ascribed to it. But the contribution to communication which it would make in this way may not offset the articulation cost involved. We are then back to the problem of weighing cost and communication, which seems inescapable if one wants to put the theory itself, rather than particular function explanations, to predictive use and empirical test.

40. *Functional load*

In situations in which cost considerations and communication considerations weigh in opposite directions, there is no way, it seems, in which one can test a theory which explains linguistic features by the fact that they represent an optimum compromise between cost and communication. Although this conclusion holds for single-case tests, however, one may claim that it does not do so for statistical tests. If contribution to communication is one important component in the criterion by which optimality is judged, as the theory asserts, then it must exert a perceptible influence on linguistic change. In any single case, this influence may happen to be offset by cost considerations. But it seems that one should nevertheless be able to detect it statistically.

To illustrate this point, take what is sometimes called the functionalists' "basic postulate", the principle according to which phonemic oppositions with a high functional load tend to be preserved in the course of linguistic change.[22] A phonemic opposition, or a distinction between two phonemes, contributes to communication by distinguishing words and, thereby, linguistic messages from one another. For any opposition, the extent of this contribution can therefore be measured by its *functional load*, roughly defined by the number of pairs of words whose members would sound identical if the two phonemes were merged. The words "see" and "she", for example, would sound identical if the opposition between the phonemes /s/ and /s/ were suppressed. Clearly, our R-evolutionary theory of language will lead us to expect that, the higher an opposition's functional load, the stronger its resistance to merger.

Historical examples which contradict this "functionalist postulate" are not difficult to find. Some oppositions with a very low functional load, for example the opposition between the voiceless /θ/ of "thin" and the voiced /ð/ of "then", turn out to be extremely stable. And other oppositions with a very high functional load, such as the one which used to differentiate "meet", "beet", etc. from "meat", "beat", etc., end up being merged. But this is not enough to refute the functionalists' claim. It is easy for them to bring in countervailing cost considerations, which turn counter-examples into further confirmations of their theory. In the first example, they may argue that the cost of maintaining the opposition is so small (due to good integration in the contrasting series of voiced and voiceless consonants) that even the opposition's small functional load is sufficient to offset it. And in the second example, they may symmetrically argue that, before the merger occurred, the cost of maintaining the opposition must have exceeded the benefit stemming from its functional load. The risk of tautology pointed out in the previous sections is clearly present here too.

Instead of looking at individual potential counterexamples, however, one could also reformulate the functionalists' postulate as a statistical hypothesis. For example, one might interpret it as a *weak point hypothesis,* which states that mergers are more likely to affect oppositions which bear low functional load than oppositions which bear high functional load. Or one might interpret it as a *least resistance hypothesis,* which states that, if a phoneme can merge with either of two neighbouring phonemes, it will merge, more often than not, with the one to which it is opposed with the lower functional load. Both these hypotheses have been tested fairly systematically with reference to the histories of a number of languages, and these tests have uniformly led to negative results. Functional load and the probability of mergers are not correlated to any significant extent.[23] Such a refutation of the functionalists' "basic postulate" seems to jeopardize the respectability of their whole approach.

However, this attempt to subject the functionalist approach to a statistical test suffers from one major defect which is sufficient to render it worthless. Testing the existence of a correlation between functional load and probability of merger can only be meaningful if other relevant variables, here the cost factors, can be assumed to be *randomized*. But the state of a language in which functional loads are measured before mergers occur, is a state on which the functionalists' R-evolutionary mechanism is supposed to have operated. Therefore, if phonemic oppositions with a very low functional load exist in that state, one should expect them to be particularly advantageous from a cost point of view. And there is no reason, therefore, why they should be any more prone to mergers than oppositions with a high functional load. In other words, the fact that one should expect a positive correlation between cost and functional load in the initial state, implies that one need not expect a negative correlation between functional load and the probability of mergers. According to the functionalists, functional load and, more generally, communicative efficiency do affect the probability of mergers and, more generally, the course of linguistic change. But this influence can only show in statistical correlations if other (relevant) things are kept "equal"—which is systematically *not* the case when the state of reference is an equilibrium state of the linguistic system.

41. Maximum differentiation

Far from breeding desperation, the failure of this statistical test to genuinely reach the functionalists' claims suggests the way in which the latter can really be put to test. If one can neither assess (without circularity) the relative weight of conflicting cost and communication considerations, nor randomize statistically either of them, one can still concentrate on situations in which one of the two dimensions can be kept constant. This can be illustrated by reference to another principle to which functionalists have paid much attention, namely the *principle of maximum differentiation,* which asserts that the distances between phonemes in the phonological space tend to be maximized. Because the notion of a (con-

tinuous) phonological space, in which distances can in principle be measured, makes more sense in the case of vowels than
in the case of consonants, the principle is often restricted (or
preferentially applied) to the former.[24]

The set of possible vowel sounds is often represented as a
triangle resting on its apex (Fig. 4.2). The coordinates of this
triangle can be given rigorously in acoustic terms or, more
intuitively, in articulation terms: the vertical dimension represents the degree of openness of the mouth when the sound is
pronounced, while the horizontal dimension represents the
degree of backwardness of the pronunciation in the mouth.
The vowel space is triangular because there is more room for a
distinction between forward and backward closed vowels (for
example, between the /i/ of "street" and the /u/ of "root")
than between forward and backward open vowels (around the
/a/ of "bar"). The average pronunciation of any vowel in a
particular dialect can be represented by a dot in this triangle.
And the distances between these average pronunciations can
be roughly measured in acoustic or articulation terms.

Figure 4.2. The vowel space

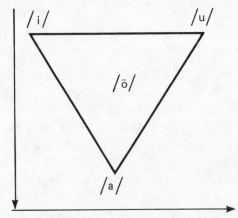

Which configuration of the vowel system represents a
locally optimal compromise between cost and communication
(within a given consonantal and non-phonological context)

seems again very difficult to determine, at least if one does not want to assert tautologically that what is present at equilibrium must have been optimal. Pressures to reduce the articulation cost push all vowels towards a neutral position in the centre of the triangle (close to the /ö/ of "blur"). Pressures to reduce the memory cost, other things being equal, promote the merger of phonemes. With a given lexicon, on the other hand, the need to keep messages as distinct as possible from one another favours variants which are as far apart from one another as possible. In other words, if satisfaction depended exclusively on cost, the R-evolutionary attractor for the /a/ phoneme, for example, would be in the middle of the space. If satisfaction depended exclusively on communication, on the other hand, this attractor would be located as far as possible in the corner of the triangle. But since satisfaction depends on both cost and communication consequences, there seems to be no way of determining *a priori* the attractor's position. As usual, therefore, no prediction and no test seem to be allowed by the functionalist approach.

In this case, however, the difficulty can be solved. With a given number of phonemes, i.e. a given memory cost, and with a given distance from the centre, i.e. a given articulation cost, there is still an infinite number of possible configurations of the vowel space. Which of these are locally optimal, according to the functionalist approach, is exclusively determined by communication considerations. With a given cost, therefore, the theory unambiguously predicts that the configuration which obtains at equilibrium is one which maximizes the distances between phonemes. In the simple case of a language (like Arabic) which has only three qualities of vowels, for example, there is a single R-evolutionary attractor, which corresponds to a situation where the vowels are /i/, /u/ and /a/, the three extreme positions in the triangle. Functionalists claim that, at equilibrium, observed languages actually display phonological configurations of this kind.[25] One may have to face here the standard difficulties connected with an arbitrary choice of context and with the criterion of "equilibrium". But this does not detract from the fact that there is room here for a genuine test of the functionalists' R-evolutionary theory of language.

A theory which can predict the state of a linguistic system at equilibrium (in a given context) can also predict changes in this equilibrium state, by reference to changes in the context which displace R-evolutionary attractors. Starting with a situation of maximum differentiation, one phoneme may move exogenously (typically for expressive reasons, as discussed in the next section) in such a way that the equilibrium configuration is disturbed. This disturbance generates push and drag chains of sound changes, which bring the system slowly back into a (new) state of maximum differentiation. *Push chains* reflect the overcrowding of areas of the phonological space into which a phoneme moves: an increase in the frequency of misunderstanding drives other phonemes away. *Drag chains*, on the other hand, reflect the under-crowding of areas of the phonological space out of which a phoneme moves: a decrease in the frequency of misunderstandings enables other phonemes to move in. As an illustration, take the evolution of the diphthong system of the dialect spoken in Martha's Vineyard (on the East Coast of the United States). At some initial point of observation, the system is in the disequilibrium state depicted below (Fig. 4.3), perhaps because of an (exogenous) merger between /uy/ and /oy/. In the space of a few decades, the system gradually achieves a new state of equilibrium, in which the phonemes are again maximally differentiated (Fig. 4.4). Both /ay/ and /oy/ are now pronounced less openly and farther back in the mouth, in such a way that /ay/ becomes /oy/ and /oy/ becomes /uy/. This is exactly what one should unequivocally expect if the functionalist theory is right.[26]

What this demonstrates is that a theory which explains linguistic features by their representing an optimum compromise between cost and communication does have testable consequences. The compromise realized by the second configuration depicted above is unambiguously optimal, re-

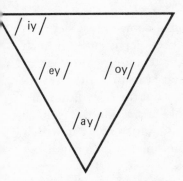

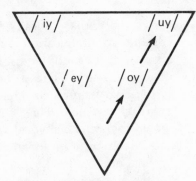

Figure 4.3 Martha's Vineyard's diphthongs: disequilibrium state

Figure 4.4. Martha's Vineyard's diphthongs: new equilibrium state

lative to the neighbouring compromise realized by the first configuration. Which of the two configurations will be present at equilibrium, therefore, can be predicted beforehand, and the theory can be subjected to a genuine test. Admittedly, as pointed out earlier (sections 38–39), there are cases in which such a test is rendered impossible by the fact that cost and communication considerations weigh in opposite directions. But if the test turns out to be favourable in those cases where it is possible, the whole approach gains credibility, and the search for function explanations and adaptational explanations within its framework becomes justified. An R-evolutionary theory of language, in other words, can no longer be dismissed as a bundle of vacuous speculations.

42. Expressive function versus communication function

It is important to stress that the theory which was being tested in the previous section is one which explains linguistic features by the fact that their presence realizes an optimal compromise between cost and communication, and *not* by the fact that their presence locally maximizes the chances of satisfaction. In other words, if the test turned out to be negative, what would be refuted is not the R-evolutionary approach as such, but only its particular ("functionalist") specification in terms of cost and communication. Suppose, for example, that a locally suboptimal compromise between cost and communication maintains itself persistently, in such a way that it cannot be discarded as a temporary situation of disequilibrium. The functionalist version of the R-evolutionary approach is refuted, but not the R-evolutionary approach as such. The "chances of satisfaction" may have dimensions which are neglected by the functionalist approach and which turn an apparently suboptimal situation into an optimal one.

One may point out, for example, that speech does not only serve to convey linguistic messages, but also to express the speaker's social standing. As recognized by functionalists and stressed by their critics, this *expressive* function of language is as likely as its communication function to affect the way in which phonetic, syntactic and semantic features are shaped.[27] It can impose a divergence from the functionalists' optimum whose extent can be appreciated in various ways. For example, one can compare the morphological and syntactic simplicity of Pidgin languages to the complicated dialect of the Brahmin caste in India, full of morphological irregularities. Whereas in the former, which have developed out of colonial languages for purely commercial purposes, the needs of communication dominate, the expression of social distinctions plays a crucial role in the latter. On a more modest scale, one can also compare the lexical system in a short-order snack-bar, where there is a premium on speed, with the colourful slang in which orders are phrased in a transport cafe.[28] Depending on the relative weight of expressive considerations in determining the chances of satisfaction associated with a linguistic feature, the positions of the R-evolutionary attractors which govern the evolution of a language may be very different indeed.

This more complex R-evolutionary theory raises exactly the same kind of problem as the simpler one examined in the previous sections. If one variant, for example of a phoneme, is better than another (neighbouring) one from an expressive angle, and worse from a communicative angle, there seems to be no way of determining which one maximizes satisfaction, save for waiting to see which one gets established. Fortunately, however, expressive consequences tend to focus narrowly but intensely on a very small number of linguistic variables at any one time. This means that, if the use of one variant of a phoneme is stigmatized while the use of the other brings prestige to its user, the latter will prevail at equilibrium, practically whatever their differential consequences from a cost-and-communication angle.[29] The variants imposed in this way can then be incorporated into the context within which the dimensions left free are being shaped by cost-and-communication considerations only. In the Martha's Vineyard example discussed in the previous section, one can conjecture that overwhelming expressive pressures have imposed the exogenous disturbance (say, a merger) which is responsible for the initial "disequilibrium" situation, but that within the context thus set the functionalists' principle of maximum differentiation is free to operate. Here again, therefore, the R-evolutionary theory is in principle testable, providing that the various components of the chances of satisfaction can be specified, and the influence of one of them isolated.

Let us sum up. The functionalist approach in historical linguistics presented and illustrated in the previous sections is given as an example of an elaborate theory which can easily be fitted into our R-evolutionary framework and can serve as a model for the reconstruction of other social-scientific explanations. However, quite apart from the difficulties which it shares with any evolutionary theory, an R-evolutionary approach raises a specific and very serious difficulty. The optimum explanations which it legitimates seem to be cluttered with an ineradicable circularity. In an NS-evolutionary perspective, whether a feature is adaptive (or locally optimal) can be established by investigating the differential chances of reproduction (or survival) of entities in which the feature is present or absent, and such an investigation is clearly different from just examining whether the feature is present at equilibrium (in a population of entities). In an R-evolutionary perspective, on the other hand, whether a feature is functional (or locally optimal) should be established by investigating the differential chances of satisfaction associated with its presence or absence in a particular entity. Practically (though not conceptually), as we have seen, this can hardly be distinct from examining whether, at equilibrium, the entity has adopted the feature. Therefore, an R-evolutionary optimum explanation of a feature's presence at equilibrium is unavoidably circular.

The way out of this circularity consists in specifying the variables in terms of which R-evolutionary optimality is judged, the components of the chances of satisfaction. When these components are in conflict—which is often the case because a cost component is usually present-, the optimum is a compromise, whose location depends on the weights given to the various components. Since these weights cannot be assessed (in a non-circular way), even specified-optimum explanations can only avoid circularity in situations in which all components but one can be kept invariant. The existence of such situations is a condition which must be fulfilled if an R-evolutionary theory is to be more than mere speculation. For an NS-evolutionary theory to be testable, on the other hand, the fulfillment of this condition and the specification of the components of optimality which it presupposes are not required, because the various components (for example, fecundity, camouflage, feeding success) are automatically aggregated into the chances of reproduction, which can be assessed directly. Compared to an NS-evolutionary approach, the restriction mentioned is the price which the R-evolutionary approach has to pay, if it is not to lose in empirical respectability what it gains in increased relevance for the social sciences.

43. R-evolutionary explanation in the social sciences

Is our R-evolutionary linguistic model more successful than our NS-evolutionary sociobiological model in providing more than an insignificant reply to the two questions which this book attempts to answer? Does it shed any more light on the deep structure of the social sciences and on the legitimacy of function explanations?

As we have seen earlier (sections 19–20), the question of whether reinforcement (individual or collective, animal or human) can legitimate function and, more generally, functional explanations, depends on whether it constitutes an *evolutionary mechanism*, i.e. on whether it articulates an element of (more or less) blind variation and an element of selection according to consequences. There is little doubt that reinforcement, as illustrated by the linguistic model, is an evolutionary mechanism in this sense. Firstly, the fact that variants may occasionally be introduced or imitated with a conscious communicative or expressive purpose and the fact that they are systematically biased towards least effort do not prevent variation from being largely *blind*. Secondly, one may want to claim that the cost associated with a linguistic feature or its contribution to communication are not sufficiently distinct from the feature, for them to be referred to as the *consequences* of its presence. As usual (see section 18), however, the consequences which are relevant to the evolutionary approach must not be viewed as "effect-events" produced by the presence of the feature, but rather as the *difference* which the feature's presence makes in a given context, when compared to its absence or to the presence of alternative features. And in this perspective, the cost of a linguistic habit or its contribution to communication are clearly consequences of its presence. This is why reinforcement, as illustrated in the linguistic model, can legitimate functional explanations, whether of the optimum or of the function kind.

As we have also seen earlier (section 21), whether an examination of the R-evolutionary approach can shed light on the deep structure of the social sciences (by exploring the residue of the action pattern) depends on whether it can legitimate *L-functional explanations*, i.e. functional explanations which do not require that the consequences by reference to which they explain be recognized by the agents involved. It has been noted above (section 33) that the registration of the causal link between the feature's presence and the consequences by reference to which it is being explained, is an essential element of reinforcement. Without such registration, the entity would not "know" which feature of its behaviour it needs to repeat, and no behaviour pattern could be reinforced. In the linguistic case, for example, if language is to be shaped by the needs of communication, the speaker must somehow perceive what it is in his speech which leads to misunderstandings. Does this mean that reinforcement can only legitimate M-functional explanations, i.e. functional explanations in which the consequences need to be "manifest" to the agents and which are therefore reducible to the action pattern?

It does not, because various factors converge to make room for R-evolutionary explanations which refer to unrecognized consequences. First of all, in the case of *immediate* consequences of the type discussed so far, registration need not mean fully conscious recognition. Because the differential consequences of the use of a phonetic variant are being felt straight away, a subconscious perception of the causal link may be sufficient for the selection of variants to be shaped by the differential consequences they have. Secondly, even if the agent is fully aware of the fact that the variant selected "locally maximizes his chances of satisfaction", he may not know *how*, through the performance of which functions, it does so. A speaker is unlikely to suspect, for example, that the way in which a particular variant of a particular phoneme minimizes the risk of ambiguities, is by maximizing the phoneme's distance from the nearest phonemes in the phonological space. Thirdly, the differential consequences by reference to which the feature's presence is explained need not be recognized all the time, but only at some *privileged moments* when alternative variants are being tried. Outside these moments, the feature's presence may be perpetuated by the sheer weight of habit. Finally, in the case of *collective* habits, not all individuals need to have gone through the reinforcement process. Some individuals may simply have picked up the functional habit by imitation, without having registered its differential consequences at any point.

In the case of functional explanations legitimated by reinforcement, therefore, it is true that some differential consequences must somehow be registered at some point by some individuals. But it is not true that all the consequences by reference to which such functional explanations can explain, must be fully consciously recognized by all the entities involved, at the time to which the explanation refers. Consequently, although reinforcement can legitimate M-functional explanations, it can also make sense of L-functional ones. Although the R-evolutionary pattern of explanation partly overlaps with the action pattern, in other words, it also covers an area which is irreducible to the latter and therefore provides a promising line along which we may be able to articulate the residue we want to explore. Because it focuses on the relevance of optimality considerations, while insisting that linguistic change is unconscious, the functionalist approach to historical linguistics, which has been discussed in this chapter, constitutes one important element of this residue, and we have seen how it can be given an R-evolutionary reconstruction. My claim is that the answers provided by this linguistic model are of far less anecdotal interest than those provided by the sociobiological model. The only way of substantiating this claim is to show how other areas of the social sciences can and must be reconstructed along similar lines. The primary purpose of the remainder of this book is to discuss a number of illustrations taken from two areas of the social sciences where L-functional explanations have been particularly popular: cultural anthropology in Chapter 5 and Marxism in Chapter 6, both broadly interpreted. Although these two chapters are meant to be more illustrative than systematic, they will also discuss a number of distinctions and difficulties, which should help to clarify the scope and limits of the R-evolutionary pattern.

5

Anthropological Theories Reconstructed

Summary

The *principle of suspicion* states that the reason which natives give for the existence of a social practice or for the form it takes, are generally false (section 44). The use of this principle prompts a distinction between two kinds of consequences associated with conformity to (or deviance from) a social practice: the *superstructural* ones, typically social and supersocial sanctions, derive from the very fact that a practice has become established, whereas the *structural* ones do not. Only the latter are relevant to an evolutionary reconstruction of anthropological theories, while the existence of the former prevents such a reconstruction from being reducible to the action pattern (section 45). The Durkheimian theory of collective rituals illustrates these points (section 46).

The scope and difficulties of an evolutionary approach in social anthropology can be explored through a discussion of *five distinctions*: between immediate and mediate reinforcement (section 47), between gratifications and penalizations (section 48), between

128

evolutionary fixation and evolutionary correction (section 49), between collective and societal reinforcement (section 50), and between evolutionary attraction and evolutionary repulsion (sections 51–52). The first and the fourth of these distinctions owe their importance to the fact that they point to the limits of the evolutionary approach; the second and the fifth owe theirs to the fact that they delineate the features of a "deviant" type of evolutionary mechanism; and the third is worth mentioning because of its misleading resemblance to our basic distinction between natural selection and reinforcement.

From the reconstruction of anthropological theories, it is possible to move to the reconstruction of more *"sociological"* theories. In particular, an evolutionary perspective can deal with social practices whose adoption (and extinction) is related to the stratified nature of a society (section 53), as well as with social practices whose production and consumption, being separate, have to meet each other on a market or a quasi-market (section 54).

Testing an evolutionary theory relying on reinforcement raises, in the anthropological domain just as in the linguistic one, very serious difficulties (section 55). However, there is room for a genuine test, even though, in case of refutation, various kinds of rescue strategies will always be available (section 56).

44. *The principle of suspicion*

Let us loosely define a *social practice* as a kind of behaviour which is both regular (or patterned) and socially induced (or governed). Whether collectively or individually performed, whether public or private, whatever is called a routine, a custom or an institution, whatever is described in terms of roles, rules or norms, can generally be considered a social practice in this sense. The existence of particular social practices and the particular form they take constitute one major set of explananda, but by no means the only one, for sociology and social anthropology. What I shall call the *principle of suspicion* states that the reasons which an agent, or a practitioner, gives for the existence of a social practice or for the form it takes, are generally false. As Radcliffe-Brown puts it: "The reasons given by the members of a community for any custom they observe are important data for the anthropologist. But it is to fall into grievous error to suppose that they give a valid explanation of the custom".[1] This principle, which can be traced back to Durkheim and Pareto, plays an important role in sociology and social anthropology. Some of its variants have even been called the "basic postulate of sociology", or the *"conditio sine qua non* of sociological knowledge".[2]

One may wonder, however, whether such a principle makes any sense. Clearly, there may be a discrepancy between why an agent says he does something and why an agent thinks he does something, between the reasons he gives and the reasons he has. But this is not what the principle of suspicion is about. What it states is that an explanation which the agent *believes* (not just claims) is right, is actually wrong. But is there not something like an "authoritative self-knowledge", which makes it impossible for a human being to be wrong about why he does what he actually does, at least providing he is neither drunk, nor drugged, nor insane? If there is, an agent's sincere statement about the reason why he performs a particular social practice or performs it in a particular way, cannot possibly be corrected by the social scientist's allegedly superior knowledge, and the principle of suspicion, it seems, cannot but appear as an absurd assertion of academic arrogance.

The principle of suspicion, however, is not about an agent's action, be it his conforming to a social practice, but about the existence of a social practice or the form it takes. Therefore, even if we agree that an agent is never wrong about why he performs a practice, he may still generally be wrong about why the practice exists. Indeed, those who defend the principle of suspicion sometimes argue that there is a systematic tendency for the answers to these two questions to diverge. According to them, the answer to the former question is complex, but uncontroversial. It has two main components. First, whatever the reason why a social practice has become established, the immediate cause of its performance is usually a combination of *inertia* and *social sanctions*. The agent performs the practice the way he does because "things have always been done that way" and/or because of the complex apparatus of social sanctions, from prestige ratings to electric chairs, which reward conformity and punish deviance. To point to these factors is usually crucial when trying to explain an agent's action, but is obviously irrelevant to the question of why inertia and social sanctions maintain the practices they actually maintain, and not others.

Second, once a social practice is established, i.e. protected by inertia and social sanctions, one can expect the following process to take place. Deviance from established practice tends to arouse some kind of vague anguish, of unfocused *awe*, which constitutes a particularly fertile soil for rationalizations which attribute the existence of the practice to two kinds of *supersocial sanctions*. On the one hand, established practices are justified/explained by reference to their intrinsic excellence, while deviance from them is said to be intrinsically disgusting. The social taboos related to corpses, faeces or sex, for instance, however hard we find it to inculcate them in our children, are frequently explained by reference to a "spontaneous" nausea, a "natural" disgust.[3] On the other hand, agents also tend to justify/explain established practices by reference to the "supernatural" consequences associated with conformity and deviance. If a Trobriander had sexual intercourse in wartime, for example, he could be sure that a hostile spear would pierce his penis. And if he had intercourse in a garden, bush pigs would be attracted by the smell of the seminal fluid and destroy the harvest.[4]

Social scientists who defend the principle of suspicion can agree that inertia and social sanctions, as well as awe and supersocial sanctions, all play a role in motivating the agent to conform and that, together, they may fully explain why the practice persists on a day-to-day basis, through the enforcement of conformity. Nevertheless, the same social scientists maintain that the "genuine reason" for the existence of a social practice, or for the form it takes, is generally distinct from the various reasons which motivate individual agents. The only way in which one can make sense of this claim, I suggest, is by distinguishing two questions, one about the existence of the practice (or the form it takes) in the short run, and one about the same in the long run. While the former can be dealt with in a purely actional perspective (as sketched above), the latter requires the use of an R-evolutionary approach.

45. Structural and superstructural consequences

This relationship which I claim exists between "suspicion" and the need for an evolutionary reconstruction leads us to a distinction which is of crucial importance to any extension of the R-evolutionary pattern beyond the linguistic case. As we have seen in the previous chapter, any R-evolutionary explanation of a feature contains an essential, though sometimes implicit, reference to the differential effects of the feature's presence on the agents' chances of satisfaction. It has been suggested in the preceding section, however, that at least some of the differential satisfactions which an agent derives from conforming to an established practice are, in various ways, the product of the very fact that the practice has become established. Reference to them cannot, therefore, contribute to the explanation of why that particular practice, rather than alternative ones, has become established. Consequently, it seems important to partition into two classes the differential consequences associated with sticking to and deviating from a social practice: those which derive from the fact that the practice is established and those which do not. The former, which basically consist in social and supersocial sanctions, I shall call *superstructural.* The latter, for lack of a better word, I shall call *structural.* Superstructural consequences constitute a protective shield for a social practice. The expectation of them is essential in securing the agents' conformity to the practice in the short run. Structural consequences, on the other hand, are the only ones which are relevant for an R-evolutionary explanation of the presence or absence of the practice in the long run.

To illustrate these points, let us start with the correlation supposedly observed between a society's sex ratio and the practice of polygamy: the higher the ratio of women to men, the more likely a society's marriage system is to allow polygamy. One might at first be tempted by an economic explanation of this correlation: the scarcer a good, the higher its price and the fewer, therefore, the number of people who can afford it.[5] Such an economic explanation is bound to fail, however, because it collapses the two levels distinguished above. Whether or not a man will want to take a second wife will depend to a large extent on such social factors as whether he will gain additional prestige or rather be sent to prison (or to hell) for having done so. These superstructural consequences cannot but play the central role in the (actional) explanation of some agent's conformity to the practice and, therefore, of the practice's persistence in the short run. However, this does not prevent us from conjecturing that, in the long run, whether polygamy or monogamy can become the established practice has something to do with the prevailing sex ratio. The latter constitutes an aspect of the practice's context which is crucial in determining the differential structural consequences of the practice's presence, for example the amounts of frustration generated by polygamy and monogamy, respectively. And it is these structural consequences, not the superstructural ones, which determine which practice corresponds to an R-evolutionary attractor.

A diagram may help to make this clear. In order to render the graphic representation easier, let us suppose, as usual, that the behaviour variable—here the set of possible marriage practices—constitutes a continuum. One can conceive of each point on this continuum as representing, say, the average number of wives which it is considered ideal for a man to have at any point in his life. In a society in which the sex ratio is about one to one, the chances of satisfaction *structurally* associated with the various possible values of the behaviour variable may be given by the continuous line in the following diagram (Fig. 5.1). Monogamy, in such a context, because it minimizes the likelihood of frustration, corresponds to the peak of the functional landscape. If the society under consideration is one in which monogamy is actually the rule, the chances of satisfaction *superstructurally* associated with the various possibilities are rather given by the broken line in the diagram. The relevant question, in drawing this second line, is no longer "What would happen if the established practice were different?", but rather "What does the agent think would happen if he deviated from the established practice?". The steepness of the broken line corresponds to the notion that the superstructure of social and supersocial sanctions provides a practice with a protective shield.

A diagram of this kind (Fig. 5.1) depicts an equilibrium situation, where the alternative whose presence maximizes the structural chances of satisfaction is also the one which maximizes the superstructural ones. In order to grasp the gist of the R-evolutionary approach to social practices and the way in which it enables us to make sense of the principle of suspicion, however, it is essential to understand what is going

Figure 5.1. Initial equilibrium situation

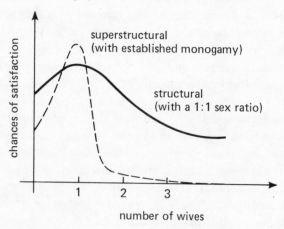

on in a situation of disequilibrium, where the two maxima do not coincide. Suppose, for example, that the sex ratio is durably increased to the level of one man to two women. This change in the relevant context presumably modifies the distribution of structural chances of satisfaction in such a way that bigamy becomes functional, i.e. corresponds to an evolutionary attractor in the altered context. Monogamy, however, does not automatically cease to be the established practice. The superstructure of social and supersocial sanctions will keep forcing the agents to be monogamous. Both for the R-evolutionary approach and for the principle of suspicion, however, it is crucial that such situations (as represented in Fig. 5.2) should be unstable. On the one hand, the structural suboptimality of the established practice must be registered at least vaguely by at least some agents, in such a way that differential structural consequences can be involved in the reinforcement process. And on the other hand, the protective shield of social and supersocial sanctions must gradually be eroded, in such a way as to make room for change. Once the new practice becomes established, however, the recognition of the differential structural consequences *may* completely disappear (as indicated in section 43 above), while a new protective shield is progressively being built (along the lines sketched in the previous section). A new equilibrium situation then emerges (Fig. 5.3).

If this kind of mechanism is deemed realistic enough, it is clear how one can make sense of the principle of suspicion. The "genuine reason" for the presence of the practice (or the form it takes) at equilibrium need not coincide, except by accident, with the reasons agents have and give for conforming to it. While the former can only be concerned with structural consequences, the latter are basically determined by superstructural ones. It is also clear how such a situation, in which the principle of suspicion is justified, necessarily legitimates L-functional explanations (by reference to currently unrecognized structural consequences), i.e. to R-evolutionary explanations which cannot be given an actional

Figure 5.2. Disequilibrium situation

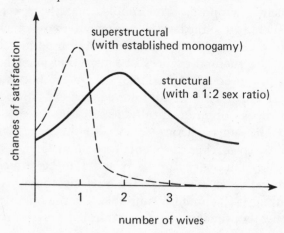

Figure 5.3. New equilibrium situation

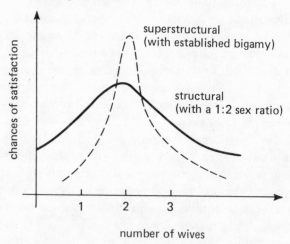

reconstruction. The R-evolutionary pattern, however, is not restricted to these situations. On the one hand, it also covers M-functional explanations (by reference to structural consequences which have been recognized all along). And on the other hand, it covers the explanation of practices, such as the linguistic habits discussed in the previous chapter, which are performed unwittingly and have very little by way of superstructural protection. Nevertheless, an appeal to the principle of suspicion is one of the most reliable clues, if one is looking for areas which are in need of evolutionary reconstruction. As the erosion and elaboration of superstructures takes considerable time, one should not be surprised to discover that these areas are more often anthropological than sociological.

46. *A general theory of collective rituals*

The Durkheimian account of religious ritual provides a typical example of a situation in which an appeal to the principle of suspicion clearly points to the need for an R-evolutionary reconstruction. In a Durkheimian perspective, explaining the universality of religious ritual by inertia and social sanctions will not do, because what we want to know is precisely why religious ritual has become universally established, i.e. protected by inertia and social sanctions. Explaining it by the supersocial sanctions invoked by the natives, on the other hand, will not do either, because such sanctions are just the product of *a posteriori* attempts to rationalize the ritual. Take, for instance, the cult of the Wollunqua snake among the Warramunga in Australia. The worshippers who perform the rituals justify their doing so by pointing to the terrible anger which Wollunqua could not help feeling if they neglected his cult. "But, says Durkheim, it is quite evident that these possible sanctions are an after-thought to explain the rite. After the ceremony has been established, it seemed natural that it should serve for something, and that the omission of the prescribed observances should therefore expose one to grave dangers. But it was not established to forestall these mythical dangers or to assure particular advantages."[6]

This suspicion towards the reasons given by the natives does not imply that religious ritual is reduced to sheer nonsense. Quite the opposite. Religious ritual, Durkheim claims, could not have survived for so long if it had not served some need, performed some function, been genuinely useful in some way or other. More specifically, for Durkheim, the "real function", the "essential raison d'être", the "main point" of religious ritual is to tighten the bonds between the individuals and the social group and so to invigorate the natives' minds. By bringing together a community of believers, religious ritual creates a climate of trust and moral strength. And it is because of the feeling of "comfort", of "moral well-being" which the believer derives from such gatherings that the latter still take place.[7] At no point, however, does this explanation require the intervention of conscious deliberation: "Religions, Durkheim stresses, fulfil needs too obscure for them to have their origin in a well-thought act of the will."[8]

Such a theory easily lends itself to an R-evolutionary reconstruction: evolutionary, since rituals are supposed to be "blindly" initiated, but selectively retained because of the consequences attached to them, and R-evolutionary because the selective retention operates directly on rituals, not via the selection of the social units which perform them (or do not). The presence of religious ritual, at least in the societies under consideration, can therefore be said to correspond to an R-evolutionary attractor, and it can be given both optimum and function explanations: religious ritual is present in the given context because, compared to its absence, its presence maximizes the natives' chances of satisfaction, and also because it performs the specific function of "morally regenerating both the individuals and the group". However, one can imagine that the context may change in such a way that religious ritual ceases to perform this function and that its presence ceases to correspond to an R-evolutionary attractor. One may conjecture, for example, that in large urban parishes the community's homogeneity has declined so dramatically that the ritual has become unable to perform any "moral regeneration". Although the superstructure of social and supersocial sanctions may keep them going for a considerable time, people will eventually stop attending mass, because the absence of religious ritual corresponds to an R-evolutionary attractor in the modified context.

This theory can easily be, and has been, extended to other types of collective rituals, from traditional wedding photographs and organized rowdiness in boarding schools to institutional ceremonies in mental hospitals.[9] Here too, one can conjecture that a certain level of homogeneity in the social group involved is a key pre-condition, if the performance of the ritual is to bring "comfort" and "moral well-being" to the participants. And one should then expect what was actually (though approximately) observed, namely that the presence or absence of traditional wedding photographs and organized rowdiness correlates with the extent to which family and classroom groups are integrated, and that institutional ceremonies (such as sports activities) involving both staff and inmates have an erratic, uncertain life in such a deeply divided community as a mental hospital. It is essential for the functional explanation of the ritual's presence, in all these cases, that the comforting character of the ritual be recognized, at least vaguely and sporadically, by the agents involved. As in the case of religious ritual, however, this recognition may only play a very small role in the actual motivation of the agents, compared to the apparatus of social and supersocial sanctions. Here again, this is what makes the principle of suspicion justifiable and an evolutionary interpretation indispensable.

47. *Immediate versus mediate reinforcement*

After these preliminary remarks and illustration, let us now explore the scope of the R-evolutionary approach and deal with some of the difficulties it raises, by introducing and illustrating five distinctions: between immediate and mediate reinforcement, between gratifications and penalizations, between evolutionary correction and evolutionary fixation, between collective and social evolution, and between evolutionary attraction and evolutionary repulsion.

An instance of the distinction between immediate and mediate reinforcement is provided by the contrast between the interpretation of the Durkheimian theory of ritual given in the preceding section and the interpretation which has become standard since Radcliffe-Brown.[10] According to the latter interpretation, the continued existence of religious ritual must be explained by the fact that it promotes the social cohesion of the social group, by asserting the solidarity which links its members to one another. The difference between the two theories which matters here is not that the former refers to the individuals' "needs", whereas the latter seems to appeal to society's "needs". What matters is rather that the consequences which are crucial in the former theory are supposed to be felt while the ritual is performed, whereas those which are crucial in the latter theory are not. The comfort which the agents derive from the ritual is felt straight away, whereas the benefits associated with the cohesion effect are not enjoyed immediately. In the latter case, no less than in the former, the possibility of an R-evolutionary mechanism is perfectly conceivable. But the fact that the causal link is less immediate makes it more likely that registration of it, if it takes place at all, will have to be fully conscious, whereas the registration of an immediate link can remain very diffuse without failing to be operative in reinforcing the practice. Because awareness can always be lost and buried under the superstructure, however, this does not in principle prevent mediate reinforcement from legitimating L-functional explanations.

Take now a very different example. A fairly large number of American tribes which depend on maize as a major item in their diet use an elaborate cooking treatment, which involves boiling corn for thirty to fifty minutes in water containing some form of alkali. It has been discovered that this kind of treatment, by breaking up glutelin in such a way that the human body can absorb it, enhances substantially the nutritional value of maize. Whatever the reasons which the natives give for conforming to this practice, it is tempting to account for its presence by pointing out this nutritional value.[11] For reasons indicated earlier (section 32), it seems wise to rule out a direct NS-evolutionary legitimation of such an explanation. At least two R-evolutionary legitimations are then possible in principle. On the one hand, one may conjecture that natural selection has so shaped the natives' innate tastes that they will like food which contains crucial nutritional elements in a digestible form. On the other hand, one may conjecture that the natives have noticed, at least sporadically, that the alkali treatment tended to make them stronger and healthier, while alternative cooking habits made them feel weaker and more vulnerable to illness. In either case, the use of the alkali treatment can constitute an R-evolutionary attractor in the space of possible ways of cooking maize. But the differential consequences which matter to the reinforcement process are much more immediate in the former case, where the selection hinges on what tastes best, than in the latter, where the selection hinges on what is better for one's health.

The difference between immediate and mediate consequences (or reinforcement), clearly, is one of degree. It only affects the logic of the explanations concerned in the following way. Whereas immediate consequences are so likely to be registered that they are bound to play a role in reinforcement, mediate consequences may remain unnoticed, and therefore inoperative, forever. This may be due to two factors. Firstly, immediate reinforcement may act so swiftly that mediate consequences are not given the chance to manifest themselves. If a new cooking habit which worsens the taste of the food is tried, it may be abandoned before its favourable consequences for the natives' health can appear. Secondly, even if mediate consequences are given time to become real, the causal link may be sufficiently subtle to escape registration. It may require an excessive amount of careful experimentation to realize, for example, that it is a reduction in the length of time for which maize is boiled, rather than a change in the weather or the intervention of evil spirits, which is responsible for a worsening of the natives' health. However, this does not mean that only the most immediate consequences affect the position of the R-evolutionary attractors. Once perceived, an adverse effect on the natives' health may weigh more than considerations of palatability. Whether it does or not depends, as usual (see section 42), on the relative weight which is being given to the various components of the chances of satisfaction. But the more mediate the consequences, the less likely they are to be taken into account.

48. *Gratifications versus penalizations*

The second distinction I want to mention is closely related to the old behaviourist distinction between positive and negative reinforcement. The latter is usually made as follows. Reinforcement is *positive* when the reinforcing consequence, i.e. the consequence whose occurrence increases the probability of occurrence of the behaviour which caused it, consists in the presentation of a stimulus, such as food, water or sexual contact. Reinforcement is *negative* when the reinforcing consequence consists in the removal of a stimulus, such as a loud noise, a bright light or an electric shock.[12] When made in this way, however, the distinction seems to be relative to the choice of words in the description of the stimulus, and therefore arbitrary. Switching off a light, for example, can be interpreted as removing light, but also as presenting darkness.

If one wants to distinguish between positive and negative reinforcement in a way which does not depend in this manner on the language used, one must postulate that there is a zero level of satisfaction, above which there is "pleasure" and below which there is "pain". Although one may be willing to concede that this zero level can shift, as the phenomenon of addiction shows, pain, in this perspective, is not just lesser pleasure, nor pleasure lesser pain. A behaviour pattern can then be said to be *positively* reinforced when, compared to alternatives, it increases pleasure, and *negatively* reinforced when, compared to alternatives, it decreases pain. If darkness is pleasurable while light is neutral for the pigeon, the latter's behaviour will be positively reinforced by switching off the light. If darkness is neutral while light is painful, its behaviour will be negatively reinforced by the same stimulus. One can extend this distinction from the case of operant conditioning to the R-evolutionary approach as a whole, by analogously distinguishing situations in which practices evolve through *gratifications* and situations in which they evolve through *penalizations*.

Compare, for example, the theory of collective ritual presented above (section 46) with the following explanation.[13] In some village, there is a strong taboo against urinating in the well. Although the natives may give all kinds of mythological justifications for this rule, it is tempting to explain its presence by the fact that it prevents the spread of some illnesses. Whereas collective ritual is claimed to be functional in that it provides the natives taking part in it with gratifications, the taboo is here suggested to be functional in that it spares the natives who respect it from penalizations. As another illustration of the same distinction, compare linguistic and technological evolution. Both have often been likened to biological evolution.[14] They both differ fundamentally from the latter however, because they are governed by reinforcement, not by natural selection. Arguably, they also differ, though less fundamentally, from one another, not only because the consequences which affect linguistic evolution are generally much more immediate than those which affect technological evolution, but also because, by and large, linguistic evolution proceeds through penalizations and technological evolution through gratifications.

The distinction, however, is often somewhat elusive, and it does not seem worthwhile discussing it in detail, as it does not affect the logic of the explanations concerned. What matters, in an R-evolutionary perspective, is not the absolute level of satisfaction corresponding to a practice, but how it compares with the levels associated with the neighbouring alternatives.

What matters is whether the presence of the practice corresponds to a peak in the functional landscape, regardless of how high this peak is. The only difference of any significance, it would seem, results from the fact that, when a practice has become established, gratifying consequences keep being produced, while penalizing consequences do not: the performance of religious ritual keeps bringing comfort to those who take part in it, whereas illnesses do not spread as long as the taboo on urinating is respected. One should therefore expect the "genuine reason" for the continuing presence of the practice to be more likely to be lost from sight in the latter case, where the presence of the practice is explained by reference to the penalizations which it does not provide, than in the former, where it is explained by reference to the gratifications which it does provide. Reinforcement through penalizations, therefore, may be more suitable than reinforcement through gratifications as a background for L-functional explanations.

There is, however, another point which is worth mentioning here, even though its importance will not appear until later (section 52). Whereas the question of which alternatives will be selected by the optimization process is exclusively a matter of differential consequences, the intensity with which R-evolutionary optimization is taking place may depend on the *absolute* level of satisfaction associated with the prevailing alternative. When this level is very low, the search for better alternatives is likely to be energetic. When it is sufficiently high, on the other hand, the relevant entity may stick forever to the same, locally suboptimal, alternative. R-evolutionary processes in which penalizations play this role of a spur to variation are analogous to other processes, which are not instances of reinforcement (through registration of a casual link and repetition of a behaviour pattern). A sleeping man unconsciously trying to find a comfortable position in his bed would provide a typical example of this kind. The common element is the fact that variation is induced by some sort of tension and will only come to an end when this tension has been removed.[15] This element is obviously absent when reinforcement operates through gratifications rather than penalizations.

49. *Evolutionary fixation versus evolutionary correction*

The third distinction which I want to make runs parallel to one alluded to earlier (section 44), between cases where what is being explained is the presence of a practice (at equilibrium) and cases where what is being explained is the form taken by a practice (at equilibrium). In one case, practices are selectively retained by what can be called a process of evolutionary *fixation*. In the other case, practices are selectively modified by what can be called a process of evolutionary *correction*.[16] In the theory of religious ritual discussed above (section 46), for example, the R-evolutionary mechanism which is assumed to operate is one of evolutionary fixation. In the conjectural explanation of the way of cooking maize (section 47), it is rather one of evolutionary correction. The distinction, however, is a very relative one. Correcting a practice, for example the cooking of maize, can easily be seen as fixing a way of performing it, for example the alkali treatment mentioned. And fixing a practice, for example religious ritual, can be seen as correcting the way in which time is being spent by the agents involved. The distinction, therefore, cannot have important implications for the logic of the explanations concerned.

Nevertheless, there seems, at least at first sight, to be an intuitive connection between evolutionary fixation and universal functionalism on the one hand, and between evolutionary correction and universal optimalism on the other. Evolutionary fixation, it seems, selects practices in such a way that, at equilibrium, only practices which serve some function are still present, while evolutionary correction modifies the form which practices take in such a way that, at equilibrium, this form is locally optimal. As in the NS-evolutionary case (section 26), however, one can apply universal optimalism to features which can just be present or absent as well as to values on a continuum, simply by regarding the presence and the absence of a feature as two neighbouring alternatives. Universal functionalism, on the other hand, applies only to features which involve a cost relative to neighbouring alternatives, and it is therefore less likely to apply to what is more naturally seen as the form of a practice than to what is more naturally seen as a practice in its own right. For example, the technique of the swing plough consists in burying the seeds by simply scraping the soil. Its persistent use in traditional Algerian agriculture can be explained by its being optimal within the given physical and economic context. It preserves perennial plants, it does not exhaust the soil, and it does not impose too heavy a work load on ill-fed animals.[17] Such a technique is most naturally viewed as the form taken by the practice of ploughing, and universal optimalism applies to it in a straightforward way: the technique would not have persisted, had it not been locally optimal. Universal functionalism, on the other hand, is not quite as relevant: one cannot say that the technique would not have persisted had it not had a function, as confidently as one can say, for example, that the practice of ploughing itself would not have survived without serving some function. However, since any practice (liable to evolutionary fixation) can, more or less naturally, be considered a form (liable to evolutionary correction) of a practice of a more abstract kind, and vice versa, this connection between evolutionary fixation and universal functionalism should not be taken too strictly.

A somewhat more worrying homology seems to link the distinction between evolutionary fixation and evolutionary correction to our key distinction between NS-evolutionary and R-evolutionary mechanisms. To illustrate this point, take the following explanation of poetry. As a literary genre, poetry is characterized throughout the world by a number of idealtypic features. One of them is semantic "impertinence", which consists for example in attributing to a substantive an adjective which ordinary language would never attribute to it.

Another is the lack of parallelism between sound and meaning, as illustrated by alliterations, pauses in the middle of a sentence, the homophonies without homosemies imposed by the rhyme, or the sound stresses without meaning stresses imposed by the rhythm. The function of these various features is to violate the "old code" in such a way that the routine functioning of language is disturbed and room is made for emotion.[18] If this suggestion is to make explanatory sense, one must be able to suggest the operation of some plausible evolutionary mechanism. This could be some sort of evolutionary fixation: of all literary traditions, only the functional ones, among them poetry as characterized above, have persisted. Or it could be some sort of evolutionary correction: literary practice has evolved in such a way as to acquire the functional features mentioned above. Or it could be both: as in the case of parlour games, sports or alphabets, evolutionary fixation and evolutionary correction, the selective retention of traditions and their selective modification, may have worked hand in hand to enforce the rule of the R-evolutionary attractors.

The difference between evolutionary fixation and evolutionary correction, as illustrated in this example, is disturbingly close to the fundamental difference between natural selection and reinforcement, as introduced earlier (section 32): features, such as semantic impertinence, seem to be selected through the selection of entities, namely literary genres, in the case of evolutionary fixation, and directly within those entities in the case of evolutionary correction. Consequently, whereas evolutionary fixation seems to imply the populational perspective associated with natural selection, evolutionary correction seems to possess the ability to account for changes in particular entities, typically associated with reinforcement. However, since the distinction between the fixation of a practice and the correction of the form a practice takes is ultimately a matter of convenience (as we have seen above), the existence of this homology undermines the claim that the distinction between NS-evolutionary and R-evolutionary processes is a clear-cut one. The only way of avoiding this consequence is to deny practices the status of "entities". The entities to which the definition of natural selection refers must be capable of death and reproduction in a *real* sense which does not cover the "extinction" and "replication" of practices. The selection of features through the selective retention of practices which they characterize can then be seen as an instance of reinforcement because, despite appearances, the selection operates within entities rather than on entities (whether individuals or groups). The relevant criterion of optimality, therefore, must be phrased in terms of the entity's chances of satisfaction, not in terms of its chances of reproduction, and R-evolutionary attractors can, after all, govern the fixation of practices as well as their correction.

50. Collective versus societal reinforcement

The fourth distinction is more important, because it points to a serious limitation of the evolutionary approach. It opposes cases in which the evolution of a social practice can be seen as the aggregation of individual R-evolutionary processes, and cases in which the evolution of a social practice necessarily involves the society as a whole. I shall speak of *collective* evolution when referring to the first set of cases, to which most of the examples discussed so far belong, and I shall speak of *societal* evolution when referring to the second set of cases, which must now be illustrated.

From Plato's *Republic* to contemporary utilitarianism, it has often been asserted that an act is morally just when it is socially useful, or at least when it conforms to a rule which is socially useful. This doctrine would have no relation whatsoever with social-scientific explanation if it were just a normative doctrine, a statement about what ought to be. But, one may argue, moral philosophers have seldom had the wish, and never had the right, to act as moral legislators. Their statements have had no other basis than the moral intuition which they share with the other members of their societies, and their task, therefore, can only have consisted in analyzing this intuition. The doctrine that a rule is morally just when it is socially useful, therefore, must be interpreted as an empirical generalization about what moral agents feel to be morally just. If such a generalization is even approximately correct, an explanation is required for this fact. The most obvious one states that the reason why particular moral rules become established as such lies in their social consequences. Of all possible rules, only the socially useful ones are selected to become moral rules. Existing moral rules, it is then possible to say, will tend to correspond to evolutionary attractors. And the explanation of moral rules by their social usefulness which is implied by this framework will clearly be an L-functional one. For conformity to the rule tends to be motivated by the agents' craving for approval, by their wish to go to Heaven, by the voice of their conscience or by the desire to behave in a noble way, rather than by a concern with social usefulness. Indeed, utilitarians sometimes note, if agents were trying to be socially useful instead of being rule fetishists, the outcome for society would be worse.[19]

This kind of L-functional explanation of moral rules is not only indirectly suggested by a long tradition of moral philosophers. It is explicitly defended by Nietzsche, for example, who seizes upon the social usefulness of common morality as a weapon in his attempt to discredit and demystify it. The justifications of morals in terms of "absolute duty" or "superterrestrial sanctions", he says, are "imaginary causes" and "nonsensical opinions". Morals are just a means by which a people tries to secure its own preservation.[20] Furthermore, social scientists often speak metaphorically of Society using moral payments as a lever to manipulate the motivation of its members to its own benefit. The behavior which it imposes upon them is not of such a nature that they find it naturally pleasant, but it is made pleasant for them by being praised as "obedience", "heroism", "altruism", etc. A judicious distribution of prestige and contempt enables Society to exploit its members' vanity, their self-esteem and their pride to its own advantage.[21] For lack of a clever and almighty moral legislator, there is no way of making explanatory sense of such formulas without attributing to their authors an L-functional explanation of moral rules very similar to Nietzsche's.

Conceivably, one can try to legitimate such an explanation by reference to the natural selection of societies, by postulating that only societies with socially useful moral rules have survived. For reasons discussed earlier (section 30), however, such an NS-evolutionary reconstruction is highly implausible. In principle, it should be much more plausible to view the presence of socially useful moral rules as resulting from selection *within* societies, rather than *of* societies. But such an R-evolutionary reconstruction is, in this case, particularly problematic. One reason for this, one might think, is that the criterion of selection which is being assumed is social usefulness and not, as usual, the individuals' chances of satisfaction. But choosing such a criterion does not mean that one should postulate the existence of a "social consciousness" which is capable of "registering" causal links between moral rules and social consequences, and of "feeling" whether these consequences are good or bad. A moral rule's contribution to the welfare or the smooth running of a society may just be its way of (locally) maximizing the chances of satisfaction of the agents of which the society is made up. Both "registration" and "feeling", therefore, can still be located at the individual level.

What makes an R-evolutionary reconstruction particularly problematic in this case is rather that the production and registration of the relevant differential consequences, which are essential to the reinforcement mechanism, cannot be achieved through individual trial-and-error. In the case, say, of linguistic rules, cooking habits or agricultural techniques, an individual agent's deviation from established practice can lead to the production and registration of the crucial differential consequences. Admittedly, the structural differential consequences may often be buried under the superstructural ones: an attempt to change an established agricultural technique may be killed by the disapproval which it arouses, rather than by the bad harvests to which it leads. But it is the possibility for (blind) individual deviations to reveal structural consequences, which enables us to postulate that the shaping of linguistic rules, cooking techniques or agricultural techniques is governed by R-evolutionary attractors. The situation is very different with our functional explanation of moral rules. Take the example of a society in which telling the truth is a moral rule. A deviant liar will probably experience negative consequences. But these will consist, for example, in guilt or punishment, i.e. in the reflection of the superstructural apparatus of social and supersocial sanctions. If one leaves these aside, the (structural) consequences for the individual deviant will rather be positive: he will benefit both from his lies and from the other people's sincerity. This state of affairs is not incompatible with our explanation, which only asserts that structural chances of satisfaction are higher in a society of truth-tellers than in a society of liars. But if this structural superiority cannot be revealed by individual variation, a trial-and-error process which involves the whole society, or a substantial part of it, is required to bring it out, and enable it to influence the shaping of moral rules. Collective evolution, in other words, is not enough, and societal evolution is needed.

Clearly, the assumption that such a societal trial-and-error process is going on to any significant extent is a very implausible one to make. And one may therefore be tempted to reject as sheer nonsense the positive theories of morality mentioned above, and to restrict legitimacy to those R-evolutionary explanations of social practices which require no more than collective reinforcement. This would include, for example, the Durkheimian explanation of ritual by reference to the comfort which it brings to those who take part in it (section 46), but it would exclude the alternative theory of ritual as a contribution to social cohesion (section 47). As we shall see in the following two sections, however, there is a way of salvaging the legitimacy of functional (and other) explanations which presuppose societal reinforcement.

51. The structuralist analysis of marriage systems

In so far as it claims to be explanatory, the structuralist analysis of kinship systems has often made use of functional explanations. The universality of the incest taboo, for example, is explained by the fact that it enables the societies which adopt it to avoid a "deadly danger for the group", a situation which would be "incompatible with the vital requirements of primitive society and of society in general". By forcing men to marry outside their families, the incest taboo prevents the social group from splitting into a number of isolated, potentially antagonistic units. And this is what accounts for its universal presence.[22] The mechanism whose operation legitimates such a functional explanation, Lévi-Strauss claims, need not involve abstract reasoning or long learning processes. All we need is "the spontaneous resolution of psycho-social tensions": the anguish which springs from collective hostility can thoroughly mar the enjoyment of a privilege. Breaking the incest taboo, in this respect, is similar to any transgression of the more general prohibition of "unilateral consumption". A Maori who is caught while secretly eating a ceremonial dish, for example, will become the subject of such mockery, anger and disgust, that he will be deterred from doing it again.[23] If the crucial "psycho-social tensions" are what this analogy suggests them to be, it is clear that they can only reflect the superstructural consequences associated with deviation from the established rule, not the structural ones. They therefore presuppose what needs to be explained, namely that the incest taboo has become established, i.e. surrounded by a protective shield of sanctions and inertia. To invoke them as part of the underlying mechanism is as irrelevant as to try to justify the functional explanation of an agricultural technique by reference to the fact that deviation from it arouses derision and hostility. Deviations which can reveal the differential structural consequences of the incest taboo must necessarily be of a societal kind.

More relevant suggestions as to the nature of the underlying mechanism can be found in connection with the structuralist analysis of a more specific kinship structure, which has been at the centre of a major methodological debate. In many primitive societies, the incest taboo takes the form of a rule prescribing or encouraging *cross-cousin marriage,* i.e. marriage with Ego's mother's brother's daughter or with his father's sister's daughter. This rule can in turn take three distinct forms. It can be *matrilateral* (if marriage with Ego's mother's brother's daugher is favoured), *patrilateral* (if marriage with Ego's father's sister's daughter is favoured) or *bilateral* (if what is promoted is marriage with a cousin who is either the former or the latter, or both at the same time). Among unilateral cross-cousin marriage systems, as it turns out, the matrilateral form is far more frequent than the patrilateral one, which can only be observed in very rare cases—if at all. Lévi-Strauss's explanation for this fact is often mentioned as the most convincing contribution of structuralism to the understanding of puzzling social phenomena, and it also constitutes a typical functional explanation of a kind which presupposes societal evolution.

First of all, Lévi-Strauss suggests, let us look at the differential structural implications of the two forms of unilateral cross-cousin marriage. In the case of a society with a matrilineal system of descent, i.e. a society in which children belong to their mother's clan, for example, these implications can be grasped by examining the following diagram (Fig. 5.4). Whereas with a matrilateral cross-cousin marriage system all marriages take place in the same direction, with a patrilateral one the direction changes at each generation. With a matrilateral system, in other words, a continuous chain of gifts and acquisitions of women binds the whole society together, whereas with a patrilateral one society is made up of a great many little systems, in which Ego's marriage is just the counterpart of, and the compensation for, his father's mar-

Figure 5.4. Structural implications of unilateral cross-cousin marriage

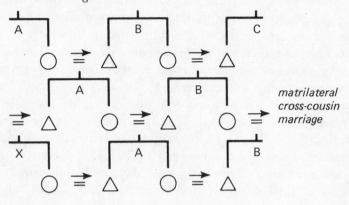

*matrilateral
cross-cousin
marriage*

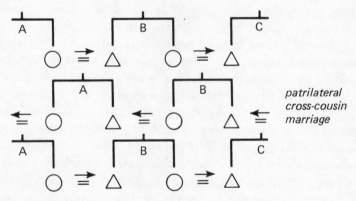

*patrilateral
cross-cousin
marriage*

Symbols used:

△ : man

◯ : woman

⌐ : filiation

= : marriage favoured by the rule

→ : direction of the circulation of women

A,B,C,... : clan to which the children belong
(After Homans & Schneider 1955, 6,11)

riage in the previous generation. On this basis, Lévi-Strauss feels entitled to conclude: as far as group solidarity is concerned, the "functional value" of the matrilateral form of cross-cousin marriage is undoubtedly far higher than that of the patrilateral form.[24]

This conclusion is not only important because it points out differential consequences which are not intuitively obvious, but above all because, according to Lévi-Strauss, it is the existence of these differential consequences which accounts for the fact that one form of cross-cousin marriage system is widespread, whereas the other hardly exists: "If, in the final analysis, marriage with the father's sister's daugher is less frequent than with the mother's brother's daughter, it is *because* the latter not only permits but favours a better integration of the group, whereas the former never succeeds in creating anything but a precarious edifice made of juxtaposed materials (. . .)."[25] Critics were quick to point out that such an explanation was "teleological", that it appealed to "final causes". However, not only does Lévi-Strauss acknowledge this, but he even asserts in this context that "structuralism is resolutely teleological; after finality had for a long time been banned by scientific thought, still full of mechanicism and empiricism, it is structuralism which gave it back its place and made it respectable again".[26] Respectability cannot be granted, however, unless it is possible to specify the nature of the mechanism through which the matrilateral system's higher "functional value" can bring about its higher frequency. As Homans and Schneider (1955, 17-18) put it, one must exhibit the way in which efficient causes play into the hands of final causes.

52. *Evolutionary attraction versus evolutionary repulsion*

As usual with social practices, both the conscious anticipation of consequences and the natural selection of societies can be dismissed for total lack of plausibility. It follows that, if matrilateral cross-cousin marriage can be given a functional explanation, the mechanism which is responsible for its predominance must be of an R-evolutionary type. This conclusion squares neatly with Lévi-Strauss's[27] own suggestion that a society's marriage system is the legacy of the same "age-old wisdom" which shapes its language and its tools. Along the same lines, Needham[28] points out how well the functional explanation outlined above fits in with Radcliffe-Brown's[29] remark that kinship systems are like languages, in so far as they are constantly made and remade by man, *without* this implying that "they are normally constructed or changed by a process of deliberation and under control of conscious purpose": just as language must function as a means of communication, a marriage system must function as a way of organizing social relations. And, even more explicitly:

"It may well be that any logically or socially possible arrangement, however contrived or however aberrant from the usual forms of social life, will be found in some society somewhere and for some time; and it is certainly conceivable, simply on this ground, that members of a certain society may have given the patrilateral prescription a trial. But even if they had and if—contrary to all theoretical expectation—it had worked, what possible reason would they have to keep it? Structurally, a matrilateral prescriptive alliance system is beautifully simple, stable and adaptive. A patrilateral system is a paradigm of instability and confusion."[30]

While primitive populations may be unable to anticipate the consequences of various possible kinship systems, Needham (1962, 116) claims, "there is little reason to think that they have difficulty in recognizing, or compunction in abandoning institutions which are unwieldy without offering acknowledged compensatory advantages".[31]

There is little doubt, therefore, that the mechanism which is claimed to operate consists in the R-evolutionary fixation of marriage systems: an element of blind variation combines with an element of selective retention guided by the recognition of differential consequences. The trouble, here again, and the key difference with the cases of language, technology or poetry, is that individual variation is not sufficient to enable structural differential consequences to be produced and recognized. If a man marries a prohibited cousin, the negative consequences which he will be made to feel cannot possibly reflect the structural consequences associated with the established marriage rule, but only the superstructure of social sanctions by which the latter is protected. As is clearly acknowledged in Needham's text quoted above, the trial-and-error which is required to reveal structural differential consequences is one which involves the whole society. But whereas individual deviations from an established practice can be assumed to happen fairly often, societal deviations can only be supposed to happen, if at all, every so many centuries. The basis which this would provide for evolutionary optimization is so narrow that societal evolution seems bound to remain a mere topic for speculation.

However, there is a way out of this difficulty. It has been noted earlier (section 48) that one potentially important difference between evolution through gratifications and evolution through penalizations is that penalizations can spur variation and so constitute an "endogenous" source of change. In other words, whether as a result of a change in its practices or of a change in its context, a society may at some point find itself in a state where its agents' chances of satisfaction, in absolute terms, are very low indeed. In such a situation of high structural tension, the society will not just wait for favourable societal mutations to happen, but it will take active steps, possibly blind in their direction, to resolve the underlying tension. Its members will protest, mobilize, innovate, until the society's practices are modified in such a way that the tension is resolved, i.e. that the absolute level of satisfaction is back to a tolerable level. Unlike the standard type of evolutionary mechanism, this variant is not exclusively concerned with relative levels of satisfaction. Because it attaches some importance to absolute levels, it may allow a system to stay forever at an "acceptable" or "tolerable" point on the slope leading to a peak in a functional landscape, whereas the standard type of evolutionary mechanism would only allow it to stabilize at the very top of the hill. Nevertheless, both cases can still be considered as varieties of evolutionary mechanisms in our sense.[32]

In our example, as a result, we do not need to make the unrealistic assumption that marriage rules are permanently submitted to spontaneous societal variation in such a way as to provide a basis for selection through the comparison of structural consequences. All we need to assume—as Needham actually suggests—is that if for any reason a society has adopted a marriage rule which leads to a high level of tension within the given context, endogenous pressure towards societal change will soon lead to its replacement. Once this replacement has taken place, the memory of the structural tension which has prompted it may of course be completely erased, and consequently nothing prevents the functional explanations legitimated by this kind of mechanism from being of an L-functional type. What is somewhat more debatable is whether locally optimal practices can still be said to constitute R-evolutionary *attractors* in the space of possible practices. Without spontaneous variation, a practice which is tolerable but suboptimal within the given context has the same claim to being present at equilibrium as has one which is locally optimal. The nature of the underlying mechanism makes it more appropriate to call R-evolutionary *repellors* the states of high tension associated with the presence of certain practices within certain contexts, and one can accordingly contrast this evolutionary *repulsion* with the standard evolutionary *attraction*. However, if one is willing to extend the concept of attractor in such a way that it may not only refer to points of the space of possible features, but also to whole areas of this space, there is no harm in calling R-evolutionary attractors the set of possibilities which do not correspond to R-evolutionary repellors. Functional explanations which assume the operation of societal evolution, such as Lévi-Strauss's explanation of the predominance of matrilateral cross-cousin marriage and, presumably, the sociological explanations of moral rules mentioned earlier (section 51), turn out, after all, to find a place in our theory of R-evolutionary attractors.

53. Stratified practices

The various distinctions discussed so far have enabled us to explore the scope of an R-evolutionary reconstruction of anthropological theories and some of the difficulties raised by such a reconstruction. I would now like to indicate briefly how the same kind of reconstruction can be naturally extended to more "sociological" theories, i.e. theories which apply *specifically* to "non-primitive" societies. One fairly typical feature of these societies, I suggest, is that the criterion of satisfaction is socially differentiated, in such a way that practices can be governed by different R-evolutionary attractors in different social groups. Another features of these societies is that, with respect to many practices, their members fall into the complementary categories of suppliers and demanders. In this section and the next one, I shall briefly examine how the explanation of practices which are affected by these two features can be accommodated into an evolutionary pattern.

The social differentiation of satisfactions can best be illustrated by reference to expressive practices. *Expressive* behaviour is the kind of behaviour which aims to influence other people's opinions about oneself, from *Potlatch* ceremonies to mate selection or name dropping. In a hierarchically organized, stratified society, expressive behaviour is often, but by no means always, *distinguishing* behaviour, in the sense that it expresses the agent's actual or claimed membership in some social group and sets him apart from the members of other, lower-ranking groups. Expressive behaviour, it would seem, is the kind of well thought-out, strategic behaviour which fits the action pattern of explanation perfectly. When taking the form of distinguishing behaviour, however, it often tends to crystallize into social practices, well protected by inertia and awe and by a superstructure of social and supersocial sanctions. Take, for instance, the teaching of Latin in nineteenth-century secondary schools. Why do parents want their son to study Latin? It may be because his father has done so, or because they believe that something vague, but definitely awful, is bound to happen to him if he does not, or because some old uncle would strongly disapprove of their taking any other course, or finally, because Latin is so beautiful, so good for the young mind, or so useful for remembering medical terms. However sincere these various kinds of accounts may be, one may nevertheless view the teaching of Latin as a conspicuous waste of time and energy, and explain its persistence by the distinguishing function it performs by setting the members of the privileged classes clearly apart from the ignorant mass of people who "do not even know Latin". Only reference to this function, one may argue, can account for the fact that the teaching of Latin was able to resist for so long the erosion of time and the pressure of efficiency.[33] As in the case of religious ritual (section 46), the discrepancy between the agents' reasons and the "genuine reason" for the retention of the practice makes a reconstruction in terms of evolutionary fixation inescapable.

As another example, take the persistence of the apparently absurd habit of wearing gowns at dinner in Oxford Colleges. If inertia is not a good enough explanation, one can examine the apparatus of formal and informal sanctions. If a student forgets his gown, the Dean may send him a note in which he is kindly requested to spare waiters, in future, the embarrassment of refusing to serve him. And if rules are loosely implemented in one College, dons from other Colleges may make deprecatory comments about the lowering of standards of good manners. If one is looking for a more profound explanation, one can also listen to the justifications adduced, more or less sceptically, by the natives themselves: the gown enables the town's shopkeepers to catch students who are

trying to get away without paying, it conceals social differences behind a uniform which only allows for academic
hierarchies, it serves to protect one's clothes. If one chooses
to dismiss there unconvincing justifications as mere rationalizations, one may alternatively point to a kind of satisfaction
which the practice provides, though possibly not to all those
who conform to it, nor at all times, nor in full clarity: the
natives concerned are proud to belong to an institution which
(many people believe) one must be rich and/or clever to join,
and they enjoy expressing their difference. Had Oxford not
been able to maintain its prestige, so this interpretation goes,
gown wearing would have offered much less resistance, and
elegant rationalizations for dropping it—modesty, convenience, etc.—would have been in ample supply. The catholic
clergy's cassock, to give another example, has not long out-
lived the recent collapse of its wearers' social status.

This last remark clearly indicates how an interpretation of
social practices as expressive practices can provide the basis
for a theory of social change. As the social context is altered,
the presence or absence of different social practices become
R-evolutionary attractors for a given social group. The spread
throughout society of a practice which used to be
monopolized by one particular group constitutes one powerful source of such attractor shifts. In nineteenth century
America, for example, the habit of wearing a corset gradually
stopped being the privilege of a small social elite, and became
increasingly widespread among middle-class women. Soon
afterwards, however, and as a result of this very spread, it
started falling into disuse among the upper strata. Why?
Simply because, in spite of all rationalizations about the
intrinsic value of the practice—it made women "so much
more elegant"—, its real raison d'être lay in the satisfaction
derived from asserting one's "distinction".[34] It is obviously
possible to try to account for such facts within the framework
of a rational, prestige-maximizing model of man. But the fact
that conformity to an expressive practice is often motivated
by considerations which have nothing to do with prestige

maximization, makes an R-evolutionary reconstruction more suitable. Such a reconstruction also provides us with the only way of making sense of the claim often made by some of the followers of Veblen's and Goblot's pioneering studies, that distinguishing practices cannot be explained as the outcome of deliberate individual strategies, but rather as the product of an "unconscious social logic".[35]

54. Market mediation

An evolutionary approach cannot only accommodate the fact that, in a stratified society, the (structural) satisfactions which govern the evolutionary fixation of practices may vary from one social group to another in the same society. It can also accommodate the complications arising from the fact that, in a differentiated society, many practices have a *production* and a *consumption* side, which are (generally) performed by different agents. Some people manufacture corsets, and others wear them. Some people teach Latin, and others learn it. Both production and consumption are indispensable to the persistence of a practice: the habit of wearing corsets will soon die out if nobody makes them, and the habit of making them cannot persist for long once people have stopped wearing them. The presence of a practice at equilibrium, therefore, can only be expected if both its production and its consumption correspond to evolutionary attractors.

However, one could argue that consumption should be given primacy for the following reason. If the chances of satisfaction associated with the consumption of a practice are sufficiently high, the *demand* they generate will (sooner or later) prompt the corresponding *supply*, by raising the chances of satisfaction (or of reproduction) associated with the production of the practice. This will happen, typically, through an increase in (potential) market prices, which makes the production of the practice more attractive: if high chances of satisfaction shift from the wearing of round hats to the wearing of square hats, the price of square hats and the profits to be gained from making them will increase. Consequently, their supply will rise, whether through the NS-evolutionary selection *of* hat-producing firms or through the R-evolutionary selection of products *within* these firms. This argument can be extended to quasi-markets, where no material payments are made. Collective rituals, for example, need organizers on the production side and participants on the consumption side. If the demand for participation in rituals is sufficiently high, it will prompt their supply, by raising the benefits associated with their organization. These benefits may here consist in prestige or allegiance, rather than in fees. What emerges is that, when the production of a practice is distinct from its consumption and when, therefore, the existence of the practice is mediated by the operation of a market or quasi-market, one can explain this existence by reference to a (sufficiently powerful) potential demand for it. The evolutionary attractor here takes the form of a "fertile soil", which is waiting for potential suppliers—manufacturers, organizers, etc.—to make the right move.

How does an R-evolutionary explanation which makes room for market mediation differ from a (purely actional) economic explanation? The crucial difference derives from the fact that, whereas the economic explanation does not discriminate between the various factors which affect demand, the R-evolutionary approach distinguishes structural and superstructural chances of satisfaction, and leaves the latter aside. There may be cases where the distinction is of little or no importance. These are the cases where the economic explanation and the R-evolutionary one coincide, and where the latter takes the form of an M-functional explanation. For example, one may want to explain the persistence of the practice of producing/using toothpaste by the demand which exists for it in a society of sugar-eaters whose teeth are not completely replaced by dentures. The satisfaction people expect from using toothpaste is sufficiently similar to the structural chances of satisfaction associated with it, for the evolutionary explanation to coincide with the actional one.

The same can be said in connection with less trivial examples, such as the persistence of prostitution in a society in which pre- and extra-marital sex is not fully liberalized, or the appearance of old peoples' homes in a society where the extended family system is replaced by the nuclear one.

There are other cases, however, where a superstructure of social and supersocial sanctions plays a major role in the agents' motivation to consume and where, therefore, the R-evolutionary explanation differs significantly from the economic one. Take, for example, the following explanation of the modern novel. Unlike lyric or epic literature, novels tell the personal story of a hero caught in a dilemma between several alternatives, none of which is cleary prescribed. Its continued existence since the 18th century can be explained by its function of expressing the frustrations associated with the stratification system of industrialized society.[36] Those who hold such a theory would have to admit that the function they point out, if it is to be operative in fixing the practice, must act through the mediation of a market: it must underlie a potential demand of sufficient intensity to make it attractive for other people to write, print and sell novels. This does not mean, however, that the functional explanation they propose collapses into an economic one. The structural demand for novels which the functional explanation points to may be buried under a superstructural demand, which is on exactly the same footing as far as the economic explanation is concerned. People may read novels because they are threatened into doing so by their teachers, or because they think that reading literature is the most noble kind of enjoyment on earth. And such motives, no doubt, are as effective as any other in feeding the market demand for novels and securing, thereby, the latter's economic viability, at least in the short run. In the long run, however, one may want to claim that what matters to the persistence of the practice, is only the structural demand to which the (L-)functional explanation mentioned above draws attention. The latter explanation, therefore, can be construed as an R-evolutionary explanation which does not reduce to the corresponding economic explanation.[37]

When the retention of a practice is mediated by a market, it has just been shown, it is possible for the consumption of that practice to be evolutionarily fixed in such a way that it can be given an L-functional explanation. This can be shown even more easily for the production of such a practice. Goffman[38] notes, for example, that atrocity tales and the ritual evocation of well-known friends and enemies are quasi-univeral features in publications which specifically address a "stigmatized" audience—racial minorities, homosexuals, the blind, the handicapped. Whether the structural demand to which the consumption of this practice corresponds is manifest (as with toothpaste) or latent (as with the novel) for the consumers, an L-functional explanation of its production can in principle be legitimated in two ways. On the one hand, the publications may have been shaped by an NS-evolutionary process: only those which displayed the right features have managed to survive, by keeping a sufficient readership. On the other hand, they may have been shaped by an R-evolutionary process: the features mentioned may first be introduced by chance, and then be retained because, for some reason, they "work" in keeping the readership happy. Admittedly, if the process is an R-evolutionary one, the production of the practice must be perceived to "work", at least at some privileged moments. But most of the time this perception may be buried under a deep layer of inertia and superstructural sanctions, in such a way that the R-evolutionary explanation (not just the NS-evolutionary one) of the quasi-universal features mentioned above can also be an L-functional explanation by reference to the structural demand of stigmatized audiences.

55. *The risk of tautology*

In the light of the various anthropological and sociological illustrations discussed in this chapter, we can now return to the central difficulty raised by the R-evolutionary approach. We have seen earlier (section 26) that the position of NS-evolutionary attractors can be determined without our needing to examine where, in the space of possible characteristics, the population concerned eventually settles. By observation or experimentation, it is in principle possible to determine which of the local variants affords the organism the greatest chance of reproduction. This enables us to explain the presence of a characteristic at equilibrium in a non-tautological fashion, to make predictions and to test the theory. As was pointed out in connection with the linguistic illustration (section 38), on the other hand, to establish the position of an R-evolutionary attractor is a much trickier business. There seemed to be no way of determining which of two neighbouring linguistic variants maximized a speech community's chances of satisfaction (within a given context), except by examining which one was eventually adopted. Consequently, prediction, testing and non-tautological explanation seemed to be ruled out.

If anything, the situation becomes even worse if we shift our attention from linguistic habits to social practices of the kind discussed in this chapter. Suppose, for example, that one wants to explain the fact that a large number of primitive societies have adopted a cross-cousin marriage system, i.e. a system which favours Ego's marriage with his father's sister's daughter or with his mother's brother's daughter or both, while a few others have adopted a parallel-cousin marriage system, i.e. a system which favours Ego's marriage with his father's brother's daughter or his mother's sister's daughter or both. The simplest explanation in an R-evolutionary perspective, consists in stating that both cross-cousin marriage and parallel-cousin marriage are functional in their respective contexts, i.e. that their presence leads to higher chances of satisfaction, in the given context, than the presence of alternative systems. Bearing in mind, in particular, that one should only be concerned with chances of satisfaction which are structurally determined, independently of the superstructure of social and supersocial sanctions, it is clear that there is no feasible way of determining which marriage system is "best" for the agents involved, except perhaps by decreeing that it must be the one which has actually been adopted. Our R-evolutionary explanation, therefore, seems bound to be vacuous.[39]

As in the case of historical linguistics (sections 40-42), the only way out of this difficulty consists in specifying the nature of the consequences which are crucial in making one alternative "better" than another. In other words, one must move away from an unspecified optimum explanation in the direction of a specific function explanation. It is important to see, however, that this move involves an additional assumption, which one will always be able to make responsible for the failure, should the more specific explanation turn out to be refuted. The standard explanation of the overwhelming predominance of cross-cousin marriage, for example, points to the cohesion of the wider social group as the key structural consequence. Whereas parallel-cousin marriage systems impose or strongly encourage clan endogamy, Lévi-Strauss shows, cross-cousin systems impose or strongly encourage clan exogamy. Exogamy weaves a network of alliances between the social units which make up the wider social group and thereby strongly contributes to the latter's cohesion.[40] Although this specification of our R-evolutionary theory may account for the fact that cross-cousin marriage is so widespread, it immediately raises the question of what one should make of the societies, however few in number, which have adopted parallel-cousin marriage. One solution consists in dismissing them as mere disequilibrium situations. Levi-Strauss's theory, like any other evolutionary theory, must be interpreted as referring to equilibrium situations, where the evolutionary mechanisms have had time to operate. Consequently, the fact that, at some point in time, some societies happen to be governed by a marriage system which does not promote the cohesion of the social group need not impair the theory's validity. However, the fact that stable parallel-cousin marriage systems have persisted for centuries in a number of Maghrebian and Arab societies renders such a strategy, if not impossible, at least unattractive.

An alternative and more fruitful strategy consists in maintaining the initial theory as a function explanation of cross-cousin marriage—the cohesion effect is what makes cross-cousin marriage locally optimal when it is—, while conceding defeat for it as a general specification of the criterion of optimality. One may argue, for example, that the cohesion of the kinship groups, i.e. of the smaller social units which make up the wider social group, is also an important factor in determining structural chances of satisfaction. This kind of cohesion is favoured by endogamy, and endogamy, as has been noted above, is encouraged by parallel-cousin marriage. Optimality, therefore, takes the form of an optimal compromise between the cohesion of the wider social group and the cohesion of the smaller units. And whether cross-cousin marriage or parallel-cousin marriage will prevail depends on the weight given, in the chances of satisfaction, to each of the two aspects of cohesion. But how do we find out which system corresponds to an optimal compromise, without looking at which one becomes established? Is this not again a way of dodging any refutation and, therefore, of making the theory tautological?

It need not be, for reasons which have already been expounded, mutatis mutandis, in the linguistic case (section 41). While keeping one of the two dimensions of the compromise constant, one can try to identify (in categorical terms) a feature of the context which is closely associated with the second dimension, and then check whether this feature correlates with the presence or absence of the two marriage systems. For example, the chances of satisfaction associated with the cohesion of kinship groups can plausibly be assumed to be much higher in a society in which land is jointly owned by the sons of a same family. Under such circumstances, the rivalry between agnates about the distribution of tasks and rewards will be a highly sensitive source of tension. Patrilateral parallel-cousin marriage, i.e. marriage with one's father's brother's daughter, alleviates this risk by strengthening the links within the agnatic group. Therefore, and despite the fact that it weakens solidarity between agnatic groups, it is plausible to say that, in the context of a regime of joint ownership, parallel-cousin marriage represents the optimal solution. As it happens, the Maghrebian societies which practice parallel-cousin marriage are precisely governed by such a regime of joint ownership. This finding seems to warrant an adaptational explanation of the difference in marriage systems by the difference in this feature of the context: parallel-cousin marriage will be adopted at equilibrium because of its local optimality in a society with joint ownership, while cross-cousin marriage will be adopted elsewhere for the same reason.[41] The same finding also seems to provide an important non-tautological confirmation of our R-evolutionary theory of marriage systems, as specified above.

56. Rescue strategies

The strength of this confirmation, however, is proportional to the extent to which the test really threatened the theory. Had no correlation been observed between marriage system and ownership system, would one have rejected the theory? Probably not, because several rescue strategies would have been possible, even if one refused to discard counterexamples on the grounds that they reflected disequilibrium situations. Firstly, it would have been possible to argue that the extent of joint ownership is not the only variable which affects the relative weight of the two kinds of cohesion in determining structural chances of satisfaction. The extent of the division of labour between kinship groups, for example, can be expected to influence positively the weight attached to the cohesion of the wider social group. The failure to control this further contextual variable, therefore, might have prevented the correlation from being statistically significant (if the division of labour happened to be more developed, on average, in societies with joint ownership). This first strategy, as depicted in Figure 5.5 under the usual assumption that all three variables are continuous, consists in increasing the number of relevant control variables.

Figure 5.5. Bidimensional control space

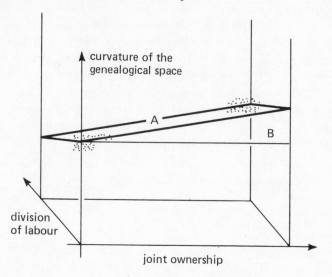

What one can call, after Lévi-Strauss, the *curvature* of the genealogical space corresponds here to the degree to which a marriage system approximates a pure parallel-cousin system and deviates from the pure cross-cousin system. The plane *A* represents the set of R-evolutionary attractors (or optimal compromises) in this space, each point of it corresponding to a combination of the two control variables, the extent of joint ownership by kinship groups and the extent of division of labour between kinship groups. The clouds of dots represent a possible configuration of the positions of actual societies along the three dimensions. Although this configuration is consistent with the R-evolutionary theory, as specified, it is of such a nature that the expected correlation between ownership regimes and marriage systems will be obscured, unless

the third variable (division of labour) is statistically controlled.

Secondly, even if one assumes that the extent of joint
ownership is the only relevant control variable, the failure to
observe a simple correlation (at equilibrium) between ownership regimes and marriage systems need not constitute a
refutation of the theory. For what matters in an evolutionary
approach is local optimality, and not global optimality. In the
space of possible marriage systems, the pure cross-cousin
type and the pure parallel-cousin one may well fail to constitute neighbouring alternatives. Blind innovations are unlikely
to shift a society from one to the other in a single step, and it
may be the case that at least some of the intermediate alternatives, which would have to be adopted on the way from one
type of system to the other, constitute solutions which are
significantly worse than either extreme, possibly because
"impure" systems introduce confusion in the network of
kinship relationships. Under such circumstances, the two
extreme types of marriage system are locally optimal at the
same time, and the resulting situation of attractor conflict can
be represented by a catastrophe surface (see section 24). For
example, with no joint ownership at all, parallel-cousin marriage may be no better than intermediate systems, and with
total joint ownership, cross-cousin marriage may be no better
than them. But, in between, there may well be degrees of
joint ownership at which both kinds of pure systems are
better than intermediate ones. As shown in Figure 5.6, this
kind of situation is compatible with the claim that the extent
of joint ownership affects the position of the attractors and is
the only variable to do so, while also being compatible with
the absence of the expected correlation. The top and bottom
curves (A_1, A_2) represent R-evolutionary attractors corresponding to each value of the control variable, while the
middle curve (W) represents "locally worst" systems. The
arrows indicate the direction of the evolutionary attraction.
The clouds of dots represent again a possible configuration of
the positions of actual societies, and the line B is the regres-

sion line corresponding to the correlation between the behaviour variable (curvature of the genealogical space) and the control variable (extent of joint ownership).

Figure 5.6. Folded behaviour space

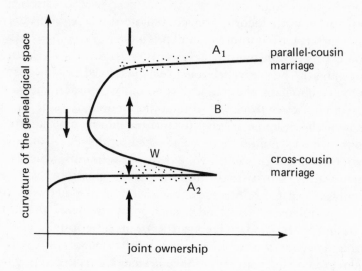

The ever present possibility of these two types of rescue strategies—adding dimensions to the control space and adding "sheets" in the behaviour space—makes any conclusive refutation of the kind considered theoretically impossible. The use of such strategies, however, prompts the formulation of further hypotheses, which can themselves be put to test. And although the sequence of refutations and reformulations is theoretically endless, it may well have pragmatic limits, beyond which the theory does not seem worth upholding. In this sense, the theory we are concerned with can be put to genuine test. Once again, however, it is important to note that the R-evolutionary theory which is being tested is never the R-evolutionary approach as such. First of all, the criterion which determines the chances of satisfaction associated with the various alternatives has to be specified. One must say, for example, that it is the marriage systems' impact on the cohesion of the kinship group, or on the cohesion of the wider social group, or on both, which determines the chances of satisfaction associated with each of them. Refutation, therefore, can always be attributed to our having picked out the wrong criterion or to our having missed out an important dimension of the right one. Secondly, no test is possible without the specified criterion or some of its dimensions being closely associated with (categorical) features of the context. Before accepting the relevance of the correlation between ownership regime and marriage system, for example, one must be able to assert that the ownership regime determines, to a significant degree, the extent to which various marriage systems influence the cohesion of kinship groups and/or the importance of this cohesion for structural chances of satisfaction. Again, refutation may be attributed to the postulated link with features of the context, rather than to the (specified) R-evolutionary theory itself.

However far-fetched these remarks may seem, they are of crucial importance for the testability and, therefore, the respectability of any R-evolutionary explanation, i.e. of practically any function or optimum explanation in the social sciences. It has been argued earlier that any explanation of the presence of a feature by the function it serves presupposes that this presence can also be explained by its being, in some sense, locally optimal (see sections 19 and 25). As has also been argued earlier, the test of an optimum explanation of this kind raises special difficulties in an R-evolutionary perspective, which it does not raise in an NS-evolutionary one. It was indispensable to tackle these difficulties, however sketchily, in order to prevent the various theories reconstructed in this chapter from providing easy prey for those who want to dismiss them as idle speculation.

6

Marxist Theories Reconstructed

Summary

Of the major types of Marxist explanations, two are potential candidates for an evolutionary reconstruction: the explanation of social practices by the class interests they serve, and the explanation of revolutionary change as the resolution of structural contradictions (section 57).

The "suspicion" which is often associated with the explanation of social practices by reference to the class interests they serve often calls only for a conspiratorial interpretation, rather than an irreducible evolutionary reconstruction (section 58). However, as can be illustrated in the case of the "structuralist" and "capital-logic" variants of Marxist State theory, conspiratorial interpretations are sometimes clearly dismissed. Unless one believes that "functional requirements" are explanatory by themselves, this implies the obligation to specify a non-conspiratorial mechanism (section 59). The most convincing way of doing so is to outline the mechanisms through which the structural constraints of a capitalist economy can

174

shape the State's policies in such a way that they necessarily maximize profitability (section 60). If one objects that not all the policies adopted by capitalist States seem to favour profitability, one can first try to argue that short-term profitability may be sacrificed to long-term profitability (section 61). If this does not work, one can also try to embed working-class resistance into the structural constraints by which the State's policies are being shaped (section 62). However, as soon as conflicting groups start behaving strategically, the very notion of an evolutionary explanation of State policies and other social practices by the class functions they serve ceases to make sense (section 63).

Explanations of structural changes by reference to underlying contradictions, on the other hand, can also be given an evolutionary reconstruction. The most plausible one assumes the operation of a mechanism through which social structures are selected in such a way that the incidence of crises is minimized (section 64). In this perspective, revolutions can be explained by changes in the position of evolutionary attractors (section 65). However, because the underlying process of trial-and-error needs to be societal, rather than just collective, it is more appropriate to speak of evolutionary repulsion than of evolutionary attraction (section 66). A wide variety of other theories of social change can conveniently be reconstructed within the same framework (section 67).

57. *Major types of Marxist explanations*

It was easy enough, one may argue, to provide an evolutionary reconstruction for those areas of the social sciences which can assume a relatively stable context and a relatively homogeneous society. It has been shown, particularly in the more sociological illustrations, how change and differentiation can be accommodated to some extent. But constant reference to "long-run equilibrium situations" and to "the typical agent's chances of satisfaction" seems to make it impossible to dispense with the kind of stability and homogeneity which is characteristic of many anthropological theories, whether restricted to primitive societies or not. Consequently, if we move into a completely different area of the social sciences—namely Marxism and related theories—

where change and conflict play a central role, it seems that the evolutionary perspective should lose much of its relevance. The aim of this last chapter is to argue that this is not the case, while at the same time exploring the limits beyond which evolutionary reconstructions become pointless.

There are two major candidates as the key explanatory concept in Marxist theory. One is class interest. The other is structural contradiction. If one chooses the former, history can be conceived of as oscillating between two extreme kinds of situations. On the one hand, there are situations in which the existing relationships of production are well established and in which, therefore, the form taken by major social practices is determined by the interests of the ruling class. On the other hand, there are situations in which the existing relationships of production are threatened and in which, therefore, the form taken by major social practices is the uncertain outcome of class struggle. Alternatively, if one chooses structural contradiction as the key explanatory concept, the crucial distinction, for purposes of explanation, will rather be between the historical processes by which a contradiction gradually expresses itself in crises and breakdown, and, on the other hand, the processes of transition, by which a new situation of correspondence (or non-contradiction) is brought about.

Between these two interpretations of the core of Marxist theory, the class-theoretical one and the historical-materialist one, there are obvious bridges. Crises, for example, may be considered decisive in the process which leads from a situation of class rule to one of class conflict may be considered essential in the process by which transition arises out of crises and breakdown. On the other hand, there are also occasional tensions between the two perspectives. The attempt to demonstrate the grip of ruling-class domination, for example, may at times clash with the attempt to demonstrate crisis tendencies, in the sense that any piece of evidence which supports the former demonstration may undermine the latter, and conversely. For our purposes, however, the important point is that, together, the two perspectives define four typical kinds of explanations, which jointly cover the bulk of Marxist explanatory practice: (1) explanations of practices by the class interests they serve, (2) explanations of practices as outcomes of the class struggle, (3) explanations of crisis tendencies by the contradictions they express, and (4) explanations of structural changes as the resolution of structural contradictions.

I shall take it for granted that explanations of the second and third types can conveniently be reconstructed within the framework of the action pattern. Whatever institutional or non-institutional form it takes, it seems that class struggle can in principle be analyzed as a complex strategical game, whose outcome can only be the object of an actional explanation. Crisis tendencies, on the other hand, are best analyzed as the unintended aggregate outcome of the subjectively rational actions of individual agents acting within a given structural framework. Consequently, if we are to find room for evolutionary explanations, and particularly for evolutionary explanations which cannot be given an actional reconstruction as well, we shall have to concentrate on the remaining two kinds of Marxist explanations: the class-theoretical explanation of social practices by reference to the interests of the ruling class, and the historical-materialist explanation of social change as governed by structural contradiction and correspondence. These two kinds of explanations will be examined in turn in the following sections.

58. Suspicion and class interest

The backbone of a great many Marxist analyses of social practices, whether they appear in sophisticated academic treatises or in popular pamphlets, consists in the delineation of the ruling-class interests which the practices serve. This kind of analysis has been applied, for example, to the activities of the School and to those of the Church, to the Press and to the Unions, to the distribution of welfare benefits and that of scientific prizes, to literary criticism and parliamentary ceremonial, to urban planning and to psychoanalysis, to the recruitment of police officers and the control of the money supply. Sometimes, the aim of the analysis is just to denounce the practice analyzed by showing that the consequences associated with it are congruent with the interests of the ruling class. An analysis of this kind in no way claims to account for the presence of the practice and is, therefore, of no interest for our purposes.

Most of the time, however, showing that a particular practice serves the interests of the ruling class or, as is often said, that if fulfils a *class function,* is clearly meant to be explanatory. Indeed, the systematic demonstration of the fact that existing social practices serve the interests of the ruling class strongly suggests that they exist because they serve these interests, just as the systematic demonstration of the fact that existing biological characteristics are adaptive strongly suggests that they exist because they are adaptive (see section 26). In some cases, however, the class function by which a particular practice is being explained refers to expected consequences rather than to those which the presence of the practice actually has. For example, a Government may decide to suppress closed-shop arrangements in the hope that this will curb the power of the working class. Even if this policy turns out to be counterproductive because it undermines Union control over the rank-and-file, it may still sound plausible to explain its presence by reference to its "class function". As we have seen much earlier (section 21), such an (unambiguously actional) explanation by appeal to expected consequences cannot possibly be given an evolutionary reconstruction. We must therefore restrict our attention to those analyses of the class functions of social practices which provide genuine functional explanations, i.e. explanations by actual consequences.

Among functional explanations, more specifically, we are looking for L-functional explanations, i.e. for functional explanations which do not suppose that the agents consciously uphold the practice because of the consequences by reference to which the practice is explained (see section 21). In other words, because we are interested in explanations which can be given an evolutionary reconstruction but no actional reconstruction, we are looking for cases where the objective rationality by which the existence of the practice is being explained does not coincide with the subjective rationality which accounts for the agents' conformity to the practice. In the anthropological illustrations, the principle of suspicion, which asserts that there is generally a discrepancy between objective and subjective rationality, was justified as follows: the real reason why a practice becomes established tends to be forgotten, and the reasons which the agent gives for his conforming to the practice tend to reflect the superstructure of social and supersocial sanctions which gets grafted onto an established practice.

Marxist explanations of a practice by the class function it serves seem to be closely associated with a similar principle of suspicion. The reasons given by the Government, the Church, the School, etc. for the practices they maintain—the good of the country, the salvation of souls, the raising of standards—do not generally coincide with what Marxists claim constitutes the real reason for their existence—the class function they serve. Often, however, the discrepancy which warrants suspicion is one between the reasons the agents give and the reasons they have for maintaining the practice, rather than one between the reasons they actually have for maintaining it and the class function by reference to which the existence of the practice is being explained. Often, in other words, what is supposed to justify suspicion is the concealing of real motives behind respectable ones. In this case, therefore, the explanation of a practice by the class function it serves must be understood as a *conspiratorial* explanation, i.e. an explanation which points to unavowed but conscious motives. If the class function refers to actual, and not just expected, consequences, there is no reason why a conspiratorial explanation could not be given an evolutionary reconstruction: the clique which controls the practice may have shaped it through a process of trial and error. But since the class functions served are clearly assumed to be recognized by the agents who control the practices, conspiratorial explanations cannot help us in our search for L-functional explanations, i.e. in our attempt to explore what cannot be reduced to the action pattern.

There are cases, however, in which Marxists explain social practices by reference to the class functions they serve, while unambiguously dismissing a conspiratorial interpretation. The latent class functions which such analyses point out can be neither mere effects, without explanatory value, nor hidden motives, whose explanatory value can be accommodated within the action pattern. We now turn to L-functional explanations of this kind, and examine whether and how they can be given an evolutionary reconstruction.

59. State theory: between conspiracy and hyperfunctionalism

The Marxist theory of the capitalist State provides a typical example of a field in which conspiratorial and non-conspiratorial class-theoretical explanations have been existing side by side. According to orthodox Marxism, from Lenin (1918: ch.1) onwards, the State, in a capitalist society, is the "Executive Committee of the Bourgeoisie", an instrument manipulated by the capitalist class. Consequently, whenever the State's policies are being explained by the class interests they serve, the functional explanations which are thus provided can safely be given a conspiratorial interpretation. This is particularly clear in the so-called Theory of State Monopoly Capitalism, the official economic theory of contemporary capitalism professed by the Russian and allied Communist parties: because of their collusion with the ruling class, Western Governments deliberately select policies in such a way as to favour the interests of the capitalist class and in particular its monopolistic fractions.[1]

For a number of reasons, however, conspiratorial explanations of this kind have become increasingly disreputable among academically sophisticated Marxists. One possible reason is of a political nature: the instrumentalist conception of the State sketched above encourages "reformism", by suggesting that a replacement of the individuals who hold the levers of power would be sufficient to alter the nature of the State's policies and that such a replacement should therefore be the main objective of the socialist movement. Another possibly important reason is methodological: conspiratorial explanations give too important a role to the intentions and actions of individual subjects in the shaping of social phenomena. But the main reason is presumably the fact that, in the critics' eyes, the policies adopted by social-democratic States, in which representatives of the working class are in power, are at least as favourable to the interests of the capitalist class as the policies adopted by other capitalist States. Unless one wants to postulate that working-class elites are systematically bribed by shrewd capitalists, the class-theoretical explanation of social practices must then be given a non-conspiratorial basis.

Non-conspiratorial theories of the capitalist State have been elaborated mainly within two traditions. On the one hand, the French "structuralists" have been concerned to stress that the capitalists' personal involvement, their voluntaristic action, plays no crucial role in shaping the nature of the State's policies. The "necessary coincidence" between the functions which the latter fulfill and the interests of the capitalist class must be located, they say, at the (objective) level of "social practices", not at the (subjective) level of "individual behaviours". As conditions change, the State's key function of ensuring the cohesion of a social formation may require it to take different forms, even a social-democratic one, even one in which the political sphere enjoys a "relative autonomy" with respect to the economic sphere. But basically, State practices will always remain such as to reproduce capitalist relationships of production and so to favour the interests of the capitalist class.[2]

The West-German "capital-logicians", on the other hand, have attempted to provide a "dialectial derivation" of the necessity of the capitalist State. When closely scrutinized, the kind of necessity they are talking about is, in effect, a functional necessity. If a capitalist system is to survive, i.e. if capital accumulation is to proceed smoothly within it, they claim, the system must possess a central institution which will perform a number of functions. Such an institution must, for example, guarantee the reproduction of waged labour and its subordination to capital in the labour process, as well as provide the monetary and legal framework required by the functioning of a complex market system. A more historically-minded variant of this State-derivation approach emphasizes the fact that the State form required by a capitalist system changes with the existing material conditions. The "autocratic-mercantilist", the "parliamentary-liberal" and the "technocratic-interventionist" States each correspond to the specific requirements of capital accumulation at different stages of capitalist development.[3]

Whether one talks in terms of structural determination or in terms of dialectical necessity, whether one stresses the State's function of maintaining cohesion or its function of promoting capital accumulation, this kind of non-conspiratorial theory of the capitalist State inevitably raises the following question. If what makes it possible to explain the State's practices by the (latent) class functions they serve is not their deliberate manipulation by the capitalists who control the State apparatus, then what is it? Not only do non-conspiratorial theories usually fail to answer this question. They hardly seem to acknowledge that there is any need to ask it. They usually content themselves with the demonstration of "functional contributions" or "functional necessities", without making any effort to suggest a (non-conspiratorial) mechanism through which the latter can acquire a causal role. Such a *hyperfunctionalist* stance has seemed inacceptable to many critics, on the grounds that black-box functional explanations, i.e. functional explanations which are not accompanied by the suggestion of a mechanism, are not legitimate.[4] As this epistemological state of affairs seems closely analogous to the one encountered in our anthropological illustrations, it is tempting, here again, to try an evolutionary reconstruction. If it works, we shall have found a way out of the dilemma between conspiracy and hyperfunctionalism.

60. Structural constraints

The question which our evolutionary reconstruction needs to answer can be restated as follows. What is the mechanism which ensures that, even when the State apparatus is apparently controlled by (uncorrupted) representatives of the working class, the State's policies are still selected in such a way that they favour the interests of the capitalist class? Following the lead of some of those who are dissastisfied with conspiratorial and hyperfunctionalist theories alike, one can focus on the way in which State policies are shaped by *structural constraints*, i.e. constraints which stem from the nature of the context, in particular the nature of the relationships of production, rather than the super-structure of social and supersocial sanctions. The argument can be broken down into two steps.[5]

First of all, regardless of their class affiliation and political faith, Governments are crucially dependent on the maintenance of as high a level of economic activity as is possible under the circumstances. This is so, firstly, because the State's capacity to finance its activities through taxation and borrowing depends on the state of the economy, and, secondly, because public support for the party in power is largely determined by the levels of income and employment. One can therefore expect that the policies which will prevail, at equilibrium, will (roughly) be such as to maximize the level of economic activity, in the context of a given international economic situation, a given endowment of natural resources, etc. This may be so, firstly, because of a (slow-action) natural selection of inflexible Governments: ruling parties whose policies do not (at least roughly) maximize the level of economic activity within the given context are swept away by bankruptcy and discontent. Secondly, and more plausibly, one may think of a reinforcement process: among the policies they try out, flexible Governments will selectively retain those which maximize their financial health and popular support. In the former hypothesis, economic-activity-maximizing policies are selected because they correspond to NS-evolutionary attractors in the space of possible practices, i.e. because they locally maximize a Government's chances of survival. In the latter hypothesis, they are selected because they correspond to R-evolutionary attractors in the space of possible practices, i.e. because they locally maximize a Government's chances of satisfaction. If either of the two mechanisms can be assumed to operate, existing practices are

Figure 6.1. Adaptive landscape

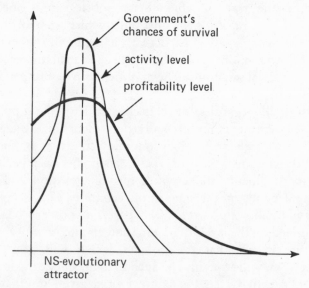

Government's chances of survival

activity level

profitability level

NS-evolutionary attractor

State policies (for example, levels of unemployment benefits)

Figure 6.2. Functional landscape

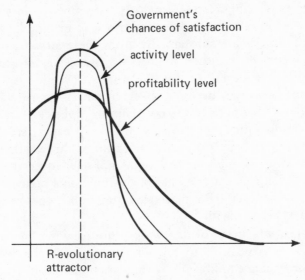

Government's
chances of satisfaction

activity level

profitability level

R-evolutionary
attractor

State policies (for example, levels
of unemployment benefits)

bound to maximize (locally) the level of economic activity—in the long run and with an unchanging context.

The second step is the crucial one. What we are concerned with is the policies of a capitalist State or, more exactly, State policies in a capitalist society, i.e. a society in which the means of production are privately owned. In such a society, the level of economic activity is largely determined by what is sometimes called *business confidence,* i.e. the set of factors which affect the capitalists' willingness to invest. Since business confidence is, in turn, basically determined by the expected level of profits, and the latter, in the long run, by the actual level of profits, one can expect the practices of a capitalist State, at equilibrium, to be such as to boost the level of profits, i.e. to favour the material interests of the (profit-taking) capitalist class. Policies which increase capitalist control over the working class, which protect business freedom, which prevent or engineer slumps at the right moment, or boost profits by any other means, correspond to evolutionary attractors (see Figures 6.1 and 6.2). Attempts to introduce policies which constitute a serious threat to profitability, i.e. attempts to deviate substantially from these attractors, will soon be corrected, either, in an NS-evolutionary interpretation, through the fall of the Government ("stubborn" left-reformist scenario), or, in an R-evolutionary interpretation, through its bashful retreat to conventional policies ("flexible" social-democratic scenario). With the former scenario, maladaptive policies (in a capitalist context) are replaced by adaptive ones through the replacement of one Government by another. With the latter scenario, dysfunctional policies (in a capitalist context) are replaced by functional ones without change of Government.

Clearly, whichever of the two evolutionary mechanisms is at work, it is possible to explain the nature of the policies which prevail at equilibrium by the class functions they serve, without any need for conspiratorial intentions on the part of those who control the State apparatus. If an NS-evolutionary mechanism is assumed to operate, it is clear that this functional explanation is an L-functional one: surviving Governments do not need to recognize that they owe their survival on the political market to the capitalist bias of their policies (see section 54). If, instead, an R-evolutionary mechanism is assumed to operate, Governments must have become at least vaguely aware of the fact that some policies are better than others at giving them financial health and popularity. But, firstly, they do not need to have discovered that what makes such policies optimal in this respect is the fact that they favour the interests of the capitalist class. And secondly, once established, the policies may become surrounded by the usual superstructure of social and supersocial sanctions, which may be as powerful in motivating conformity as the recognition of the structural consequences associated with the practices. Consequently, whether by appealing to the natural selection of Governments or to the selective retention of policies by existing Governments, it seems possible to make sense of an

L-functional explanation of policies by the class functions they serve. Without needing the help of any conspiracy, the structural constraints determine the position of the evolutionary attractors, and, whoever is in power, these attractors govern, in the long run, the nature of the State's policies.

61. *The irrelevance of long-term consequences*

There is an obvious objection to this kind of class-functional explanation of State policies, in our evolutionary interpretation as well as in a conspiratorial one. As Marx (1867: ch. 8) himself documented abundantly in his discussion of the "Factory Acts", State policies are sometimes durably imposed against the resistance of most or even all fractions of the capitalist class. How can this fact be reconciled with the claim that persisting State policies are necessarily such as to favour the capitalists' interests? The simplest solution to this difficulty consists in distinguishing immediate and mediate consequences, short-term and long-term interests. State policies which become established may fail to favour the capitalists' short-term interests. But when longer-term consequences are taken into account, the overall balance of costs and benefits (compared to local alternatives) must be positive from the capitalists' point of view. The "Factory Acts", for example, by reducing the length of the working day, do depress profitability in the short term. But they also prevent an excessive exploitation of the working class, which would put the reproduction of labour-power at risk. Thereby, they protect the foundation of long-term profitability and so favour the interests of the capitalist class.

In principle, there seems to be no problem involved in accommodating such long-term considerations into a conspiratorial perspective. The capitalist State can be viewed, to use Engels' expression, as an "ideal collective capitalist", more long-sighted and provident than individual capitalists, and therefore able to weigh the importance of long-term consequences. More serious problems arise as one attempts to accommodate long-term considerations into a perspective which focuses on the role of structural constraints in the way sketched in the previous section. The difference, however, is not due to the fact that one perspective attributes to Governments the active desire to favour capitalist interests, while the other does not. It is rather due to the fact that the conspiratorial perspective calls for an interpretation in terms of consequence-anticipation (though it does not in principle rule out an evolutionary interpretation), while the structural perspective calls for an evolutionary reconstruction (while not excluding the possibility of consequence anticipation).

Why should an evolutionary perspective, whose relevance is anyway restricted to the explanation of which policies are adopted in the long term, have more difficulties in accommodating long-term consequences? Why should evolutionary mechanisms be short-sighted? Note, first of all, that the short-sightedness we are concerned with here is not the one which arises directly from the fact, pointed out much earlier (section 19), that evolutionary mechanisms are mechanisms of local optimization, while consequence-anticipation allows for global optimization. Local optimization implies that the choice horizon is limited to neighbouring alternatives. Unlike deliberate decision-makers, evolutionary processes cannot adopt indirect strategies. They cannot move to a neighbouring position in which the entities involved are worse off (in terms of chances of reproduction or satisfaction), in order to be able to move from there to a more remote position in which the entities would be better off than in the initial position. Because of this feature, evolutionary processes may deserve to be called "myopic" or "short-sighted", but this has nothing to do with their inability to take long-term consequences into account.[6]

What underlies this inability, in the case of R-evolutionary processes, has already been briefly indicated earlier (section 47). Firstly, it can be argued that the long-term consequences of a policy which is functional in the long term, but dysfunctional in the short term, will never be actualized, because the deviation which introduces that policy will be corrected before the latter has had time to produce its long-term effects. Suppose, for example, that a tough monetarist policy is, in the long term, more favourable to profitability and to economic activity (in a given context) than is a mellow Keynesian one. The latter may nevertheless correspond to the R-evolutionary attractor, if evolutionary correction is so swift as to not give a tough policy a real chance. With a slacker correction mechanism, differential long-term consequences could, in principle, be brought about and taken into consideration. But the slacker the mechanism, the less powerful the evolutionary approach in predicting the policies actually adopted, since non-equilibrium policies will be allowed to stay around for a considerable time.

Secondly, even with long time lags in the correction process, long-term consequences may still be prevented from having any impact on the position of R-evolutionary attractors, because their connection with the policy by which they are produced may be much less readily recognizable than that of short-term consequences. Suppose, for example, that part of the troubles of the British economy are due to a lack of mobility on the part of the active population, and that this lack of mobility is itself due to the Council Housing system, which, as it is currently organized (without full transferability of entitlements) puts a significant premium on immobility.[7] The causal link between housing policies and long-term profitability may be subtle enough to remain unperceived or, if it is perceived, to remain controversial. And it may therefore fail to contribute anything to the R-evolutionary shaping of the State's policies.

One might think that an NS-evolutionary perspective, which takes policies to be shaped by the selective elimination of Governments, avoids both these difficulties. The action of an NS-evolutionary mechanism is slower and should therefore allow longer-term consequences to be actualized. And it does not require that the Governments should recognize differential consequences for these to influence the shaping of governmental policies. However, in the NS-evolutionary scenario suggested above (section 60), a Government's survi-. val was supposed to depend crucially on its popularity, which in turn was supposed to depend on the level of economic activity secured by the Government's policies. This assumes that, if not the Governments themselves, at least the general public, on whose support they depend, is able to register the causal link between the presence or absence of a particular kind of Government and its impact on the level of activity. Consequently, if a policy's functionality is of a long-term kind, and if, therefore, the voting public is unlikely to register the link between the policy and its crucial consequences, the very limited plausibility of the NS-evolutionary scenario will be further impaired.

62. *Working-class resistance and legitimation*

What emerges from the discussion of the previous section is that appealing to the capitalists' long-term interests in order to account for a policy which does not seem to serve their short-term interests, though not entirely absurd, is very problematic in a non-conspiratorial perspective. The long-term consequences of a policy may never be given a chance to be produced, let alone to be recognized, and it cannot therefore be taken for granted that they can take any significant part in the R-evolutionary (or NS-evolutionary) process by which policies are selected. Furthermore, particularly in advanced capitalist societies, there are undoubtedly a large number of State policies which do not seem to promote either short-term or long-term profitability. One possible example is the provision of comparatively high and permanent unemployment benefits, which seems to have the "dysfunctional" effect of reducing pressure on wages and work discipline, and of making large layers of the labour force permanently unsuitable for work.

We could of course try to dismiss such policies—which include the major part of the Welfare State—as "disequilibrium" measures, which can only last for so long as their impact on economic activity has not been fully realized. Short of accepting this heroic strategy, however, we are forced to admit that the interests of the working class, and not just those of the capitalists, play a role in determining which policies will be adopted at equilibrium. Does this mean that we have to give up our class-functional explanations, for which an evolutionary reconstruction has been provided above, and shift to straightforward actional explanations in terms of class struggle? Few Marxists have found this conclusion very attractive, as class-struggle explanations are hardly different, in their structure if not in their tone, from the mainstream liberal-pluralist theory of the State, the major target of Marxist State theory. If one agrees to translate such concepts as "class fraction" and "struggle" into, say, "pressure group" and "bargaining", the explanations generated by the two approaches are formally identical.

At first sight, there is an obvious way to avoid such an actional reduction, strongly suggested by our evolutionary approach. We have seen all along that the positions of evolutionary attractors are always relative to a given context, i.e. to the value taken by relevant control variables. The suggestion, then, is that the extent to which working-class resistance constitutes a threat to the smooth functioning of the capitalist economy could be considered a crucial control variable. In the situation considered above (Fig. 6.1 and 6.2), the value of this variable was tacitly assumed to be very low: the working class was supposed to be poorly organized and powerless. In a different situation, however, the context may be very different. The labour movement may be sufficiently powerful and militant to be able to disrupt production through strikes and other forms of unrest if it does not approve of the policies introduced or maintained by the Government (see Fig. 6.3). Consequently, the policy—for example, the level of unemployment benefits—which genuinely maximizes the capitalists' profits may be very remote from the one which one should expect to prevail if the strength of the labour movement were negligible (see Fig. 6.4).

Figure 6.3. The unrest effect

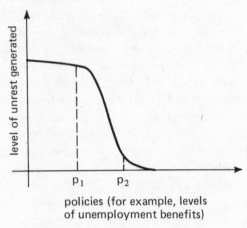

Figure 6.4. Potential and actual profitability

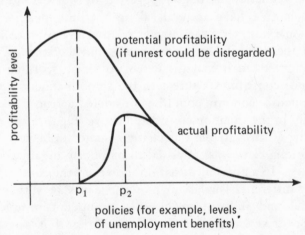

As usual (see section 24), diagrams which depict adaptive or functional landscapes for different values of a control variable can be aggregated into a single diagram. The projection of the crest line on the horizontal plane then represents the set of

Figure 6.5. Working-class strength as a control variable

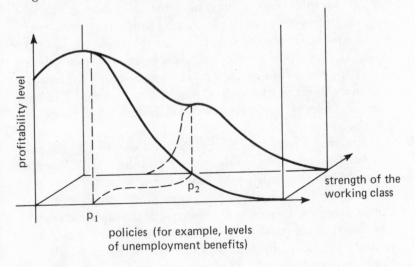

policies (for example, levels
of unemployment benefits)

policies which correspond to evolutionary attractors in the
various contexts (Fig. 6.5).

In this way, it seems possible to accommodate the fact that
the policies which prevail at equilibrium are often far from
maximizing *prima facie* profitability, while maintaining a
class-functional explanation of these policies. In a situation in
which working-class strength is not negligible, the fact that
some policies generate labour unrest must be taken into
account in determining which policies are most favourable to
the interests of the capitalist class. This point fits in nicely
with the structuralists' emphasis on the State's role in pre-
serving social cohesion, or with the distinction which is often
made between two major functions of the capitalist State: on
the one hand, it must provide the conditions for profitable
capital accumulation, and on the other hand, it must secure
the legitimation of the capitalist system in the workers' eyes.[8]
The policies which one can expect to prevail at equilibrium
will then be those which strike an optimal compromise between accumulation and legitimation, with the latter component gaining increasing weight as the working class grows

stronger. In this perspective, generous social legislation need not be interpreted as a way of protecting the capitalists' long-run interest, for example by preventing the exhaustion of the stock of labour power. It can be understood as a capitalistically optimal solution, even in the short run, in a context in which "going too far", by jeopardizing the State's legitimacy in the workers' eyes, would disrupt society's cohesion and, thereby, generate a steep fall in the level of capitalist profits.

It has often been objected that the kind of move which has just been sketched makes the theory tautological. Whatever policy seems to impair profitability and to benefit the working class can be interpreted as serving a function of legitimation and thereby favouring the interests of the capitalist class.[9] The theory under attack, however, is in principle less difficult to test than formally similar theories referring to a compromise between cost and communication (section 38) or between two forms of social cohesion (section 55). For the two components between which a compromise has to be struck in this case are not directly components of the Government's (unobservable) chances of satisfaction, but only of the level of genuine profitability, which only affects the Government's chances of satisfaction via business confidence, the level of economic activity, and popularity or financial health. It is in principle possible (though difficult in practice) to check non-tautologically, for example, whether a given level of unemployment benefits maximizes genuine profitability—i.e. whether it constitutes the lowest level compatible with the absence of major labour unrest—whereas the only way of checking whether it maximizes the Government's chances of satisfaction would be to examine (tautologically) whether it actually becomes established. It seems, therefore, that our evolutionary perspective enables us to make sense of attempts to explain State policies by their serving the interests of the ruling class in a society in which the means of production are privately owned, even in a context in which working-class strength has ceased to be negligible.

63. *Where the evolutionary approach breaks down*

What emerges from the previous section, it would seem, is the conclusion that situations in which interests conflict can successfully be dealt with in an evolutionary perspective. Not only were the policies under consideration of such a nature that they affected the capitalists' and the workers' chances of satisfaction in opposite directions. But the selection of the policies by the Government also depended on the actions taken by both capitalists and workers. In order to determine the position of the evolutionary attractors, in situations of this kind, one did not need to wonder which policies locally maximized the capitalists' and the workers' chances of satisfaction. One only needed to make a hypothesis about the factors (here, the level of economic activity) which determined the chances of satisfaction (or survival) of the policies' immediate controllers, and then assess the consequences of the various possible policies in terms of these factors. In the process, the impact on these factors of the capitalists' and the workers' reactions to the various policies had to be taken into account, and it could therefore be said that the policies eventually adopted were the outcome of a struggle between classes with conflicting interests.

The trouble is that this kind of situation is a very unstable one. Just as one has supposed that Governments will realize, sooner or later, what are the consequences associated with the various possible policies, one should also suppose that both capitalists and workers will realize, sooner or later, that the way in which they react to the Government's policies has in turn some influence on the Government's action (and probably also on each other's reaction to the latter). Instead of simply reacting, by investing or withdrawing, by working or striking, to the policies introduced by the Government, they will rather try to use the means at their disposal to make the Government's preference schedule agree with their own. For example, if the workers are exclusively interested in very high unemployment benefits, they will stage major unrest in reaction to any governmental policy which does not satisfy their request, in such a way that the Government's attempt to maximize its own chances of satisfaction by maximizing the level of economic activity will make it select a policy which maximizes the workers' chances of satisfaction.

What this means is a shift from a *parametric* to a *strategic* context, i.e. from a context in which consequences can be univocally determined to one in which this is not possible because the choice of the consequences which will be actualized depends on the reaction they are likely to prompt. Since an evolutionary approach is essentially dependent on the possibility of drawing functional (or adaptive) landscapes, i.e. of determining and assessing the differential consequences associated with various alternatives in a given context, one may think that the introduction of strategic contexts makes the application of an evolutionary framework impossible. This is not strictly true, however. One side's power may be so overwhelming that it is able to impose its own preferences on any other individual or group concerned by the practice. This supposes that one side can significantly affect the other sides' chances of satisfaction, while its own chances of satisfaction cannot significantly be affected by the other sides' actions. R-evolutionary attractors can then unambiguously be defined as corresponding to those practices which maximize the dominant side's chances of satisfaction. In other words, we are then back to a situation in which, for all practical purposes, no conflict of interests needs to be taken into account.

In a situation of genuine conflict, however, all sides are able to use sanctions against each other, i.e. to affect each other's chances of satisfaction. For example, capitalists can stop investing and so create unemployment—which workers do not like—and workers can stop working and so reduce profits—which capitalists do not like. Under such circumstances, the most than can be said (under some plausible conditions) is that the outcome of the conflict will be somewhere "inbetween" the two sides' optima—which is just a rough way of saying that it is predictable only to the extent that there is no conflict about it. There are two ways in which one might think it possible to carry the evolutionary approach further than this. On the one hand, one might be tempted to say that what prevails at equilibrium is the optimal outcome for each side, given the constraints imposed by the other one. But this is precisely the kind of statement which is made impossible by the fact that the "other side" 's behaviour forms part of a strategic context, not a parametric one. On the other hand, one might be tempted to say that what prevails at equilibrium is the optimal outcome, when judged by reference to the aggregated chances of satisfaction of all the individuals or groups involved. However, not only would such an attempt run into the difficulty of comparing the intensities of chances of satisfaction for different individuals or groups—a difficulty which is strictly parallel to the standard problem of the "interpersonal comparison of utilities". It would also have to weight each side's chances of satisfaction according to the power which it can exert on the others. But as soon as power is used strategically, and unless one side's power is overwhelming, there is no meaningful way of performing such an operation.

What this means is that we have found here a point where the evolutionary approach breaks down, even more radically than in the case of long-term consequences. When an established policy is recognized as corresponding to a compromise between conflicting interests—which is usually expressed in the concession that it serves a function of "legitimation" to the benefit of the ruling class—functional explanations by reference to the interests of the ruling class need not be abandoned straight away. As long as the working class exerts its power "unwittingly"—and can therefore be considered a part of a parametric context—the scenario sketched above (section 60), if plausible, enables us to make sense of the proposition that established policies will tend to be locally optimal, as far as the interests of the ruling class are concerned. But as soon as both sides become aware of the feedback impact of their behaviours on the choice of policies—which cannot take long—it becomes as absurd to explain the compromise policy by its function of serving the capitalists' interests as by its function of serving the workers' interests. No optimality principle can then guide our explanations and predictions of which policies will become established. Unless one side's power is overwhelming, the process by which policies are selected will be essentially contingent upon the subtlety of each side's strategies, its intransigeance, its willingness to enter coalitions, its dexterity in manipulating threats—as well as upon mere luck. Evolutionary attractors must here give way to saddle points, and the tools of game theory must be brought in.[10]

In the previous sections, I had done my utmost to make sense, by means of an evolutionary reconstruction, of some Marxists' L-functional explanations of social practices by the class interests they serve. In this section, I have then tried to show why the legitimacy of this kind of explanation, and of its evolutionary reconstruction, stopped short of genuine class conflict. This argument, which was formulated above with reference to Marxist State theory, could be repeated *mutatis mutandis* with reference to the class-theoretical analysis of any other type of social practice. Indeed, it could be repeated whenever the presence or absence of a practice, or the form it takes, affects differently the chances of satisfaction of different individuals and groups. It could be repeated, in other words, whenever there is a conflict of interests over a practice, whether inside a family, a firm, a Trade Union or society at large. Instead of doing so, however, I would now like to turn from the first to the second interpretation of the explanatory core of Marxist theory, from the class-theoretical perspective to the historical-materialist one, and to examine whether the latter makes any more room for evolutionary reconstructions than the former.

64. Contradiction, correspondence, crisis

Historical materialism attempts, on the one hand, to explain changes in the nature of the relationships of production in particular societies by reference to changes in the level of development achieved by their productive forces. And it attempts, on the other hand, to explain changes affecting a society's laws, its political institutions, its ideologies, by reference to modifications of its relationships of production. In either case, the key explanatory concept is that of *structural contradiction*. Contradictions between various structures of a society are viewed as the "source", the "motor" the "internal cause" of social change. This clearly presupposes that social reality is governed by a tendency towards *correspondence*, or non-contradiction, between the structures involved. A contradiction can only be the source of a change in a society's relationships of production, for example, because the latter tend to *adjust* to the level of development of the productive forces, according to some "law of correspondence".[11] Such adjustments, however, need not happen straight away. They may involve considerable time lags. Consequently, the laws of correspondence must be interpreted as equilibrium laws.

As presented above, it is clear that the basic propositions of historical materialism can be reformulated in terms of attractors, or locally stable equilibrium states. The level of development of the productive forces, for example, can be viewed as the control variable, and the form taken by the relationships of production as the behaviour variable. Each level of development of the productive forces can then be said to determine one or more attractors in the space of possible relationships of production. However, this does not entail that historical materialism can be reformulated in terms of *evolutionary* attractors. This point is easily understood if one considers for a moment Hegel's theory of history, as interpreted by Althusser. Not unlike Marx, Hegel distinguishes a number of "spheres" or "levels" which together encompass a society's whole reality. One of these spheres, the *Volksgeist*, is given a privileged status, in the sense that the other spheres adjust to it with some delay. It is therefore possible to speak here of a control variable determining attractors in the behaviour space of the subordinate spheres. For Hegel, however, what determines the position of an attractor has nothing to do with the objective consequences attached to that position. Once the *Volksgeist,* the people's self-consciousness, has changed, the various spheres of that people's concrete life— civil society, law, religion, art, the educational system—, change accordingly, as a result of the new *Volksgeist* "expressing itself" in them.[12] The mechanism here, if any, is certainly not evolutionary in our sense (section 19), and Hegelian attractors, therefore, are not evolutionary attractors.

With historical materialism, the situation is very different. Whether capitalist relationships of production are in contradiction or in correspondence with the level achieved by the forces of production, for example, has to be decided in the light of the differential consequences associated with their presence in the given context (as characterized by the level of development of the productive forces). If capitalist relationships impede the development of the productive forces by inducing an increasingly serious sequence of crises of overproduction, while socialist relationships would (in the same context) prevent crises from happening and promote the development of the productive forces, one will want to say that the capitalist society under consideration is in a state of contradiction and that correspondence would be restored by a transition to socialism. If this example is at all typical, it is clear that the attractors postulated by historical materialism are evolutionary attractors, i.e. that the equilibration process through which they exert their action involves the production of differential consequences by the available alternatives. This mechanism of equilibration could in principle take the form of natural selection or of reinforcement, and the attractors could accordingly be NS-evolutionary or R-evolutionary. In the former case, however, one would have to consider the society whose modification is being explained as a collection of smaller units, each of which can alter (independently of the others) its relationships of production, its legal system, its political institutions, etc. Changes in the society under consideration would then just be the sum total of the mutations and differential survivals of its constituent units. Even leaving aside the fact that the features which historical materialism attempts to explain can often be located only at the level of a total society, such a mechanism is sufficiently remote from what the theory's proponents have in mind for it to be safely discarded.[13] This means that we are left with reinforcement, and hence that the attractors postulated by the theory will be such as to (locally) maximize, not some entity's chances of reproduction or survival, but rather the (structural) chances of satisfaction of the members of the society concerned (or of whoever else controls the latter's relationships of production, its legal system, etc.).

As this remains exceedingly vague, we can return to the example of the transition to socialist relationships of production, in search for suggestions as to what determines the relevant chances of satisfaction. The example suggests two possibilities. On the one hand, if what makes capitalist relationships of production contradictory under the circumstances is the fact that they impair the development of the productive forces, the degree to which such a development is promoted will constitute a good approximation of the (structural) chances of satisfaction associated with a particular form of relationships of production. On the other hand, if what makes capitalist relationships of production contradictory when the productive forces have reached a certain level is rather the fact that they lead to the outbreak of crises, the extent to which a society is made crisis-prone by a particular form of relationships of production (in the context of a given level of development of the productive forces) will largely determine the (structural) chances of satisfaction associated with that form. Both interpretations are defensible on exegetical grounds. However, if the trans-cultural claims of historical materialism are to be accommodated into an R-evolutionary perspective, whatever is said to determine the underlying criterion of optimality must find a place among universally shared human desires. Consequently, since it seems less wildly implausible to assume a universal "preference" for the avoidance of crises than for the development of productive forces, I shall choose the second interpretation and reject the first one.[14] Structural correspondence or non-contradiction, in other words, characterizes a system whose crisis-proneness is locally minimized, rather than one in which productive forces develop at (locally) maximum speed.

But what is a *crisis*? It is obviously important, given the choice which has just been made, that one should not define the concept in a way which would either restrict it to a particular mode of production—for example, if a crisis were just a "sudden interruption of the process of capital accumulation"—or make it circularly dependent on the concept of contradiction—for example, if a crisis were just a "condensation of contradictions".[15] For our purposes, it will be sufficient to define it, very loosely, as a situation of material hardship for a significant part of a society. Admittedly, such a vague concept of crisis and the associated concept of contradiction cannot be very useful for an historical-materialist crisis theory, i.e. for an attempt to explain crises by reference to the underlying contradictions, unless both concepts are specified in such a way that a particular kind of crisis is being explained by reference to a particular structural contradiction of the society considered. No such specification is needed, however, to make sense of historical materialism as a general theory of macrosocial change.

65. *An evolutionary theory of revolutions*

Although I shall here restrict myself to the case of relationships of production, I shall define a *revolution* as any major "structural" change, whether it affects a society's relationships of production, its legal system, or its political institu-

Figure 6.6. Functional landscape with the productive forces at level I

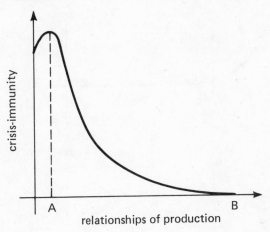

Figure 6.7. Functional landscape with the productive forces at level II

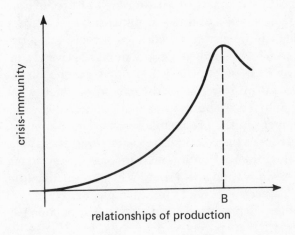

tions, etc. What has been said in the previous section enables us to formulate an evolutionary theory of revolutions in this sense. If one is willing to make a number of simplifying assumptions, this theory can be given the usual intuitive

Figure 6.8. The development of the productive forces as a control variable

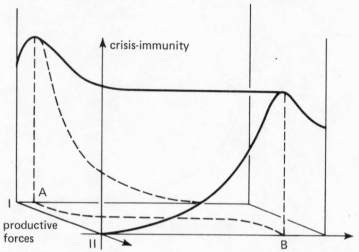

representation by means of functional landscapes. Suppose, first of all, that forms of relationships of production can be contrasted along continuous dimensions. Capitalism, for example, can be distinguished from socialism in terms of the extent to which means of production are privately or collectively owned (or controlled). And it can be distinguished from feudalism in terms of the extent to which workers are free to sell their labour on a market. For a given level of development of the productive forces—and assuming that no other aspect of the context is relevant—one can associate with each value of such continuous variables, the system's degree of success in warding off crises. When productive forces have reached a certain level I, for example, purely capitalist relationships of production (A) may perform much better in this respect than purely socialist ones (B) (Fig. 6.6). When productive forces have reached a higher level II, on the other hand, the opposite may be the case (Fig. 6.7).

If one further supposes that the level of development of the productive forces—whether one means by this the degree to which the production process is socialized or the extent of technological progress—can also be represented along a continuous dimension, two-dimensional diagrams of the kind illustrated above can conveniently be aggregated into a three-dimensional one (Fig. 6.8).

Figure 6.9. An attractor curve for revolutions

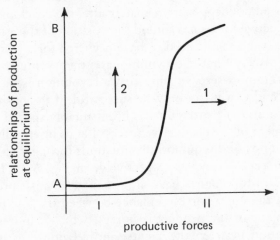

If one can suppose that crisis-immunity is a good indicator of the structural chances of satisfaction associated with each kind of relationships of production (for a given level of development of the productive forces), this kind of diagram represents what has been called earlier a functional landscape (section 34), and the projection of the crest line on the horizontal plane represents the set of functional states, or R-evolutionary attractors, of the system concerned. For each level of development of the productive forces, this projection indicates the states of correspondence, in which the relationships of production can stabilize, whereas all other possible states are (unstable) states of contradiction (Fig. 6.9). If the slope of the curve is very steep in the area between pure forms A and B, this indicates that, as productive forces keep developing, revolutions are likely to be rather abrupt, as there is hardly any level of development of the productive forces for which the relationships of production can settle in a state which is not, say, either purely capitalist *(A)* or purely socialist *(B)*.

It is important to stress, however, that the relationship represented by this curve is only an *equilibrium* relationship and hence that, even in this case, the revolution, the structural change need not happen immediately after the development of the productive forces has shifted the position of the attractor. Nor does such a shift need to have occurred for a revolution to take place. What the evolutionary theory illustrated in these diagrams asserts, is only that a revolution is bound to happen, and that it can only be successful, if the position of the R-evolutionary attractor has been suitably shifted by the development of the productive forces. Let us briefly illustrate the two kinds of disequilibrium situations (brought about by moves of types *1* and *2*, respectively, in Fig. 6.9). Firstly, Marxist anthropologists have argued that, in most primitive societies, there is a correspondence between the low level of development of the productive forces, which requires close collaboration between the agents, and relationships of production organized around kinship structures. However, the appearance of a new kind of productive forces, connected to irrigation and terrace cultivation, introduces a contradiction, which could only be solved by the adoption of new relationships of production. The correspondence will eventually be restored by the rise of the Toltec or Inca states, but a long time may elapse, with a high incidence of crises, before such revolutions take place.[16] Secondly, Marxists point out that in the past there have been various attempts to suppress class inequalities: for example, the city of Tabor and the communist State in eleventh-century Yenan. However, the level of development of the productive forces was then insufficient to enable the whole society to perform accumulation functions, and the attempts to establish a classless society were therefore bound to fail. In the meantime, however, it was possible for revolutions to take place and for their outcomes to persist for some time, before the development of the productive forces had made a new kind of relationships of production functional.[17] Historical materialism, as reconstructed above, is a comparative-static theory of change, and is therefore compatible with the temporary persistence of such situations of contradiction.

66. *Contradictions as evolutionary repellors*

Our evolutionary reconstruction of the historical-materialist theory of structural change may be criticized on several accounts. Firstly, it may be criticized on the grounds that it is fragmentary: it has only dealt with the case of relationships of production. One can argue, however, that with given relationships of production, an evolutionary reconstruction of class-theoretical Marxism (as presented in sections 58-63) becomes relevant, and provides us with what we need to make sense of the historical-materialist explanation of legal systems, political institutions and other non-economic structures. Secondly, our reconstruction may be criticized on the grounds that it is oversimplified, not only as an account of historical reality, but also as an interpretation of the Marxist theory of history. Most conspicuous are its neglect of the (non-evolutionary) feedback influence of the nature of the relationships of production on the development of the productive forces, its restriction of relevant control variables to the development of productive forces, and its assumption that for any given value of this control variable, there is only one attractor in the space of possible relationships of production. The last two complications, however, can easily be accommodated, along the lines sketched in the preceding chapter (section 56), by adding dimensions to the control space and introducing catastrophe surfaces in the behaviour space. And the first complication can be dealt with by distinguishing a *fast* dynamics, which adjusts fairly swiftly the relationships of production to the level reached by the productive forces, and a *slow* dynamics, which effects more gently the passage of the productive forces from one level to another. Such a distinction enables us to keep talking of evolutionary attractors, while conceding that the control variable is not exogenously given.[18]

The main objection, however, is that, even if one concedes that our reconstruction could be made less fragmentary and less simplistic, it would still fail to achieve its aim. It would fail to *make sense* of historical materialism by suggesting the operation of a plausible mechanism. The reasons for this failure have already been suggested in the previous chapter (section 50). The kind of evolution which is required for our reconstruction to work is societal, not collective. The differential consequences associated with a particular form of relationships of production, like those associated with moral rules or kinship systems, can only be actualized and recognized through a trial-and-error process which involves whole societies, not just individuals. And whereas individual deviations from established practice can be assumed to occur as a matter of course and thus provide a suitable raw material for the evolutionary fixation or correction of practices, societal deviations cannot be assumed to do so without undermining the very notion of a society's equilibrium state, the only state on which an evolutionary approach has any grip. As argued earlier (section 52), however, there is a way of getting round this difficulty. It consists in supposing that R-evolutionary processes, unlike NS-evolutionary ones, make room for endogenously induced deviations. If, due to a change in a practice or to a change in its context, structural chances of satisfaction become excessively low in absolute terms, not just suboptimal, the entity affected starts innovating blindly, until a state is reached in which structural chances of satisfaction reach an acceptable level again. True, the evolutionary process would then just be "satisficing", and not "optimizing". And it would be a case of evolutionary repulsion, rather than of evolutionary attraction (see section 52). But this alteration of our basic framework may enable us both to express better what is assumed in historical materialism and to make it sound more plausible.

Let us illustrate this point by reference to the process by which capitalism is supposed to be replaced by socialism. According to historical materialism, the contradiction between the development of the productive forces and the capitalist form of the relationships of production expresses itself in crises of overproduction. In order to show how the growth of the productive forces is bound, under capitalism, to generate such crises, one of the following two arguments is generally used. According to the *underconsumptionist* argument, the growth of the mass of means of production is bound to create a deepening gap between the quantity of commodities produced and the quantity which exploited workers (who form the majority of the population) can afford to consume. According to the *falling-rate-of-profit* argument, on the other hand, the increase in the value of the means of production used by the capitalists, relative to the amount of surplus value which is being produced, is bound to depress the rate of profit (over capital advanced) and so to induce a fall in the rate of accumulation. It is usually conceded that crises of overproduction generated in either of these two ways have a curative effect: they lead to the economic destruction of part of the existing means of production. What this means, however, is only that one should expect crises to be cyclical, none of them automatically leading to the final breakdown. But this does not rule out the possibility of increasingly severe crises, providing that the trend (increase in the mass or in the value of the means of production) persists, once the curative effects of the crisis have disappeared.

Clearly, such crisis processes do not make capitalism impossible, nor its replacement by socialism automatic—as a rigid breakdown theory would have it. As Sweezy (1942, 214) puts it, their impact rather consists in making capitalism "very onerous". Increasingly severe crises of overproduction, and the resulting falls in output and employment levels, create intolerable hardships for a large proportion of the population. These hardships will induce protests, mass movements, explorations, innovations in various directions, until the society's relationships of production are modified in such a way that correspondence is restored. If, given the level of development of the productive forces, only socialism can achieve this result, one can expect that, sooner or later, it will replace capitalism. Such a scenario presupposes that the society's members perceive, more or less distinctly, that the source of their troubles lies in the existing relationships of production, rather than, say, in their cooking habits. And it does not exclude that the elaboration and implementation of alternative models of society should be a deliberate and purposeful process. But what determines, "in the final analysis", where a society will settle, is the level of development of the productive forces and the objective landscape of differential consequences which it associates with the various possible forms of relationships of production. This is what determines the position of the evolutionary attractor (or at least of the complement of the evolutionary repellors), i.e. which attempt will in the end be successful. And once a particular form of relationships of production has become established and protected by a superstructure of social and supersocial sanctions, nobody needs to remain aware of its differential consequences, however decisive they were in its selection. This is why historical materialism can provide L-functional explanations.[19]

67. A general framework for the explanation of structural change

With the kind of scenario sketched in the preceding section, a state of *contradiction* (or non-correspondence) is most conveniently defined as a state which gives rise to crises (rather than one which does not minimize the incidence of crises), and a *crisis* situation as a situation of intolerable hardship (rather than just of hardship) for a significant part of society. Structural change can then be explained "endogenously" as triggered off by a crisis, which itself expresses an underlying contradiction. However, we have seen repeatedly that an R-evolutionary explanation can only avoid circularity if the nature and determinants of the relevant entities' chances of satisfaction are specified. Similarly, in this special case where variation is endogenously generated, the explanation of a change can only fail to be tautological if the nature and determinants of "intolerable hardships" are specified. Otherwise, all one would be saying is that the change occurred because the situation was one of intolerable hardship (i.e. of excessively low chances of satisfaction), and the only possible evidence for this would be that the change actually occurred.

Nonetheless, the approach outlined by these general concepts provides an abstract framework into which a wide variety of theories of social change, not just historical materialism, can easily be fitted.[20] Take, as a first example, Montesquieu's *De l'Esprit des Lois,* as interpreted by Althusser (1959, 38–50). Montesquieu distinguishes, more or less clearly, between the *principle* of a Government, which stems from the "spirit" of a nation, its "folkways", and the *nature* of that Government, as laid down in its constitution. In *pure* forms of Government, the principle and the nature are "in agreement", and the total Government is "at peace". In *impure* forms, the principle and the nature are "contradictory", and the Government tries "blindly" to reduce this contradiction "until, with the help of circumstances, a new agreement takes shape". Consequently, the principle of a Government can be viewed as being, "in the last analysis", the cause of its nature. As in the case of historical materialism, we are here given a functional explanation of the form taken at equilibrium by the "subordinate" structure. And as in the case of historical materialism again, the R-evolutionary mechanism by reference to which such an explanation can be legitimated is not one of optimization on the basis of permanent variation, but rather one of "selective settlement", steered by crises and innovatory reactions to crises.

As a second example, take the so-called *functionalist* theory of social change. After it had nearly become a commonplace that such a theory was a theoretical impossibility, Lockwood (1964, 249–250) convincingly argued that room could be made for a "functionalist" treatment of change, if one was careful to distinguish system integration from social integration. In the language which we have been using so far, this distinction can be made as follows. Arguably, a theory which claims to provide functional explanations of social practices is bound to be concerned with equilibrium states. But these equilibrium states are not defined as states in which a society's members conform to established practices (social integration). They are rather states of mutual compatibility between the society's various structures and of compatibility between these structures and the society's environment (system integration). Whereas the former kind of equilibrium state is basically maintained by a shield of superstructural consequences, i.e. by the machinery of social and supersocial sanctions, the latter is maintained by a landscape of structural consequences i.e. of consequences which are associated with the presence of a practice because of the context in which it appears. Whereas a cybernetic model of change may be appropriate in the former case—where homeostatic reactions respond to temporary disturbances—, an evolutionary model is appropriate in the latter—where adaptational adjustments respond to parametric alterations of the context. Consequently, whereas the first approach only allows for a very poor theory of change, restricted to the specification of "invariance thresholds", beyond which conformity cannot be maintained, the second approach provides a basis for a genuine theory of change, which can be cast in an evolutionary framework.

As functionalists, like Marxists, have tended to focus on practices which require societal evolution for their differential consequences to be felt, it is not surprising to see that they have emphasized the role played by "structural tensions", "structural strain", "dysfunctions", "dysnomia", etc. in the genesis of social change.[21] A typical example is the general model of institutional change proposed by Smelser (1968, 205–207, 269–276). The starting point is a disturbance arising from a (contextual) change in some aspect of the social system. Agents, as a result, become increasingly dissatisfied with the way in which certain institutionalized roles are performed and organized. This dissatisfaction soon expresses itself in the form of anger, anxiety, hostility, utopian visions, prophecies of doom, protests, conflicts of all kinds. Attempts are then made, whether blindly or otherwise, to set up new institutions which might put an end to the initial dissatisfaction. This will only be possible when the impetus element— the tension which triggers off the change—encounters a mobilization element—the innovating initiative of leaders, entrepreneurs, prophets, etc. The analogy between this scenario and the one described earlier in terms of contradiction, crisis and revolution is obvious enough. Historical materialism and the functionalist theory of change seem to require precisely the same variety of evolutionary reconstruction.[22]

This should, however, be qualified as follows. A number of typical functionalist explanations of social change do not require societal evolution, but only collective evolution. This is the case, for example, with Durkheim's explanation of the substitution of organic for mechanical solidarity by reference to an increase in a population's moral density, or with Parsons' explanation of the substitution of the nuclear for the extended family by reference to the progress of industrialization.[23] In both explanations, structural tension is clearly assumed to play an important role in the underlying mechanism: the tension which arises from remaining unspecialized in a morally dense population in one case, the tension which arises from conforming to extended-family patterns of life in the midst of high geographic and social mobility in the other. But there is no need here for the whole society to change its ways in order to reveal which practices generate more tension and which less. Individual experimentation is enough to make this realization possible and thus to legitimate an R-evolutionary reconstruction of Durkheim's or Parsons' explanation. In other words, societal evolution is not required, and the intervention of tensions, or crises, in the generation of variation, is not indispensable, although it may conceivably play some role. What this means is that some functionalist theories of change, because they can rely on permanent individual variation, can be reconstructed with the help of the standard notion of R-evolutionary attractor. It is only when societal trial-and-error is essential, that functionalist theories, like historical materialism, must give a crucial role to crises and can then be more conveniently reconstructed in terms of evolutionary repulsion (away from states of contradiction). However, in the realm of so-called "social structures", this condition is met often enough for the the framework illustrated by historical materialism to provide a general framework for the explanation of "structural change".

Conclusion

Summary

Our inquiry has led to three main outcomes. Firstly, it has demonstrated the legitimacy of function and, more generally, functional explanations in the social sciences. As one can also show that such explanations are neither necessarily untestable, nor necessarily conservative, their rehabilitation is complete (section 68). Secondly, our inquiry has generated a tentative map of the social sciences in the form of a list of major explanation patterns—the action pattern, the NS-evolutionary pattern, the R-evolutionary pattern (section 69). Finally, by disclosing a network of similarities and differences, it has contributed to the emergence of an evolutionary "paradigm" (section 70).

68. How respectable are functional explanations?

In this book, I have endeavoured to answer two questions about social-scientific practice. Firstly, what is the deep structure of the social sciences? Secondly, how is it possible for function explanations to be legitimate in the social sciences? Let us now summarize the outcome of this inquiry, starting with the second question.

Function explanations, it has been argued, are most fruitfully viewed as explanations of persistent features by the fact that the context is such that the feature's presence has certain

215

differential consequences and that these consequences are "good". If one excludes the possibility of perfect foresight, function explanations and optimum explanations, with which they are closely connected and jointly form the set of functional explanations, can only make sense in an evolutionary perspective. An evolutionary mechanism is a mechanism which combines blind variation with selection according to consequences (chapter 2). There are two basic types of such mechanisms: natural selection, which selects features through the selection of the entities which they characterize, and reinforcement, which selects features directly. In the social sciences, mechanisms of the first type, or NS-evolutionary mechanisms, cannot legitimate more than an insignificant number of functional explanations, even if one allows features to be culturally, rather than genetically, transmitted, and if one allows selection to operate on societies and subsocieties, rather than organisms (chapter 3). Mechanisms of the second type, or R-evolutionary mechanisms, on the other hand, provide a much more promising basis for the legitimacy of functional explanations, as is first argued in connection with the way in which languages are shaped (chapter 4). However, as was subsequently argued in connection with the R-evolutionary reconstruction of a number of anthropological and Marxist theories, the legitimacy of social-scientific functional explanations becomes very shaky when the consequences to which they refer are of a long-term nature (sections 47 and 61), when they cannot be revealed by individual variation (sections 50 and 66) and when they affect in opposite directions the interests of different groups (section 63). Despite these reservations concerning long-term, societal and conflictual "functionalism", a substantial number of social-scientific function or optimum explanations can be legitimated through their insertion into an R-evolutionary perspective (chapters 5–6).

In order to make function explanations and, more generally, functional explanations respectable, however, it may not be enough to show that they are legitimate, in the sense that they assume the operation of a type of mechanism which is, in principle, plausible. It is also important that they should constitute genuinely testable hypotheses. The testing of any functional explanation, we have seen, involves two steps, corresponding to the two causal claims which such an explanation makes. On the one hand, one must check whether, in a given context, the presence of the feature actually has the (differential) consequences by reference to which it is being explained. And on the other hand, one must check whether the feature is present at equilibrium because the context is such that its presence has these consequences. We have also seen that this second step can be dispensed with if one can establish that the features (of the kind investigated) which are present at equilibrium are systematically such that their presence has the differential consequences mentioned (section 26). In the case of NS-evolutionary functional explanations, neither step presents a special difficulty, because both an entity's chances of reproduction (in the case of optimum explanations) and specific contributions to it (in the case of function explanations) can in principle be observed. In the case of R-evolutionary functional explanations, on the other hand, a special problem arises from the fact that there is no direct way of observing an entity's chances of satisfaction. R-evolutionary optimum explanations, therefore, are at risk of being tautological, the selection of a feature being taken as the only evidence for its optimality. The only way of avoiding this risk is to specify the criterion of optimality in such a way that its application can be checked in a non-circular fashion. The conclusive testing of both specified-optimum and function explanation may then still raise quite formidable difficulties (see sections 38–42, 55–56). But this would by no means make them stick out among other social-scientific explanations.

Legitimacy-in-principle and testability-in-principle, however, do not necessarily add up to respectability. If functional explanations are to be respectable, it seems that one should also be able to show that they are not intrinsically conservative. For the widespread conviction that they are so has been a powerful factor in discrediting functional explanation in an increasingly radical profession. If anything, however, it looks as if the analysis provided in this book has made things worse in this respect. Both function and optimum explanations have been shown to imply that the features whose presence is being explained have "good" consequences, that they are more "beneficial" than alternative features. Nothing could highlight this point more strikingly than the analogy sketched earlier (section 50) between sociological "functionalism" and ethical "utilitarianism". Both answer why-questions about social practices (rules, norms, institutions, etc.), and both do so by drawing attention to the differential consequences of the practices' presence, and more precisely by showing how "good" these consequences are. Admittedly, a society's chances of survival or its members' chances of satisfaction, which define what should be meant by "good" in the former case, may diverge somewhat from "happiness for the greatest number" (or related notions), in terms of which utilitarian "goodness" is to be judged. But the two sets of criteria are sufficiently vague and sufficiently akin to one another, for us to suspect that any functional explanation of a social practice comes very close to providing, *ipso facto*, a utilitarian justification for it. How could social-scientific explanatory practice be more tightly geared to the preservation of the *status quo*? How could it be more slavishly conservative?

Even if one is dealing with a world in which evolutionary processes have operated in such a way that functional explanations can be given for all social practices, however, systematic discrepancies will crop up between what is (at equilibrium) and what ought to be (from a utilitarian point of view). Firstly, evolutionary processes are processes of local optimization (section 19). When there are several local optima, functionalism can only predict that one of them will prevail, while utilitarianism can pick out among them the global optimum, and advocate it. Secondly, (R-evolutionary) functionalism cannot take it for granted that differential consequences which can only appear in the long run or through societal mutation will be taken into account in the selective fixation and correction of social practices (sections 50 and 61). This restriction is of no relevance to utilitarianism, which endeavours to determine the optimal alternative, however hard to detect the consequences which make it optimal. Finally, inasmuch as functionalism applies to a conflict situation, it will have to predict the presence of those practices which are optimal for the powerful (section 63). And whatever criterion utilitarians choose for the sake of aggregating conflicting preferences, on the other hand, it can certainly not be the relative power of individuals and groups. These are three reasons why the fact that a practice can be explained functionally does not imply that it can be given a utilitarian justification.

Furthermore, even in situations where none of these sources of discrepancies is relevant, the justification suggested by a functional explanation is always relative to a given context, and can therefore also serve as a foundation for social criticism. Often, the functional explanation of a social practice—from cross-cousin marriage to the wearing of gowns—carries the connotation that its presence is less silly, less absurd, wiser than one might think. The value thus ascribed to the practice, however, stems from its propensity to produce certain consequences in a particular social context, not from an intrinsic property it may possess or from supersocial sanctions allegedly associated with it. Consequently, the justification suggested by a functional explanation is often at the same time a demystification. The superiority of the practice is made contingent upon the state in which the context happens to be, and as soon as this context starts changing, the functional-utilitarian approach may become as keen to denounce suboptimality as it was to celebrate optimality. For functional explanations cannot be given for whatever practice happens to be present, but only for practices which are present "at equilibrium", i.e. after evolutionary processes have had time to operate. As Campbell (1975,

1104) puts it, the wisdom produced by such processes is a "wisdom about past worlds". Practices which are present in a "disequilibrium" situation may be as silly, as absurd, as unwise as they seem to be, and the criticism of them which is suggested by the functional explanation of their presence in a different context may form part of the mechanism through which optimality is being restored. Marxist-inspired revolutions illustrate this point.

Let us conclude. A substantial part of this book has been devoted to showing how function explanations and, more generally, functional explanations can be legitimate in the social sciences. A few sections were devoted to showing that they do not need to be tautological. And we have just seen that they do not need to be conservative either. Why should social scientists still feel ashamed of openly using functional explanations?

69. *A tentative map of the social sciences*

This rehabilitation of functional explanation, however, is only one of the three main outcomes of our inquiry into some aspects of social-scientific practice. The second one is a tentative answer to the question of the deep structure of the social sciences as specified in the first chapter, i.e. a list of the patterns of intelligibility to which social-scientific explanations conform. More precisely, our inquiry was set up as an attempt to establish whether there were any legitimate social-scientific explanations which did not conform to the action pattern and, if so, whether the mechanisms whose operation they assumed were still of an individualistic and psychological nature. The results of this inquiry can be summarized in the following table (Table C.1), where "+", "−", and "(−)" indicate that explanations which assume the operation of a mechanism of the type mentioned in the corresponding row satisfy, fail to satisfy, or fail to satisfy with some qualifications, the principle mentioned in the corresponding column.

Of the four forms of natural selection distinguished in

Table C.1. Evolutionary explanations and methodological principles

Type of mechanism		Principle		
		Actionalism	Psychologism	Individualism
Natural selection	biological characteristics	individuals	−	−	+
		groups	−	−	−
	cultural traits	individuals	−	(−)	+
		groups	−	(−)	−
Reinforcement	"latent"	collective	−	+	+
		societal	−	+	(−)
	"manifest"	collective	+	+	+
		societal	+	+	(−)

chapter 3 (section 22), the first two are irrelevant because their operation can only legitimate the explanation of biological characteristics, while the third one can be disregarded because of its intrinsic precariousness. Only the fourth form is then left to provide us with an NS-evolutionary pattern of explanation in the social sciences. Any explanation conforming to such a pattern, i.e. any explanation of the presence of a cultural trait by reference to the natural selection of societies or subsocieties, clearly transgresses the principle of methodological individualism. It also transgresses the principle of methodological psychologism, at least in so far as its selection component is concerned, but not its transmission or variation components. Finally, it unambiguously transgresses the principle of methodological actionalism. However, to the extent that this pattern only covers a very small part of social-scientific practice, as has been argued above (sections 30–32), these various refutations cannot shed much light on the deep structure of the social sciences.

Explanations which assume the operation of some form of reinforcement, on the other hand, play a much more prominent role in social-scientific practice. Some of them, however, can fairly conveniently be accommodated by the action pattern (see section 21). In the case of functional explanations —the most typical form of R-evolutionary explanations— these correspond to manifest-functional (or M-functional) explanations, i.e. explanations which assume that the agents who maintain the feature which is being explained do so in view of the consequences by reference to which the feature is being explained. Consequently, what one could call "manifest" reinforcement is irrelevant to the exploration of the residue of the action pattern. However, not all functional explanations assuming reinforcement are M-functional. As has been argued earlier (sections 43–44), although the consequences by reference to which the feature is being explained must be recognized by someone, in some way and at some point, this recognition may be completely absent from the agents by whom the feature is maintained at a particular time, as well as buried under a superstructure of social and supersocial sanctions. There is room, in other words, for latent-functional (or L-functional) explanations, i.e. for functional explanations by reference to consequences of which the agents involved need not be aware. Such explanations, on which the last three chapters have concentrated, cannot be accommodated by the action pattern in the same way as M-functional explanations can, and one must therefore conclude that they constitute a further transgression of methodological actionalism. This "latent" reinforcement can be either societal or collective, depending on whether or not variation in the whole society or subsociety is required for the reinforcing consequences to be revealed. L-functional explanations assuming collective reinforcement, for example those encountered in diachronic linguistics, are compatible both with methodological psychologism and methodological individualism. L-functional explanations assuming societal reinforcement, for example those encountered in historical materialism, are also compatible with methodological psychologism: variation, transmission and selection are taking place through the agents' minds. But, even though differential consequences must eventually be recognized and assessed by individuals, they are not compatible with methodological individualism, since variation needs to occur on a societal scale.

The outcome of this discussion is a tentative classification of (non-black-box) explanations proposed by social scientists. Some explanations, admittedly, are not very clear about the nature of the mechanism which they suppose to be at work, and other explanations clearly assume the simultaneous operation of two or more distinct mechanisms. Lévi-Strauss's explanation of the universality of the incest taboo would be an example of the former, and an explanation of the production techniques used at equilibrium by capitalist firms which relies on the conjunction of consequence-anticipation and competitive elimination, would be an example of the latter. However, once these two categories of explanations have been subjected to an adequate treatment ("reconstruction" in the former case and "decomposition" in the latter), every social-scientific explanation can be ascribed to a single pattern of explanation, unless the same type of mechanism can be construed in two different ways—as we have seen is the case with "manifest" reinforcement. The classification emerging from the previous discussion can then be depicted by the thickly drawn circles in the following diagram (Fig. C.1). The areas to the right of the dotted lines contain the explanations which transgress methodological psychologism and methodological individualism, respectively.

Figure C.1. Major patterns of social-scientific explanation

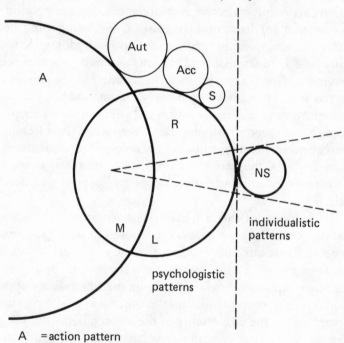

```
A   = action pattern
R   = R-evolutionary pattern
(M  = "manifest", L = "latent"
NS  = NS-evolutionary pattern
Aut = authority pattern
Acc = accommodation pattern
S   = structuration pattern
```

Although I believe that the three patterns of explanation which have been explored (to various extents) in this book, cover the bulk of social-scientific explanations, I do not claim that this list is exhaustive. Indeed, I shall briefly suggest the existence of three additional patterns. First of all, one will have noticed that the explanation of beliefs has hardly ever been mentioned in this whole book. If what a society or subsociety believes has an impact on its chances of survival, nothing prevents the presence of a belief, any more than the presence of a practice, from being the object of an NS-evolutionary explanation. However, because beliefs are not "chosen" by a believer in the same way as actions or practices are "chosen" by an agent or a practitioner, their explanation cannot be accommodated either by the action pattern or the R-evolutionary one. Social-scientific explanations of beliefs rather seem to fall under two other patterns which are, very roughly, to each other what the action pattern is to the R-evolutionary one. On the one hand, just as the social upkeep of practices is often explained by reference to the machinery of social and supersocial sanctions, as controlled by reference groups, the social upkeep of belief systems is often explained by the pressure of social and supersocial authorities, as controlled by what Berger and Luckmann[1] call "plausibility structures". On the other hand, the form taken by "distorted" belief systems—prejudices, rumours, myths, ideologies, Durkheimian "prenotions", Freudian "illusions" —is often explained by reference to the interests, needs, desires to which the beliefs are accommodated. We may call *authority pattern* and *accommodation pattern*, respectively, the patterns to which these two sets of belief explanations conform. Finally, the explanation of cultural forms by their "structural homology" with other cultural forms or other aspects of social life, as illustrated in the work of Panofsky, Francastel and Goldman for example, does not seem to be reducible to any of the patterns mentioned so far. We can call *structuration pattern* the corresponding pattern of

explanation, as defined by the underlying mechanism of
mental structuration. All three additional patterns are individualistic, psychologistic, but not actionalistic. They are
represented by the thinly drawn circles in Figure C.1.

I propose this list of six explanation patterns as a rough
outline of the deep structure of the social sciences. By way of
a challenge to counterexamples, I claim that there is no
legitimate explanation in the social sciences which cannot be
reconstructed in such a way that it fits into one of the six
patterns.

70. *The emergence of a paradigm*

Through a systematic investigation of what is asserted and
assumed in a wide variety of social-scientific explanations,
our inquiry has produced an answer to the "grammatical"
questions formulated in the first two chapters. By doing so, it
has led to the outcomes described in the preceding two
sections: a rehabilitation of functional explanations and a
sketch of the deep structure of social-scientific explanatory
practice. In the process, it has involved the exploration of two
patterns of explanation, the NS-evolutionary one (sections
30–31) and, in considerably greater detail, the R-evolutionary
one (sections 33–67). This leads to a third outcome: a contribution to the emergence of a paradigm, i.e. of a "standard
way of doing things".

In order to make such a contribution, this book has not
itself proposed any new explanation, nor has it tried to dictate
new rules about how to explain. In the case of disciplines
where the confusion arising from stigmatization prevents the
"way things are done" from being standardized, an attempt
to reveal similarities between the ways things are being done
in very different areas of those disciplines may enable these
"ways things are done" to become standard, i.e. it may enable
a paradigm to emerge. By bringing out underlying
similarities, it is possible to spread widely the respectability
gained in one particular area, whether as a result of a careful

study of the mechanism at work or of the integration of a large number of facts, and one can thus encourage the pursuit of a similar approach in other areas, where respectability is much shakier. On the other hand, by bringing out such similarities, one can also clarify the nature of the difficulties which are intrinsic to the approach, by showing how they apply throughout the areas in which it is used, and thus make it possible for them to be dealt with otherwise than by arrogant ignorance or insecure overconfidence. In this way, the systematic description of similarities (and differences) can have a (modestly) normative impact: it can generate a new outlook on what should be done and what not.

This is, I hope, what this book has achieved, by weaving a network of analogies (and disanalogies) between evolutionary explanations, both at the level of their logic and of their morphology. Around the (R-)evolutionary pattern of explanation, a new set of "standard ways of doing things" can emerge. Such an evolutionary paradigm, as sketchily outlined in the second half of this book, does not only consist in a formal framework, our "theory of (R-)evolutionary attractors", which can be widely used as a tool for the integration of existing explanations. It also provides a set of heuristic suggestions for the formulation of new explanations, as well as for the investigation of their microfoundations. If any one of them is ever taken up, this book will not have been written in vain.

Notes

Introduction

1. When writing "he", "him" or "his", I obviously mean "he or she", "him or her" or "his or her".

2. An analogous distinction between "logic in use" and "reconstructed logic" is made by Kaplan (1964, 3–11). See also Chomsky (1965, 4, 24–25) for the analogous linguistic distinction.

3. See Bourdieu and Sayad's (1972) general critique of the language of rules.

4. See for example Labov's (1966, 93–94) perceptive remarks.

5. This is one possible interpretation of the "rubbish that lies in the way to knowledge" in Locke's (1689, 58) "underlabourer" conception of philosophy.

6. Although, for brevity's sake, appearances may sometimes be allowed to suggest the contrary in subsequent discussions.

Chapter 1

1. Typical examples are provided by Lazarsfeld (1970, ch. 3) and Touraine (1973, ch. 1), respectively.

2. For a recent analysis of this kind, see Achinstein (1977b).

3. Suggested by Samuelson (1948, 651–652).

4. A sophisticated defense of a "Humean" concept of causality is presented by Mackie (1965, 1974, ch. 1–3).

5. Von Wright (1971, ch. 2, 1973) discusses logical and epistemological aspects of such a "production" concept of causation.

6. See, for example, Lewis' (1973) defense of a counterfactual concept of causation, and Kim's (1973) critical note.

7. Suggestive remarks about these "pragmatic" aspects of explanation have been made by Scriven (1963, 409–410) and Runciman (1969, 166–167) in terms of "contrast classes", by Mackie (1965, 21–25) in terms of "causal fields" and by Putnam (1978, 42–44) in terms of "explanation spaces".

8. This is the case when statistical relationships are allowed in. For example, if there is a positive correlation between variables A and B, and another positive correlation between variables B and C, it does not necessarily follow that there is a positive correlation between A and C. This conclusion does follow, however, if both A and C can be assumed to be causally dependent on B. For details, proofs and further examples, see for example Costner & Leik (1964).

9. See footnote 3 above.

10. This distinction between three concepts of understanding parallels to some extent Habermas' (1965, 1968) and Apel's (1977) distinction between three cognitive interests. Related distinctions between "hermeneutic" and "causal-motivational" understanding are discussed by Abel (1948, 85–88; 1975, 99–102) and Keat & Urry (1975, 167).

11. Along these lines, see, for example, Hanson (1958, ch. 3), Mischel (1966), Kuhn (1971), Toulmin (1972, ch. 2) etc.

12. Along these lines, see Harré (1964, ch. 1; 1970, ch. 4), Apostel (1974, part 4), Bhaskar (1975, ch. 3), Keat & Urry (1975, ch. 2), etc.

13. A typical formulation of this position can be found in Cohen (1978, 285–286).

14. See especially Weber (1913, 437–439; 1922, 1–11).

15. See for example Popper (1944, 140–142; 1945, 94–95), Jarvie (1964, 196–197).

16. See for example Homans (1967, 33–64; 1970, 316–321), Heath (1976, 7–18).

17. See Harsanyi (1968). Systematic attempts to integrate some specific aspects of the social sciences into this framework have been made by March & Simon (1958) for organization theory and by Hawthorn (1970) for the sociology of fertility.

18. The validity of this claim would justify a conception of sociology as an application of (an ideal) psychological theory to the social domain—a conception held for example by Freud (1933, 194) and Homans (1967, 62).

19. As we shall see later (section 69), however, psychological mechanisms can conceivably be non-individualistic (in some sense), and the claim that individualism is weaker than psychologism must be qualified accordingly.

Chapter 2

1. This definition will be modified below (section 19).

2. See, for example, Wright (1976a, 112–113) and Achinstein (1977a, 359) for a discussion of this point.

3. This terminology is suggested by Cohen (1978, 259).

4. See, for example, Durkheim (1895, 89, 109), Emmet (1958, 56–57), Homans (1964, 809–811), Jarvie (1964, XVII, 156, 195–198), Cohen (1968, 47–48), MacLachlan (1976, 236–237, 239–240). In a way, this argument is just another version of what Bennett (1976, 36) calls "Spinoza's challenge", i.e. of the claim that *"causas finales nihil, nisi humana esse figmenta"*. The label *"logical mistake argument"* is somewhat of a misnomer, unless it is interpreted as referring to what I have called above (section 6) the *logic* of explanation.

5. The way in which this and subsequent verbal formulations attempt to paraphrase causal claims, and particularly embedded causal claims of type (1), is unavoidably defective. (See Cohen 1978, 259–261 for a discussion of this problem.) In particular, one must bear in mind that the underlying causal concept is the one discussed in sections 6–7 above.

6. An argument which is essentially similar to the one presented in this paragraph can be found in Taylor (1964, 15–17) and Cohen (1978, 258–264). One could at this point introduce the notion of "teleological law", a universally quantified version of (1) (see Taylor 1964, 9–10; Bennett 1976, 38–42; Woodfield 1976, 75–81). One does not need to, however, because the notion of "law" has only played a minor role in the discussion of explanation and causality presented previously (sections 6–7).

7. As in Achinstein's (1977a) comprehensive discussion, for example.

8. Such analysis has been proposed by Wright (1973; 1976a, ch. 2).

9. See, for example, Nagel (1977, 284) and Achinstein (1977a, 348).

10. Type-(5) counterexamples have been a standard objection to the "etiological" view (see e.g. Grim 1974, 62–64; Boorse 1976, 75–76; Wright 1976b, 156; Achinstein 1977a, 348; Purton 1979, 14–15). Type-(4) counterexamples are discussed by Woodfield (1976, 83) in another context. What he calls the "double-edge objection" (Woodfield 1976, 83–88) provides a further, but more artificial, class of counterexamples of the latter kind.

11. The standard analyses of functional language in physiology are by Nagel (1956 and 1961, ch. 12) and Hempel (1959).

12. See especially Radcliffe-Brown (1922, 233–234, 257, 401–405).

13. The difficulties connected with this postulate of indispensability have been one of the favourite themes in the discussion on "functionalism". See e.g. Merton (1949, 86–90), Hempel (1959, 310–314), Isajiw (1968, 36–39), etc.

14. Some classic analyses of punishment and burial ceremonies by Durkheim (1912, 583–584 and 571–574, respectively), Radcliffe-Brown (1952, 210–211 and 1922, 285–286, respectively), Malinowski (1926, 85–86 and 1948, 52–53, respectively), and Parsons (1951, 309–315 and 304–306, respectively), can easily be fitted into this framework.

15. See, for example, Emmet (1985, 60–70), Cancian (1960, 204–207), Rudner (1966, 105–111), Ryan (1970, 184–187), Lessnoff (1974, 127–130).

16. My definition of "cybernetic", which covers all cases of negative feedback, may be judged excessively broad. As will be noted later (section 17), a restriction of the term to those cases where there is a negative-feedback *device* would make an appeal to "cybernetics" which is more specifically, but not more widely relevant to the legitimation of function explanations.

17. This point is suggested by Merton (1949, 104) but has hardly been taken up since. Cohen (1976, 255–256, 296) rejects it explicitly, on the grounds that there are numerous counterexamples (e.g. the function of the adoption of a bill). Here, I shall consider such counterexamples as "marginal", just as I have excluded from the "hard core" of function statements those which do not ascribe *actual* consequences to the item's presence (section 14).

18. A similar terminology is used in the literature on "catastrophe models". See, for example, Zeeman (1977, ch. 1).

19. Early explicit proponents of this "benefit theory" of functions

include Durkheim (1895, 96, 118) and Freud (1899, 52). More recent variants can be found in Hinde (1975, 3–5), Woodfield (1976, 130–134) or Cohen (1978, 263–264).

20. As pointed out by Halfpenny (1981), incidentally, function explanations involve three levels (feature, specific consequence, criterion) in this optimization perspective, just as they involve three levels (feature, functional imperative, welfare) in the welfare perspective. Together with the resemblance between the most plausible interpretations of the welfare of an entity (survival or proper working) and of the criterion of evolutionary selection (reproduction or satisfaction), this similarity has certainly helped to muddle the debate about "functionalism".

21. Clearly, this means that we are here concerned with a specific variety of cybernetic mechanisms (in the broad sense in which they have been defined above): *cybernetic mechanisms*, because a negative feedback loop is involved (and hence it is possible to give a consequence explanation of the reaction which restores an equilibrium state); *specific variety*, because the feedback loop involves the consequences associated with various states of the system (and hence it is also possible to give a consequence explanation of the equilibrium states themselves).

22. Elster (1979, 16–17) points out this connection between consequence-anticipation/consequence-feedback and global/local optimization.

23. See, for example, Delattre (1971, ch. 3) and Opp (1979).

24. The distinction between "evolutionist" and "evolutionary" is elaborated by Toulmin (1972, 321–324, 333–336), and that between "logic" and "dynamics" of development by Habermas (1976, 154–155). It follows from this paragraph that there is hardly more than a superficial connection between the subject-matter of this book and the social or cultural evolutionism vindicated or discussed by Childe (1951), White (1959), Ginsberg (1961), Burrow (1966), Parsons (1966), Service (1971, 1975), or even Steward (1955).

25. Such a "filtering" conception of evolution is proposed, for example, by Toulmin (1972, 135, 337), Wimsatt (1972, 12–13, 67) and Campbell (1974, 421–422). The notion of an uncoupled/fully coupled continuum is introduced by Toulmin (1972, 337–338). Harré's (1979, 364–367) "Darwinian/Lamarckian spectrum" is closely parallel.

26. See especially Popper (1972, 65–71, 256–284).

27. The related distinction between latent and manifest functions was originally introduced by Merton (1949, 114–120). The importance of stating clearly whether recognition or anticipation is the distinguishing feature has repeatedly been stressed, from Levy (1952, 95–98) onwards. The former interpretation has been chosen here.

Chapter 3

1. See Tinbergen (1951, 164).

2. For our purposes, it is harmless to disregard the complication arising

in cases where diversity in the population is adaptive as such. The "adaptive polymorphism" of snails subjected to search-image predation is one typical example. The phenomenon of "heterosis", i.e. the fact that, for some genes, heterozygous organisms have higher chances of reproduction than homozygous ones, is another typical example.

3. Also used, for example, by Gerard & al. (1956, 13–15), Goudge (1961, 104–105) and Wilson (1975, 24). This kind of representation obviously oversimplifies the relationship between characteristics and genes: no pleiotropism, no polygeny, no distinction between dominant and recessive genes. For our purposes, however, such complications do not need to be taken into account.

4. This close connection between biological function explanations and adaptiveness is stressed, for example, by Wimsatt (1972, 6–8) or Ruse (1973, 182–185).

5. See Tinbergen (1956).

6. The heuristic value of these two principles is often vigorously defended. In the case of behavioural characteristics, see, for example, Klopfer and Hailman (1972, 101) and Hinde (1975, 7) for the former, Tinbergen (1965, 521, 526–527, 531) for the latter.

7. This statement (and consequently, the two principles) should be qualified to take into account both the possibility of adaptive diversity and that of complex relationships between genes and characteristics (see footnotes 2 and 3 above). As noted in the previous chapter (section 19), on the other hand, the distinction between optimization and satisficing (or between "survival of the fittest" and "survival of the fit") is not crucial here.

8. See Tinbergen & al. (1962).

9. See Kettlewell (1974) for a survey of the literature.

10. See Smith (1975, ch.12) or Wilson (1975, ch.5) for a summary presentation.

11. For a critical discussion of "reciprocal altruism", see for example Hamilton (1975, 150–151) and Wilson (1975, 120–121).

12. See again Smith (1975, ch.12) or Wilson (1975, ch.5) for a concise discussion.

13. See Pratt (1975, 371–372; 1978, 127–129).

14. A comprehensive survey of the literature can be found in Bischof (1975).

15. See, for example, Malinowski (1927, 199–200), Lévi-Strauss (1949, 19–22,34–35), Fox (1967, 68–71). An opposite view is defended by Bischof (1975, 59–63), on the basis of some (flimsy) evidence from Israel and Taiwan.

16. As is often noted without any suggestion of a mechanism. See e.g. Ruse (1974), Blurton Jones (1978).

17. The term is indirectly suggested by Cloak (esp. 1977, 50), although his use of it is substantially broader than mine. (See also Cloak 1975.) The distinction between the natural selection of (innate) biological characteristics and the natural selection of (acquired) cultural traits constitutes one possible interpretation of the Darwinian/Lamarckian opposition (see e.g. Ruse 1974, 433).

18. See Blurton Jones & Sibly (1978) for a quantitative discussion. A similar suggestion has been made by Durham (1976, 105–106).

19. See for example Malinowski (1944, 144; 1948, 62), Radcliffe-Brown (1952, 8–9), Bredemeier (1955, 173), Dore (1961, 69–71), etc. Such suggestions converge with some of the attempts to elaborate analogically a theory of cultural evolution. See especially Gerard & al. (1956, throughout), Sahlins (1960, 233–235), Hayek (1967, 68–70).

20. See Malinowski (1927, 249–252) and Lévi-Strauss (1949, 48,549), respectively, for typical statements. The example is developed by Beck (1975, 48–51).

21. This kind of difficulty has been stressed e.g. by Emmet (1958, 101–102), Rapoport (1967, 133–134), Harsanyi (1968, 306–307), Ruyle (1973, 213–214), Sztompka (1974, 145).

22. The original formulation of this model is due to Alchian (1950). Further developments can be found in Winter (1974; 1975), Nelson & Winter (1974), Nelson & al. (1976), etc. The relevance of the model to the debate on functionalism is discussed, for example, by Lessnoff (1974, 121) and Elster (1979, 31–33).

23. See Alchian (1950, 214–217) and Nelson & Winter (1974, 899–900).

24. See Wilson (1975, 4).

25. See Perrow (1967, 202–203).

26. See Worsley (1957, 245–246). The possibility of such an NS-evolutionary approach to sects is hinted at by Ruyle (1973, 206) and Wilson (1975, 561).

27. This is, for example, Smith's (1961, 91–92) and Elster's (1979, VIII,1–2) position—a challenge which the rest of this book aims to take up.

Chapter 4

1. See Skinner (1953, 62–75) for a classic presentation.

2. The parallelism between (psychological) learning through reinforcement and (biological) evolution through natural selection has often been pointed out. See, for example, Skinner (1953, 90) and Lorenz (1965, 103).

3. The term "register" is suggested in this sense by Bennett (1976, 46–48).

4. To contrast NS-optimality and R-optimality as "adaptiveness" and "functionality" is misleading, in so far as it suggests an unwarranted parallelism with the distinction between (comparative-static) adaptational explanations and (static) functional explanations, both of which are equally at home in an NS-evolutionary and in an R-evolutionary perspective. Nevertheless, this choice of words seemed the most convenient one to make.

5. See Fisher & Hinde (1949), Hinde & Fisher (1951).

6. See Miyadi (1964).

7. See Wilson (1975, 169).

8. This point is made more fully by Durham (1977, 61–62).

9. See, however, Malinowski (1944, 134–135,141–142), or Spiro (1966, 106–107). These suggestions converge with Bourdieu's (1972, 177–179) conception of the way in which a "class habitus" is shaped, as well as with some of the attempts to work out a theory of cultural evolution on the model of evolutionary biology: see especially Murdock (1956, 330), Hayek (1967, 101), Ruyle (1973, 53–55), Corning (1974, 278–280), Langton (1979, 297–308).

10. Analogies between linguistic and biological evolution are systematically developed by Gerard & al. (1956, 15–25), Stevick (1963, 164–167) and Toulmin (1972, 342–348).

11. The former version is suggested by Darwin (1871, 465), the latter by Jespersen (1941, 6–7), who also emphasizes the importance of blunders and slips in the origin of linguistic changes (see *ibid.* 22,86–87). One recent textbook on historical linguistics (Samuels 1972) is entirely organized around the opposition between "inertial variation" and "systemic selection".

12. See, for example, Cherry (1957, 102–103), Andersen (1973, 789), Heath (1975, 90).

13. See especially Jespersen (1922, ch.14–15), Jakobson (1931), de Groot (1931), Jespersen (1941) and Martinet (1955). "Functionalism", in this sense, must be clearly distinguished from "functionalism" as an approach to syntax which stresses the structural role of syntagms in a sentence (see e.g. Martinet 1962, ch.2 and Heller & Macris 1967) or as an attempt to highlight the diversity of functions served by language (see e.g. Halliday 1977).

14. The first aspect of cost (slurred pronunciation) was given prominence in the traditional, "Neo-Grammarian" approach to linguistic change. The second aspect of cost (systemic simplicity) has been emphasized, under the heading of "rule loss", by generativists (for example Kiparsky 1968 or King 1969, ch.4–5).

15. See de Groot (1931, 138–139).

16. See especially Jespersen (1922, 166, 282–283, 286–287 and 1941, 17–18, 22–23), Martinet (1955, 42, 47–51, 59, 141 and 1960, 209–210), Hockett (1965, 202–203), Andersen (1973, 773, 777).

17. See, for example, Jakobson (1931, 265), Martinet (1960, 209 and 1962, 159–160), Juilland (1967, 354–357), Samuels (1972, 178).

18. Functionalists are aware of these implications: see de Groot (1931, 139–140) and Martinet (1960, 185), respectively, for approximate formulations of our two principles. Universal functionalism, in its strengthened form, also implies Jespersen's (1922, 267–268 and 1941, 24–25) "principle of value" or Martinet's (1960, 184–185 and 1962, 139–140) "principle of proportionality", which assert, roughly, that *in the average* the energy spent on a linguistic unit is proportional to the amount of information it conveys.

19. See, for example, Anderson (1973, 157–158).

20. See Samuels' (1972, 80–84) brief survey of the controversy surrounding this question.

21. See Martinet (1955, 151). The argument of this section can easily be extended to more complex examples, such as Heath's (1975) interesting explanation of non-case-related third-person personal-pronoun differentiation and of "strict complex identification rules" by their function of reference clarification.

22. See Jakobson (1931, 259) and Martinet (1955, 27, 42, 49–50). The question of how to measure functional load has been widely discussed: see e.g. Hockett (1967).

23. See King (1967, 836–848).

24. See de Groot (1931, 121) and Martinet (1955, 60–62 and 209–210). The question of whether the phonological space is continuous or discrete, however, has been the centre of a heated controversy: see e.g. King (1969, 109–119) and Andersen (1972, 11–18) for representative statements of the two views.

25. See Martinet (1955, 62).

26. See Labov (1965, 537–538). For further discussion and illustrations of push and drag chains, see especially Martinet (1955, 50–52, 59–62, 85–87, 180–181).

27. See, for example, Martinet (1962, 140) and Bourdieu (1977, 25), respectively.

28. See Ervin-Tripp (1969, 75–77 and 51–53).

29. As demonstrated by Labov (1965; 1966; etc.).

Chapter 5

1. Radcliffe-Brown (1952, 142).

2. See, for example, Bouthoul (1957, 191), Bourdieu & al. (1968, 38–40), Touraine (1973, 15, 40, 76–79), as well as Durkheim (1912, 3) and Pareto (1916, §§154, 166, 177–178).

3. See Bataille (1957, 63–65).

4. See Malinowski (1929, 414–416).

5. See Becker (1974, 17–20).

6. Durkheim (1912, 540).

7. See Durkheim (1912, book III).

8. Durkheim (1912, 245).

9. See Bourdieu (1965, 38–41, 52–55, 343–344), Testaniére (1967) and Goffman (1961, 90–105), respectively.

10. See Radcliffe-Brown (1952, 148–150) and, for example, the "Neo-Durkheimian" analyses of political ritual reviewed by Lukes (1975). Some passages in Durkheim's work (esp. 1912, 610–611) actually support this second interpretation better than the first one.

11. See Katz & al. (1974), as discussed by Durham (1978, 14–16).

12. Skinner (1953, 72–75).

13. Suggested by Pareto (1916, §154).

14. See ch. 4 fn. 9 on linguistic evolution, and, for example, Marx (1867,

361–362) and Popper (1972, 262) on the evolution of tools, or Gerard & al. (1956, 15) and Rapoport (1967, 122–123) on the evolution of cars.

15. This common element is at the core of what Harré (1979, 349–359) calls a "dialectic" process.

16. This constitutes one possible interpretation of the opposition between Darwinian and Lamarckian evolution (see e.g. Cohen 1978, 291–292). Alternative interpretations have been mentioned previously (ch. 2 fn. 25 and ch. 3 fn. 17).

17. See Bourdieu (1958, 64).

18. See Cohen (1966, 223–225).

19. See Smart (1956, 175; 1973, 49–51.

20. See, for example, Nietzsche (1878, 900, 903–904; 1882, 210; 1889, 975–976; 1890, 481, 786).

21. See, for example, Durkheim (1912, 92, 295, 542–453) and Radcliffe-Brown (1922, 254–255, 315), but also Goffman (1967, 58, 258–260) or Bourdieu (1972, 196–197).

22. See Lévi-Strauss (1949, 48, 60, 549–551, 560, 565).

23. See Lévi-Strauss (1949, 49–50, 67–73).

24. See Lévi-Strauss (1949, 511–517).

25. Lévi-Strauss (1949, 517). The emphasis is mine.

26. Lévi-Strauss (1965, 14; 1971, 615).

27. Lévi-Strauss (1965, 15).

28. Needham (1962, 28).

29. Radcliffe-Brown (1952, 62).

30. Needham (1962, 118).

31. Needham (1962, 116). Along the same lines, see also Needham (1962, 26–27), Lévi-Strauss (1965, 14), Spiro (1965, 109–110).

32. If interpreted in this manner, the distinction between "satisficing evolution" and "optimizing evolution" would cease to be dependent on the way in which the behaviour variable is categorized (see section 19).

33. See Veblen (1899, 252–257), Goblot (1925, 84–87).

34. See Veblen (1899, 106–109, 129–130).

35. See typically, Bourdieu (1966, 221–223; 1977, 24–26) and Baudrillard (1970, 80–31; 1972, 75–78). A rational-prestige-maximizing model of changes affecting distinguishing practices is proposed in Van Parijs (1977, 152–154). Veblen's own perspective, on the other hand, is explicitly evolutionary: see especially Veblen (1899, 47–49, 69, 94–95, 118–119, etc.)

36. See Da Gloria & Desaunay (1967, 50–52).

37. A similar argument applies, for example, to Merton's (1949, 126–135) classic functional explanation of the American political machine. As is sometimes pointed out (e.g. by Ryan 1970, 189–191), such an explanation makes essential reference to the costs and receipts involved for the machine's personnel and its customers. But it does not follow, as has been shown in the other examples, that Merton's explanation is reducible to an economic one.

38. Goffman (1963, 37–38).

39. For a discussion on this point, see Ruyle (1977, 54) and Durham (1977, 60–61).

40. See Lévi-Strauss (1949, 80–97, 116–117, 166–167, etc.).
41. This explanation is suggested by Bourdieu & Sayad (1972, 121–123).

Chapter 6

1. See, for example, Comité Central (1971). A largely similar position is defended by Mandel (1962, Vol. 3, 214–218).
2. See, for example, Poulantzas (1968; 1969) and Althusser (1970).
3. See, for example, Altvater (1972) for the "capital-logic" variant, and Hirsch (1974) for the "historically-minded" variant. Texts from both variants are collected in Holloway & Picciotto (1977).
4. Along similar lines, see, for example, Miliband (1970, 259), Gold & al. (1975, 38–39), Block (1977, 28), Jessop (1977, 358, 364), Gough (1979, 156), etc.
5. This is a simplified version of an argument which is put forward by Offe & Ronge (1976, 55–56, 65–66) and Block (1977, 15–19). The Marxist argument against left-wing reformism in contemporary Britain often rests on an analogous analysis. See, for example, Glyn & Harrison (1980, ch. 5).
6. Contrary to what is implied, it seems, in Elster's (1979, 35) forceful critique of "long-term functionalism".
7. As argued by Jay (1976, 16).
8. See, for example, Offe (1972, 94–100), Habermas (1973, 84), O'Connor (1973, 6, 70), etc.
9. See, for example, Clarke (1977, 20), Elster (1978, 146) and Maravall (1979, 283), for typical objections of this kind.
10. Elster (1981) argues convincingly that such a move is of crucial importance.
11. This point is emphasized by Godelier (1968, 80–82, 97–98, 288–290).
12. See Althusser (1965, 100–103, 208–210; 1968, 115–120).
13. Cohen's (1978, 292–293) suggestion of a mechanism of this kind presupposes the existence of capitalist relationships of production. Only the latter, through the competition between firms, can provide a plausible basis for a sufficiently efficient NS-evolutionary mechanism.
14. See, however, Cohen (1978, ch. 6) for a systematic development of the first interpretation.
15. See, for example, Howard & King (1975, 212–213) and Poulantzas (1976, 22–23), respectively.
16. See Godelier (1968, 90–92).
17. See Mandel (1962, Vol. 1, 226–227).
18. These three "complications" are discussed somewhat more thoroughly in Van Parijs (1978, 206–212 and 1979a, 89–95).
19. The scenario sketched above is not fundamentally different from Habermas' idea that societies can be viewed as answering "systemic problems", "evolutionary challenges", by mobilizing the practical knowledge stored in their *Weltbilder*. See especially Habermas (1976, 158–163, 175–178).
20. From Veblen's (1899, ch. 8) conception of "inner relations" as

adjusting through "stress" to the state of the "outer relations", to Touraine's (1973, ch. 7) conception of a society's *fonctionnement* adjusting, through "crises", to its *historicité*.

21. See, for example, Malinowski (1945, 60), Merton (1949, 107–108), Parsons (1951, 180, 491), Radcliffe-Brown (1952, 43, 181–183), Moore (1963, 10–11), etc.

22. The similarity between functionalist and Marxist theories of social change is pointed out, for example, by Emmet (1958, 91), Lockwood (1964, 249–252) and Sztompka (1974, 168–178).

23. As summarized in Durkheim (1895, 92–93) and Parsons (1951, 177–178), respectively.

Conclusion

1. Berger and Luckmann (1966, 154–158).

Bibliography

In references to all items except periodical articles, two dates are given. The first one, which immediately follows the author's name, is the date of first publication and is used to identify the item in the text and the notes (e.g., Veblen 1899). The date at the end of the bibliographical reference relates to the edition used for citation.

Abel, T. 1948. "The operation called Verstehen", *Understanding and Social Inquiry* (F. R. Dallmayr & T. A. McCarthy eds.), University of Notre Dame Press, Notre Dame (Illinois), 1977, 81–92.

Abel, T. 1975. "Verstehen I and Verstehen II", *Theory and Decision* 6, 99–102.

Achinstein, P. 1977a. "Function statements", *Philosophy of Science* 44, 341–367.

Achinstein, P. 1977b. "What is an explanation?", *American Philosophical Quarterly* 14, 1–15.

Alchian, A. A. 1950. "Uncertainty, evolution, and economic theory", *Journal of Political Economy* 58, 211–221.

Althusser, L. 1959. *Montesquieu, la Politique et l'Histoire*, P.U.F., Paris, 1964.

Althusser, L. 1968, "L'objet du *Capital*", *Lire le Capital* Vol. 1 (by L. Althusser & E. Balibar), Maspero, Paris, 1968, 87–184.

Althusser, L. 1970. "Idéologie et appareils idéologiques d'Etat", *Positions* (by L. Althusser), Editions Sociales, Paris, 1976.

Altvater, E. 1972. "Zu einigen Problemen des Staatsinterventionismus", *Probleme des Klassenkampfes* 3, 1–53.

Andersen, H. 1973. "Abductive and deductive change", *Language* 49, 765–793.

Anderson, J. M. 1973. *Structural Aspects of Language Change*, Longman, London, 1973.

Apel, K. O. 1977. "Types of social science in the light of human cognitive interests", *Philosophical Disputes in the Social Sciences* (S. C. Brown ed.), Harvester Press, Brighton (Sussex), 1979, 3–50.

Apostel, L. 1974. *Matière et Forme. Introduction à une épistémologie réaliste*, Communication & Cognition, Ghent, 1974.

Ayala, F. J. 1970. "Teleological explanations in evolutionary biology", *Philosophy of Science* 37, 1–15.

Bataille, G. 1957. *L'Erotisme*, Gallimard, Paris, 1957.

Baudrillard, J. 1970. *La Société de Consommation*, Denoël, Paris, 1970.

Baudrillard, J. 1972. *Pour une Economie Politique du Signe*, Gallimard, Paris, 1972.

Beck, M. C. 1975. *Functional Analysis in Social Science*, University of Reading, B.A. Dissertation, 1975.

Becker, G. S. 1974. "A theory of marriage: part II", *Marriage, Family Human Capital, and Fertility* (T. W. Schultz ed.), University of Chicago Press, Chicago, 1974, 11–26.

Bennett, J. 1976. *Linguistic Behaviour*, Cambridge University Press, Cambridge, 1976.

Berger, P. L. & Luckmann, T. 1966. *The Social Construction of Reality*, Doubleday, New York, 1967.

Bhaskar, R. 1975. *A Realist Theory of Science*, Harvester Press, Hassocks (Sussex), 1978.

Bischof, N. 1975. "Comparative ethology of incest avoidance", *Biosocial Anthropology* (R. Fox ed.), Malaby Press, London, 1975, 37–67.

Block, F. 1977. "The ruling class does not rule: notes on the Marxist theory of the State", *Socialist Revolution* 33, 6–28.

Blurton Jones, N. 1978. "Introduction" to *Human Behaviour and Adaptation* (V. Reynolds & N. Blurton Jones eds.), Taylor & Francis, London, 1978, 3–9.

Blurton Jones, N. & Sibly, R.M. 1978. "Testing adaptiveness of culturally determined behaviour", *Human Behaviour and Adaptation* (V. Reynolds & N. Blurton Jones eds.), Taylor & Francis, London, 1978, 135–157.

Boorse, C. 1976. "Wright on functions", *Philosophical Review* 85, 70–86.

Bourdieu, P. 1958. *Sociologie de l'Algérie*, P.U.F., Paris, 1974.

Bourdieu, P. 1965. *Un Art Moyen. Essai sur les usages sociaux de la photographie*, Editions de Minuit, Paris, 1965.

Bourdieu, P. 1966. "Condition de classe et position de classe", *European Journal of Sociology* 7, 201–233.

Bourdieu, P., Passeron, J.C. & Chamboredon, J.C. 1968. *Le Métier de Sociologue*, Mouton & Bordas, Paris, 1968.

Bourdieu, P. 1972. *Esquisse d'une Théorie de la Pratique*, Droz, Genève, 1972.

Bourdieu, P. & Sayad, A. 1972. "Stratégie et rituel dans le mariage kabyle", *Esquisse d'une Théorie de la Pratique* (by P. Bourdieu), Droz, Genève, 1972, 71–151.

Bourdieu, P. 1977. "L'économie des échanges phonétiques", *La Langue Française* 34, 17–34.

Bouthoul, G. 1957. "Les sciences sociales", *Panorama des Idées Contemporaines* (G. Picon ed.), Gallimard, Paris, 1968, 183–252.

Bredemeier, H.C. 1955. "The methodology of functionalism", *American Sociological Review* 20, 173–180.

Burrow, J. 1966. *Evolution and Society. A study in Victorian social theory* Cambridge University Press, Cambridge, 1966.

Campbell, D.T. 1965. "Variation and selective retention in socio-cultural evolution", *Social Change in Developing Areas. A reinterpretation of evolutionary theory* (H.R. Barringer, G. L. Blanksten & R. W. Mack eds.), Schenkman, Cambridge (Mass.), 1965, 19–49.

Campbell, D. T. 1974. "Evolutionary epistemology", *The Philosophy of Karl Popper* (P. Schilpp ed.), The Library of Living Philosophers, La Salle (Ill.), 1974, 413–459.

Campbell, D. T. 1975. "On the conflicts between biological and social evolution and between psychology and moral tradition", *American Psychologist* 30, 1103–1126.

Cancian, F. M. 1960. "Functional analysis of change", *Theory in Anthropology* (R. A. Manners & D. Kaplan eds.), Routledge & Kegan Paul, London, 1968, 204–212.

Cherry, C. 1957. *On Human Communication*, M.I.T. Press, Cambridge (Mass.), 1966.

Childe, V. G. 1951. *Social Evolution*, Watts & Co., London, 1951.

Chomsky, N. 1965. *Aspects of the Theory of Syntax*, M.I.T. Press, Cambridge (Mass.), 1972.

Clarke, S. 1977. "Marxism, sociology, and Poulantzas' theory of the State", *Capital and Class* 2, 1–31.

Cloak, F. T. 1975. "Is a cultural ethology possible?", *Human Ecology* 3, 161–182.

Cloak, F. T. 1977. "Comment", *Human Ecology* 5, 49–52.

Cohen, G. A. 1978. *Karl Marx's Theory of History*, Oxford University Press, Oxford, 1978.

Cohen, G. A. 1980. "Functional explanation: reply to Elster", *Political Studies* 28, 129–135.

Cohen, J. 1966. *Structure du Langage Poétique*, Flammarion, Paris, 1966.

Cohen, P. S. 1968. *Modern Social Theory*, Heinemann, London, 1975.

Comité Central du Parti Communiste Francais, 1971. *Le Capitalisme Monopoliste d'Etat*, Editions Sociales, Paris, 1971.

Corning, P. A. 1974. "Politics and the evolutionary process", *Evolutionary Biology* Vol. 7 (T. Dobzhansky, M. K. Hecht & W. C. Steers eds.), Plenum Press, New York, 1974, 253–294.

Costner, H. L. & Leik, R. K. 1964. "Deductions from 'axiomatic theory' ", *American Sociological Review* 29, 819–835.

Da Gloria, G. & Desaunay, G. 1967. "Deux mécanismes de régulation sociale: télévision et participation politique", *Sociologie du Travail* 9, 48–63.

Darwin, C. 1871. *The Descent of Man and Selection in Relation to Sex*, Appleton, New York, 1913.

De Groot, A. W. 1931. "Phonologie und Phonetik als Funktionswissenschaften", *Travaux du Cercle Linguistique de Prague* 4, 116–147.

Delattre, P. 1971. *Système, Structure, Fonction, Evolution*, Maloine-Doin, Paris, 1971.

Dore, R. P. 1961. "Function and Cause", *The Philosophy of Social Explanation* (A. Ryan ed.), Oxford University Press, London, 1973, 65–81.

Durham, W. H. 1976. "The adaptive significance of cultural behaviour", *Human Ecology* 4, 89–121.

Durham, W. H. 1977. "Reply", *Human Ecology* 5, 59–68.

Durham, W. H. 1978. "The coevolution of human biology and culture",

Human Behaviour and Adaptation (V. Reynolds & N. Blurton Jones eds.), Taylor & Francis, London, 1978, 11–32.

Durkheim, E. 1895. *Les Règles de la Méthode Sociologique*, P.U.F., Paris, 1947.

Durkheim, E. 1912. *Les Formes Elémentaires de la Vie Religieuse*, P.U.F., Paris, 1968. (English Translation: Allen & Unwin, London, 1915.)

Elster, J. 1978. *Lecture Notes on Marxism*, Historisk Institut, Oslo, 1978.

Elster, J. 1979. *Ulysses and the Sirens. Essays on rationality and irrationality*, Cambridge University Press, Cambridge, 1979.

Elster, J. 1980. "Cohen on Marx's theory of history", *Political Studies* 28, 121–128.

Elster, J. 1981. "Marxism, functionalism and game theory", *Marxist Perspectives* 4, forthcoming.

Emmet, D. 1958. *Function, Purpose and Powers*, Macmillan, London, 1958.

Ervin-Tripp, S. M. 1969. "Sociolinguistics", *Advances in the Sociology of Language* Vol. 1 (J. A. Fishman ed.), Mouton, Paris & The Hague, 1971, 15–81.

Fisher, J. & Hinde, R. A. 1949. "The opening of milk bottles by birds", *Function and Evolution of Behaviour* (P. H. Klopfer & J. P. Hailman eds.), Addison-Wesley, Reading (Mass.), 1972, 366–373.

Fox, R. 1967. *Kinship and Marriage*, Penguin Books, Harmondsworth, 1967.

Freud, S. 1899. *Die Traumdeutung*, Deuticke, Vienna, 1950.

Freud, S. 1933. *Neue Folge der Vorlesungen zur Einführung in die Psychoanalyse*, Fischer, Frankfurt, 1967.

Gerard, R. W., Kluckhohn, C. & Rapoport, A. 1956. "Biological and cultural evolution", *Behavioral Science* 1, 6–34.

Ginsberg, M., "Social evolution", *Darwinism and the Study of Society* (M. Banton ed.), Tavistock Publications, London, 1961, 95–127.

Glyn, A. & Harrison, J. 1980. *The British Economic Disaster*, Pluto Press, London, 1980.

Goblot, E. 1925. *La Barrière et le Niveau. Etude sociologique sur la bourgeoisie française moderne*, P.U.F., Paris, 1967.

Godelier, M. 1968. *Rationalité et Irrationalité en Economie*, Maspero, Paris, 1968.

Goffman, E. 1961. *Asylums*, Penguin Books, Harmondsworth, 1968.

Goffman, E. 1963. *Stigma*, Penguin Books, Harmondsworth, 1968.

Goffman, E. 1967. *Interaction Ritual*, Penguin Books, Harmondsworth, 1972.

Goffman, E. 1969. *Strategic Interaction*, Blackwell, Oxford, 1970.

Gold, D., Lo, C.Y.H. & Wright, E. O. 1975. "Recent developments in Marxist theories of the State", *Monthly Review* 27.5, 29–43.

Goudge, T. A. 1961. *The Ascent of Life. A philosophical study of the theory of evolution*, Allen & Unwin, London, 1961.

Gough, I. 1979. *The Political Economy of the Welfare State*, Macmillan, London, 1979.

Grim, P. 1974. "Wright on functions", *Analysis* 35, 62–64.

Habermas, J. 1965. "Erkenntnis und Interesse", *Technik und Wissenschaft als "Ideologie"* (by J. Habermas), Suhrkamp, Frankfurt, 1971, 146–168.

Habermas, J. 1968. *Erkenntnis und Interesse,* Suhrkamp, Frankfurt, 1971.

Habermas, J. 1973. *Legitimationsprobleme im Spätkapitalismus,* Suhrkamp, Frankfurt, 1975.

Habermas, J. 1976. *Zur Rekonstruktion des Historischen Materialismus,* Suhrkamp, Frankfurt, 1976.

Halfpenny, P. 1981. "Two-variable and three-variable functional explanation", *Philosophy of the Social Sciences* 11, forthcoming.

Halliday, M.A. K. 1977. *System and Function in Language. Selected essays,* Oxford University Press, London, 1977.

Hamilton, W. D. 1975. "Innate social aptitudes of man: an approach from evolutionary genetics", *Biosocial Anthropology* (R. Fox ed.), Malaby Press, London, 1975, 133–155.

Hanson, N. R. 1958. *Patterns of Discovery,* Cambridge University Press, Cambridge, 1969.

Harré, R. 1964. *Matter and Method,* Macmillan, London, 1964.

Harré, R. 1970. *The Principles of Scientific Thinking,* Macmillan, London, 1972.

Harré, R. 1979. *Social Being. A theory for social psychology,* Blackwell, Oxford, 1979.

Harsanyi, J. C. 1968. "Individualistic and functionalistic explanation in the light of game theory", *Problems in the Philosophy of Science* (I. Lakatos & A. Musgrave eds.), North-Holland, Amsterdam, 1968, 305–321.

Hawthorn, G. 1970. *The Sociology of Fertility,* Collier & Macmillan, London, 1970.

Hayek, F. A. 1967. "Notes on the evolution of systems of rules of conduct", *Studies in Philosophy, Politics and Economics* (by F. A. Hayek), Routledge & Kegan Paul, London, 1967, 66–81.

Heath, A. 1976. *Rational Choice and Social Exchange,* Cambridge University Press, Cambridge, 1976.

Heath, J. 1975. "Some functional relationships in grammar", *Language* 51, 89–104.

Heller, L. G. & Macris, J. 1967. "Perspectives in functionalism", *Word* 23, 288–299.

Hempel, C. G. 1959. "The logic of functional analysis", *Aspects of Scientific Explanation and Other Essays in the Philosophy of Science* (by C. G. Hempel), The Free Press, New York, 1965, 297–330.

Hinde, R. A. & Fisher, J. 1951. "Further observations on the opening of milk bottles by birds", *Function and Evolution of Behaviour* (P. H. Klopfer & J. P. Hailman eds.), Addison-Wesley, Reading (Mass.), 1972, 373–377.

Hinde, R. A. 1975. "The concept of function", *Function and Evolution in Behaviour* (G. Baerends, C. G. Beer & A. Manning eds.), Oxford University Press, London, 1975, 3–15.

Hirsch, J. 1974. *Staatsapparat und Reproduktion des Kapitals,* Suhrkamp, Frankfurt, 1974.

Hockett, C. F. 1965. "Sound change", *Language* 41, 185–204.

Hockett, C. F. 1967. "The quantification of functional load", *Word* 23, 300–320.

Holloway, J. & Picciotto, S. (eds.) 1977. *The State and Capital: A Marxist Debate*, Arnold, London, 1977.

Homans, G. C. & Schneider, D. M. 1955. *Marriage, Authority and Final Causes. A study of unilateral cross-cousin marriage*, The Free Press, Glencoe (Ill.), 1955.

Homans, G. C. 1964. "Bringing men back in", *American Sociological Review* 29, 809–818.

Homans, G. C. 1967. *The Nature of Social Science*, Harcourt, Brace & World, New York, 1967.

Homans, G. C. 1970. "The relevance of psychology to the explanation of social phenomena", *Explanation in the Behavioural Sciences* (R. Borger & F. Cioffi eds.), Cambridge University Press, Cambridge, 1970, 313–328.

Howard, M. C. & King, J. E. 1975. *The Political Economy of Marx*, Longman, London, 1975.

Isajiw, W. W. 1968. *Causation and Functionalism in Sociology*, Routlege & Kegan Paul, London, 1968.

Jakobson, R. 1931. "Prinzipien der historischen Phonologie", *Travaux du Cercle Linguistique de Prague* 4, 247–267.

Jarvie, I. C. 1964. *The Revolution in Anthropology*, Routledge & Kegan Paul, London, 1964.

Jay, P. 1976. *Employment, Inflation and Politics*, Institute of Economic Affairs, London, 1977.

Jespersen, O. 1922. *Language*, Allen & Unwin, London, 1922.

Jespersen, O. 1941. *Efficiency in Linguistic Change*, Munksgaard, Copenhague, 1941.

Jessop, B. 1977. "Recent theories of the capitalist State", *Cambridge Journal of Economics* 1, 353–373.

Kaplan, A. 1964. *The Conduct of Inquiry. Methodology for Behavioral Science*, Chandler, San Francisco, 1964.

Katz, S. H., Hediger, M. L. & Valleroy, L. A. 1974. "Traditional maize processing techniques in the New World", *Science* 184, 765–773.

Keat, R. & Urry, J. 1975. *Social Theory as Science*, Routledge & Kegan Paul, London, 1978.

Kettlewell, B. 1974. "The evolution of industrial melanism in Lepidoptera", *Evolution. The Modern Synthesis* (by J. Huxley), Allen & Unwin, London, 1974, xl-xlix.

Kim, J. 1973. "Causes and counterfactuals", *Causation and Conditionals* (E. Sosa ed.), Oxford University Press, London, 1975, 192–194.

King, R. D. 1967. "Functional load and sound change", *Language* 40, 831–852.

King, R. D. 1969. *Historical Linguistics and Generative Grammar*, Prentice-Hall, Englewood Cliffs (New Jersey), 1969.

Kiparsky, P. 1968. "Linguistic universals and linguistic change", *Universals in Linguistic Theory* (E. Bach & R. T. Harms eds.), Holt, Rinehart & Winston, New York, 1972, 170–202.

Klopfer, P. H. & Hailman, J. P. (eds.) 1972. *Function and Evolution of Behaviour*, Addison-Wesley, Reading (Mass.), 1972.

Kuhn, T. S. 1963. "The function of dogma in scientific research", *Scientific Change* (A. C. Crombie ed.), Heinemann, London, 1963, 347–369.

Kuhn, T. S. 1971. "Les notions de causalité dans le développement de la physique", *Les Théories de la Causalité* (J. Piaget ed.), P.U.F., Paris, 1971, 7–18.

Labov, W. 1965. "On the mechanism of linguistic change", *Directions in Sociolinguistics* (J. J. Gumperz & D. Hymes eds.), Holt, Rinehart & Winston, New York, 1972, 512–538.

Labov, W. 1966. "Hypercorrection by the lower middle class as a factor of linguistic change", *Sociolinguistics* (W. Bright ed.), Mouton, The Hague, 1966, 84–113.

Langton, J. 1979. "Darwinism and the behavioral theory of sociocultural evolution", *American Journal of Sociology* 85, 288–309.

Lazarsfeld, P. F. 1970. *Main Trends in Sociology*, Allen & Unwin, London, 1973.

Lenin, V. I. 1918. *The State and Revolution*, Progress, Moscow, 1970.

Lessnoff, M. 1974. *The Structure of Social Science*, Allen & Unwin, London, 1974.

Lévi-Strauss, C. 1949. *Les Structures Elémentaires de la Parenté*, Mouton, Paris, 1967. (English translation: Eyre & Spottiswoode, London, 1969.)

Lévi-Strauss, C. 1965. "The future of kinship studies", *Proceedings of the Royal Anthropological Institute* 1965, 13–22.

Lévi-Strauss, C. 1971. *L'Homme Nu*, Plon, Paris, 1971.

Levy, M. J. 1952. *The Structure of Society*, Princeton University Press, Princeton (New Jersey), 1952.

Lewis, D. 1973. "Causation", *Causation and Conditionals* (E. Sosa ed.), Oxford University Press, London, 1975, 180–191.

Locke, J. 1689. *An Essay concerning Human Understanding*, Collins, Glasgow, 1977.

Lockwood, D. 1964. "Social integration and system integration", *Explorations in Social Change* (G.K. Zollschan & W. Hirsch eds.) Routledge & Kegan Paul, London, 1964, 244–257.

Lorenz, K. 1965. *Evolution and Modification of Behaviour*, Methuen, London, 1966.

Lukes, S. 1975. "Political ritual and social integration", *Essays in Social Theory* (by S. Lukes), Macmillan, London, 1977, 52–73.

Mackie, J. L. 1965. "Causes and conditions", *Causation and Conditionals* (E. Sosa ed.), Oxford University Press, London, 1975, 15–38.

Mackie, J. L. 1974. *The Cement of the Universe*, Oxford University Press, London, 1974.

McLachlan, H. V. 1976. "Functionalism, causation and explanation", *Philosophy of the Social Sciences* 6, 235–240.

Malinowski, B. 1926. *Crime and Custom in Savage Society*, Routledge & Kegan Paul, London, 1970.

Malinowski, B. 1927. *Sex and Repression in Savage Society*, Routledge & Kegan Paul, London, 1960.

Malinowski, B. 1929. *The Sexual Life of Savages in North-Western Melanesia*, Routledge & Kegan Paul, London, 1968.

Malinowski, B. 1944. *A Scientific Theory of Culture and Other Essays*, University of North Carolina Press, Chapel Hill, 1973.

Malinowski, B. 1945. *The Dynamics of Cultural Change*, Yale University Press, New Haven (Conn.), 1945.

Malinowski, B. 1948. *Magic, Science and Religion, and Other Essays*, Souvenir Press, London, 1974.

Mandel, E. 1962. *Traité d'Economie Marxiste*, Union Générale d'Edition, Paris, 1969, 4 Vol.

Maravall, J. M. 1979. "The limits of reformism. Parliamentary socialism and the Marxist theory of the State", *British Journal of Sociology* 30, 267–290.

March, J. G. & Simon, H. A. 1958. *Organizations*, Wiley & Sons, New York, 1958.

Martinet, A. 1955. *Economie des Changements Phonetiques*, Francke, Bern, 1955.

Martinet, A. 1960. *Eléments de Linguistique Générale*, Armand Colin, Paris, 1960.

Martinet, A. 1962. *A Functional View of Language*, Clarendon Press, Oxford, 1962.

Marx, K. 1867. *Das Kapital* Vol. 1, Dietz, Berlin, 1962.

Merton, R. K. 1949. "Manifest and latent functions", *Social Theory and Social Structure* (by R. K. Merton), The Free Press, New York, 1968, 73–138.

Miliband, R. 1970. "Reply to Nicos Poulantzas", *Ideology in Social Science* (R. Blackburn ed.), Fontana & Collins, London, 1975, 253–262.

Miyadi, D. 1964. "Social life of Japanese monkeys", *Function and Evolution of Behaviour* (P. H. Klopfer & J. P. Hailman eds.), Addison-Wesley, Reading (Mass.), 1972, 384–388.

Moore, W. E. & Tumin, M. 1949. "Some social functions of ignorance", *American Sociological Review* 14, 787–795.

Moore, W. E. 1963. *Social Change*, Prentice-Hall, Englewood Cliffs (New Jersey), 1963.

Murdock, G. P. 1956. "How cultures change", *Man, Culture and Society* (H. L. Shapiro ed.), Oxford University Press, London, 1971, 247–260.

Nagel, E. 1956. "A formalization of functionalism", *Systems Thinking* (F. E. Emery ed.), Penguin Books, Harmondsworth, 1972, 297–329.

Nagel, E. 1961. *The Structure of Science*, Routledge & Kegan Paul, London, 1974.

Nagel, E. 1977. "Functional explanations in biology", *Journal of Philosophy* 74, 280–301.

Needham, R. 1962. *Structure and Sentiment*, University of Chicago Press, Chicago, 1969.

Nelson, R. R. & Winter, S. G. 1974. "Neo-classical versus evolutionary theories of economic growth", *Economic Journal* 84, 886–905.

Nelson, R. R., Winter, S. G. & Schuette, H. L. 1976. "Technical change in an evolutionary model", *Quarterly Journal of Economics* 90, 90–118.

Nietzsche, F. 1878. *Menschliches, Allzumenschliches, Werke* Vol. 1 (by F. Nietzsche), Hauser, München, 1956, 435–1008.

Nietzsche, F. 1882. *Die Fröhliche Wissenschaft, Werke* Vol. 2 (by F. Nietzsche), Hauser, München, 1956, 2–274.

Nietzsche, F. 1889. *Götzendämmerung, Werke* Vol. 2 (by F. Nietzsche), Hauser, München, 1956, 939–1033.

Nietzsche, F. 1890. "Aus dem Nachlass der Achtziger Jahre", *Werke* Vol. 3 (by F. Nietzsche), Hause, München, 1956, 415–925.

O'Connor, J. 1973. *The Fiscal Crisis of the State*, St. Martin's Press, New York, 1973.

Offe, C. 1972. *Strukturprobleme des kapitalistischen Staats*, Suhrkamp, Frankfurt, 1975.

Offe, C. & Ronge, V. 1976. "Thesen zur Begründung des Konzepts des 'kapitalistischen Staats' und zur materialistischen Politikforschung", *Rahmenbedingungen und Schranken staatlichen Handelns* (C. Pozzoli ed.) Suhrkamp, Frankfurt, 1976, 54–70.

Opp, K. D. 1979. "Social evolution: learning theory applied to group action", *Theory and Decision* 10, 229–243.

Pareto, V. 1916. *Trattato di Sociologia Generale*, Comunità, Milan, 1964, 2 Vol.

Parsons, T. 1951. *The Social System*, The Free Press, New York, 1951.

Parsons, T. 1966. *Societies. Evolutionary and comparative perspectives*, Prentice-Hall, Englewood Cliffs (New Jersey), 1966.

Perrow, C. 1967. "A framework for the comparative analysis of organizations", *American Sociological Review* 32, 194–208.

Popper, K. R. 1944. *The Poverty of Historicism*, Routledge & Kegan Paul, London, 1974.

Popper, K. R. 1945. *The Open Society and its Enemies* Vol. 2, Routledge & Kegan Paul, London, 1969.

Popper, K. R. 1972. *Objective Knowledge. An evolutionary approach*, Oxford University Press, London, 1974.

Poulantzas, N. 1968. *Pouvoir Politique et Classes Sociales*, Maspero, Paris, 1968, 2 Vol.

Poulantzas, N. 1969. "The problem of the capitalist State", *Ideology in Social Science* (R. Blackburn ed.), Fontana & Collins, London, 1975, 238–253.

Poulantzas, N. (ed.) 1976. *La Crise de l'Etat*, P.U.F., Paris, 1977.

Pratt, V. 1975. "Functionalism and the possibility of group selection", *Studies in the History and Philosophy of Science* 5, 371–372.

Pratt, V. 1978. *The Philosophy of the Social Sciences*, Methuen, London, 1978.

Purton, A. C. 1979. "Biological function", *Philosophical Quarterly* 29, 10–24.

Putnam, H. 1978. *Meaning and the Moral Sciences*, Routledge & Kegan Paul, London, 1978.

Quadagno, J. S. 1979. "Paradigms in evolutionary theory: the sociobiological model of natural selection", *American Sociological Review* 44, 100–109.

Radcliffe-Brown, A. R. 1922. *The Andaman Islanders*, The Free Press, New York, 1964.

Radcliffe-Brown, A. R. 1952. *Structure and Function in Primitive Society*, Routledge & Kegan Paul, London, 1971.

Rapoport, A. 1967. "Mathematical, evolutionary and psychological approaches to the study of total societies", *The Study of Total Societies* (S. Z. Klausner ed.), Praeger, New York, 1967, 114–143.

Rudner, R. 1966. *Philosophy of the Social Sciences*, Prentice-Hall, Englewood Cliffs (New Jersey), 1966.

Runciman, W. G. 1969. "The sociological explanation of 'religious' beliefs", *European Journal of Sociology* 10, 149–191.

Ruse, M. 1973. *The Philosophy of Biology*, Hutchinson, London, 1973.

Ruse, M. 1974. "Cultural evolution", *Theory and Decision* 5, 413–440.

Ruyle, E. E. 1973. "Genetic and cultural pools: some suggestions for a unified theory of biocultural evolution", *Human Ecology* 1, 201–215.

Ruyle, E. E. 1977. "Comment", *Human Ecology* 5, 53–55.

Ryan, A. 1970. *The Philosophy of the Social Sciences*, Macmillan, London, 1970.

Sahlins, M. D. 1960. "Evolution, specific and general", *Theory in Anthropology* (R. A. Manners & D. Kaplan eds.), Routledge & Kegan Paul, London, 1968, 229–241.

Samuels, M. L. 1972. *Linguistic Evolution*, Cambridge University Press, Cambridge, 1975.

Samuelson, P. A. 1948. *Economics*, McGraw-Hill, New York, 1973.

Scriven, M. 1963. Review of Nagel's *The Structure of Science*, *Review of Metaphysics* 16, 403–424.

Service, E. R. 1971. *Cultural Evolutionism*, Holt, Rinehart & Winston, New York, 1971.

Service, E. R. 1975. *Origins of the State and Civilization. The process of cultural evolution*, Norton, New York, 1975.

Simon, H. A. 1957. *Models of Man*, Wiley & Sons, New York, 1957.

Skinner, B. F. 1953. *Science and Human Behaviour*, The Free Press, New York, 1965.

Smart, J. J. C. 1956. "Extreme and restricted utilitarianism", *Theories of Ethics* (P. Foot ed.), Oxford University Press, London, 1968, 171–183.

Smart, J. J. C. 1973. "An outline of a system of utilitarian ethics", *Utilitarianism. For and against* (by J. J. C. Smart & B. Williams), Cambridge University Press, Cambridge, 1973, 3–74.

Smelser, N. J. 1968. "Toward a general theory of social change", *Essays in Sociological Explanation* (by N. J. Smelser), Prentice-Hall, Englewood Cliffs (New Jersey), 1968, 192–280.

Smith, A. D. 1973. *The Concept of Social Change. A critique of the functionalist theory of social change*, Routledge & Kegan Paul, London, 1973.

Smith, J. M. 1961. "Evolution and history", *Darwinism and the Study of Society* (M. Banton ed.), Tavistock Publications, London, 1961, 83–93.

Smith, J. M. 1975. *The Theory of Evolution*, Penguin Books, Harmonsworth, 1975

Spiro, M. E. 1965. "Causes, functions and cross-cousin marriage", *Theory in Anthropology* (R. R. Manners & D. Kaplan eds.), Routledge & Kegan Paul, London, 1968, 105–115.

Spiro, M. E. 1966. "Religion: problems of definition and explanation", *Anthropological Approaches to the Study of Religion* (M. Banton ed.), Tavistock Publications, London, 1966, 85–126.

Stevick, R. D. 1963. "The biological model and historical linguistics", *Language* 39, 159–169.

Steward, J. L. 1955. *Theory of Culture Change. The methodology of multilinear evolution*, University of Illinois Press, Urbana (Ill.), 1971.

Sweezy, P. M. 1942. *The Theory of Capitalist Development*, Monthly Review Press, New York, 1970.

Sztompka, P. 1974. *System and Function*, Academic Press, New York, 1974.

Taylor, C. 1964. *The Explanation of Behaviour*, Routledge & Kegan Paul, London, 1964.

Testanière, J. 1967. "Chahut traditionnel et chahut anomique dans l'enseignement du second degré", *Revue Française de Sociologie* 8, 17–33.

Tinbergen, N. 1951. *The Study of Instinct*, Oxford University Press, London, 1974.

Tinbergen, N. 1956. "On the functions of territory in gulls", *Ibis* 98, 401–411.

Tinbergen, N., Broekhuysen, G. J., Houghton, J. C. W., Kruuk, H. & Szulec, E. 1962. "Egg-shell removal by the black-headed gull: a behaviour component of camouflage", *Function and Evolution of Behaviour* (P. H. Klopfer & J. P. Hailman eds.), Addison-Wesley, Reading (Mass.), 1972, 135–151.

Tinbergen, N. 1965. "Behavior and natural selection", *Ideas in Modern Biology* (J. A. Moore ed.), The Natural History Press, Garden City (New York), 1965, 519–542.

Tinbergen, N. 1972. "Functional ethology and the human sciences", *Proceedings of the Royal Society of London* B-182, 385–410.

Toulmin, S. 1972. *Human Understanding* Vol. 1, Oxford University Press, London, 1972.

Touraine, A. 1973. *Production de la Société*, Le Seuil, Paris, 1973.

Van Parijs, P. 1977. "Triadic distributions and contrepied strategies. A contribution to a pure theory of expressive behaviour", *Journal for the Theory of Social Behaviour* 7, 129–160.

Van Parijs, P. 1978. "Théorie des catastrophes et matérialisme historique", *Revue Française de Sociologie* 19, 195–220.

Van Parijs, P. 1979a. "From contradiction to catastrophe", *New Left Review* 115, 87–96.

Van Parijs, P. 1979b. "Functional explanation and the linguistic analogy" *Philosophy of the Social Sciences* 9, 425–443.

Veblen, T. 1899. *The Theory of the Leisure Class*, Allen & Unwin, London, 1970.

Weber, M. 1913. "Ueber einige Kategorien der verstehenden Soziologie",

Methodologische Schriften (by M. Weber), Fischer, Frankfurt, 1968, 427–474.

Weber, M. 1922. *Wirtschart und Gesellschaft,* Mohr, Tübingen, 1972.

White, L. 1959. *The Evolution of Culture,* McGraw-Hill, New York, 1959.

Wilson, E. O. 1975. *Sociobiology: the New Synthesis,* Harvard University Press, Cambridge (Mass.), 1975.

Wimsatt, W. C. 1972. "Teleology and the logical structure of function statements", *Studies in the History and Philosophy of Science* 3, 1–80.

Winter, S. G. 1964. "Economic 'natural selection' and the theory of the firm", *Yale Economic Essays* 4, 225–272.

Winter, S. G. 1975. "Optimization and evolution", *Adaptive Economic Models* (R. H. Day & T. Groves eds.), Academic Press, New York, 1975, 73–118.

Woodfield, A. 1976. *Teleology,* Cambridge University Press, Cambridge, 1976.

Worsley, P. 1957. *The Trumpet Shall Sound. A study of 'Cargo' cults in Melanesia,* Paladin Books, London, 1970.

Wright, G. H. von 1971. *Explanation and Understanding,* Routledge & Kegan Paul, London, 1971.

Wright, G. H. von 1973. "On the logic and epistemology of the causal relation", *Causation and Conditionals* (E. Sosa ed.), Oxford University Press, London, 1975, 95–113.

Wright, L. 1973. "Functions", *Philosophical Review* 82, 139–168.

Wright, L. 1976a. *Teleological Explanations,* University of California Press, Berkeley, 1976.

Wright, L. 1976b. "Reply to Grim", *Analysis* 36, 156–157.

Zeeman, E. C. 1977. *Catastrophe Theory,* Addison-Wesley, Reading (Mass.), 1977.

Index

Revolutions, 202–206
R-evolutionary (or reinforcement-evolutionary): attractor, 95, 98–99, 109, 141, 158, 166, 184, 227; explanation, 95, 124–125; pattern, 95, 127, 136–137
Ritual, 137–139
Ronge V., 237
Rudner R., 230
Rules, x, 19–20
Runciman W. G., 228
Ruse M., 232
Ruyle E. E., 233, 234, 236
Ryan A., 230, 236

Sahlins M. D., 233
Samuels M. L., 234
Samuelson P. A., 228
Sanctions, social versus supersocial, 131
Satisfaction, chances of, 97–98, 124, 132, 166, 194; structural versus super-structural, 133–135, 163
Satisficing, 20, 49–50, 208, 232, 236
Sayad A., 228, 237
Schneider D. M., 154, 155
Scriven M., 228
Sects, 91
Selection, 51–52. (*See also* natural selection, kin selection, group selection)
Service E. R., 231
Sibly R. M., 233
Simon H. A., 20, 229
Skinner B. F., 21, 233, 235
Smart J. J. C., 236
Smelser N. J., 213
Smith J. M., 232, 233
Social practice, 129–131
Social sciences: chaotic appearance of, 2–3; deep structure of, 3, 23, 54, 92, 125, 223–226; scope of, 24; specific features of, xi–xii
Sociobiological model, 61, 91, 127
Sociobiology, 61, 77–81, 92
Spinoza B., 229
Spiro M. E., 234, 236
Stability, 43, 67
State theory, 180–198
Static explanation, 42
Statistical test, 116–117, 170–171
Stevick R. D., 234

Stigmatization, xi–xii, 226
Steward J. L., 231
Structural constraints, 182–187
Structuralism: evolutionary, 107; in Marxism, 181, 193; in social anthropology, 25, 152, 155
Structuration pattern, 225
Survival, 34, 35, 59, 87, 231
Suspicion, principle of, 129–132, 179–180
Sweezy P. M., 209
System functionalism, 60, 87–91, 104
Sztompka P., 233, 238

Taylor C., 230
Teleology, 106, 155, 230
Testability: of causal claims, 9; of NS-evolutionary explanations, 75–77, 216–217; of R-evolutionary explanations, 111–124, 166–173, 194–195, 216–217
Testanière J., 235
Theory, 17, 21
Tinbergen N., 231, 232
Total societies, 87–89
Toulmin S., 229, 231, 234
Touraine A., 24, 228, 235, 238
Trial-and-error, 51
Tumin M., 32

Understanding, types of, 13–14, 24, 229
Urry J., 229
Utilitarianism, 148, 218–219

Van Parijs P., 236, 237
Veblen T., 162, 236, 237

Weber M., 21, 229
Welfare, 34–35, 231
Welfare view, 34–36
White L., 231
Wilson E. O., 232, 233
Wimsatt W. C., 231, 232
Winter S. G., 233
Woodfield A., 230, 231
Working-class strength, 190–198
Worsley P., 233
Wright G. H. von, 228
Wright L., 229, 230

Zeeman E. C., 230